God bless you,
Wade + Tracy!
May the windows of heaven
open over your lives!

The Beliefs of the Catholic Church

25 Questions

Comparing Doctrines, Practices, and Traditions to Scripture

MIKE SHREVE (B.Th., D.D.)

The Beliefs of the Catholic Church
25 Questions Comparing Doctrines, Practices, and Traditions to Scripture

Copyright © 2023 Mike Shreve

ISBN: 978-1-949297-71-3   LCCN: 2023909965

Available also as an e-book.

Unless otherwise noted, all Scripture references are from the NEW KING JAMES VERSION®. Copyright © 1982 by Thomas Nelson, Inc. Used by permission. All rights reserved.

Scripture quotations marked (ESV) are from THE HOLY BIBLE, ENGLISH STANDARD VERSION®, Copyright© 2001 by Crossway, a publishing ministry of Good News Publishers. Used by permission.

Scripture quotations marked (NCB) are from THE NEW CATHOLIC BIBLE®. Copyright © 2019 Catholic Book Publishing Corp. Used by permission. All rights reserved.

Scripture quotations marked (CJB) are from the COMPLETE JEWISH BIBLE, Copyright© 1998 by David H. Stern. Published by Jewish New Testament Publications, Inc. www.messianicjewish.net. Distributed by Messianic Jewish Resources Int'l. www.messianicjewish.net. All rights reserved. Used by permission.

Scripture quotations marked (KJV) are from the King James Version of the Bible. Public domain. Those scriptures marked (KJV/A) are very close to the King James Version, however, the author has carefully substituted his own more modern words for the archaic English.

Scripture quotations marked (MEV) are taken from THE HOLY BIBLE, MODERN ENGLISH VERSION. Copyright© 2014 by Military Bible Association. Published and distributed by Charisma House.

Scripture quotations marked (TLV) are taken from the Holy Scriptures, Tree of Life Version. Copyright © 2014, 2016 by the Tree of Life Bible Society. Used by permission of the Tree of Life Bible Society.

Scripture quotations marked (DRA) are taken from the Douay-Rheims Version of the Bible (1899 American Edition) public domain.

Cover design and internal layout by Elizabeth Shreve

Contact information:

Mail: Mike Shreve, P.O. Box 4260, Cleveland, TN 37320

Email: mikeshreve@shreveministries.org

Ministry website: www.shreveministries.org

Comparative religion website: www.thetruelight.net

Catholicism website: www.toCatholicswithlove.org

Ordering Information

Individuals and church groups may order books from Mike Shreve's two websites, or from the publisher. For bulk orders, contact the publisher listed below. Retailers and wholesalers should order from our distributors. Refer to the Deeper Revelation Books website for distribution information, as well as an online catalog of all our books.

Published by:

Deeper Revelation Books

Revealing "the deep things of God" (1 Cor. 2:10)

P.O. Box 4260, Cleveland, TN 37320

Phone 423-478-2843

Website: www.deeperrevelationbooks.org

Email: info@deeperrevelationbooks.org

Deeper Revelation Books assists Christian authors in publishing and distributing their books. Final responsibility for design, content, permissions, editorial accuracy, and doctrinal views, either expressed or implied, belongs to the author. One of our core values is to strive for excellence so that every book we publish is an act of worship toward God.

*Serving as an altar boy at the Catholic Church
at Mayport Naval Base, north of Jacksonville, Florida
(second from left). I will always respect Father Biddle
for his kindness, his gentleness, and his sacrificial
service. He was a very positive role model in my life.*

DEDICATION

I dedicate this book to the sincere nuns and priests who helped shape my values at an early age, whose lifestyle of self-sacrificing service to others will never be forgotten. I also dedicate it to every sincere Catholic who loves God, embraces the cross, believes in the resurrection, and longs for heaven—I love you; I respect you, and I want to be a blessing in your life.

TABLE OF CONTENTS

Introduction

My years as a Catholic and the turning point in my life

There are approximately 2.6 billion professing Christians in the world, a larger slice of the global population pie than any other religion. Of all the varieties of the Christian faith, Catholicism is the largest, with about 1.3 billion adherents (approximately 16.5% of the world population). Their influence is felt on every continent, even in some of the most remote areas. Millions have heard the Good News of the birth, death, and resurrection of our Savior through priests and nuns willing to sacrifice their lives to shine the light of God's goodness in a world that leans so often toward badness. That is commendable!

I love Catholics. I respect Catholics. I admire the commitment often found in Catholic organizations to things that truly matter—like justice for the oppressed, care for the poor, conservative family values, and the pro-life movement.

I am not an angry, former Catholic who was hurt by the church or its leadership. I have only good memories. My grandmother was a fervent Catholic who prayed the rosary every day. Nana's last words to my father were, "Andy, I'll rise with Jesus!" I believe she knew the Lord and had a real assurance of salvation. Most importantly, I believe she is in heaven right now.

As an infant, I was baptized in the Catholic Church and raised by parents who were fervent in their devotion to its principles. I attended Catholic parochial schools until I was about twelve. The nuns who taught me were some of the most humble, self-sacrificing individuals

I have ever known. Well, to be honest, a few were somewhat fierce to deal with, especially when assignments were ignored or discipline was needed, but looking back, I realize now that their stern demeanor was probably necessary. They would most likely—unanimously—say that I was a little challenging to deal with, too (imagine a smiley face inserted here).

As an altar boy, I served under priests who were real role models of sincerity, consecration, gentleness, discipline, and devotion to God. They may not have believed in some of the biblical principles I presently embrace, but I respected them deeply—and they were very real in their love for God and their commitment to serving others. I am indebted to all of those who impacted my life in a positive way, especially Father Biddle, the Navy Chaplain at Mayport Naval Base, just north of Jacksonville, Florida, back in the 1960s.

Falling away, then finding my way

Unfortunately, around the age of thirteen, I dropped out of church altogether, primarily because of a lack of interest in religious matters. Several years later, I began playing keyboard in a rock band that performed all over the state of Florida (which was not a good thing, but I learned some very important life-lessons). Then off to Florida State University, in Tallahassee, to pursue a major in either oceanography or orchestration. But all those hopes and dreams came to a screeching halt when I had a near-death experience during my freshman year.

After that unplanned, near-departure from this world, my priorities changed radically. Even educational pursuits seemed shallow and meaningless when measured against eternity. So, I dropped out of college with a dual purpose in mind: to search for truth and for God until I found both. Intentionally, I wiped the religious slate clean and began at what I hoped was an unbiased starting point.

Like so many in that "flower child generation" (the latter 60s), I was greatly influenced by the Far Eastern and New Age megatrends that swept through the western world. I got so involved in yoga that I began teaching it at four universities and also running a yoga ashram in the Tampa, Florida, area. (I cover this phase of my life in greater depth in a free, downloadable, 64-page mini-book titled, *The Highest Adventure: Encountering God,* available in multiple languages on my comparative religion website: www.thetruelight.net. I pray it is a blessing to you.)

Reverting back to a Bible-based worldview arrived at the front door of my life unanticipated. Larry, a former college friend, after being out of touch for six months, sent me a letter with an update on his spiritual condition. While attending Florida State University, we both embraced a more pluralistic worldview, convinced that all religions were equally legitimate paths to the same "Ultimate Reality." Then one astonishing day, as Larry walked into a church, he heard an audible voice declare, "Jesus is the only way." At that precise moment, he claimed the Spirit of God came upon him, filled his heart powerfully, and he was "born again." I was stunned for two reasons. First, I was very acquainted with Larry's belief system, and this new Bible-based approach was a complete departure from it, and second, I had no idea what he meant by being "born again." No one had ever mentioned that intriguing concept to me before.

Even though I initially dismissed his claims, that letter kindled a fire in my heart. For several weeks, my mind swirled with various questions comparing Far Eastern religions to the Christian worldview. Finally, I decided to pursue the answers in prayer. I dedicated an entire day to Jesus, reading the Bible and seeking Him, from early in the morning until late in the afternoon, asking the Lord if this "born again" experience was real to give me a sign. I expected something supernatural to happen: a voice, a vision, a supernatural visitation— something truly undeniable. But God decided to respond in His own unique way, as He usually does.

The divinely orchestrated turning point

In the early evening of that same day, I was hitchhiking to the University of South Florida to teach a yoga class, but still focused on getting an answer to the questions echoing inside. (By the way, at that point, part of my spiritual discipline included a commitment to own no material things, so I had to hitchhike or walk everywhere.) With my thumb stuck out, standing on the side of the road, I was still praying, "Jesus, this is Your day! If You're truly the only way to eternal life, show me. Give me a sign."

Whenever I share the details of how God answered that petition, I overflow with gratitude. Remembering how He orchestrated a pivotal meeting with the right person, at the right place, at the right time is still so awe-inspiring to me.

Unknown to me, an interdenominational prayer group in Tampa had been praying for me for several weeks that I would have an encounter with the Lord Jesus. One of the members of that group just happened to be about two miles away from me when I stepped out on the road to catch a ride, and he just happened to be a former student of yoga himself. (Isn't that a prime example of something I call "sacred synchronicity"?)

Kent was a college student, walking in a laundromat with an armful of dirty clothes, ready to take care of a boring, but needful task. He was somewhat startled when the Spirit of God emphatically spoke to his heart, "Don't go in there. Get back in your van and start driving. I have a job for you to do."

Those were all the instructions the Holy Spirit gave. Even though Kent was a new Christian and not used to God interrupting his plans, thankfully, he obeyed that impulse. He had no idea that he was about to meet someone he and his prayer group had been praying for almost a month. As he drove, whenever he felt an impression, he turned, and eventually, was led to the very spot where I was standing with my hand extended. (I don't call that a coincidence—I call it a "God-incidence.")

Even though he had a cardinal rule never to pick up hitchhikers, Kent felt that nudge from God again—so he pulled over. When I opened the door and looked in, my heart jumped—because on the ceiling of his 1960s Volkswagen Van, Kent had taped a picture of Jesus. I knew it was my answer. I knew this was my sign. I was full of anticipation, waiting for something to happen. After a few normal, introductory statements, the man at the wheel blurted out, "Friend, can I ask you a question?" I quickly responded, "Sure."

He bluntly asked, "Have you ever experienced Jesus coming into your heart." I immediately replied, "No, but when can I?" He looked at me incredulously, never imagining I would give in so quickly. He offered, "You can come to our prayer meeting tonight." I countered, "I don't want to wait for a prayer meeting. I've been praying all day. If I can find Jesus, I want to find Him right now." Thrilled over my openness and eagerness, Kent pulled into the first available parking lot.

After sharing his own personal conversion story, he opened his Bible and began quoting passages and promises he claimed would radically change my life. For about thirty minutes, we read the Scripture and talked. One passage in the Gospel of John was a major focus:

> *There was a man of the Pharisees*
> *named Nicodemus, a ruler of the Jews.*
> *This man came to Jesus by night and said to Him,*
> *"Rabbi, we know that You are a teacher come from*
> *God; for no one can do these signs that*
> *You do unless God is with him."*
> *Jesus answered and said to him, "Most assuredly,*
> *I say to you, unless one is born again, he*
> *cannot see the kingdom of God."*
> *Nicodemus said to Him, "How can a man be born*
> *when he is old? Can he enter a second time into*
> *his mother's womb and be born?"*
> *Jesus answered, "Most assuredly, I say to you, unless*
> *one is born of water and the Spirit, he cannot*
> *enter the kingdom of God.*
> *That which is born of the flesh is flesh, and*
> *that which is born of the Spirit is spirit.*
> *Do not marvel that I said to you,*
> *'You must be born again.'"*
> *(John 3:1-7)*

My newfound friend assured me that same experience could be mine. I could be "born again." Jesus Christ would dwell in my heart through faith (a promise found in Ephesians 3:17). All I had to do was ask, believing. If I did, I could encounter Him in a real way and have a genuine relationship with the Savior of my soul. It didn't take long for me to decide. At that point, I was so thirsty for God. As soon as he finished talking, I nodded my head and said, "I'm ready. Let's pray."

We knelt together in the back of that van and sought God. As I poured out my soul, I felt a spiritual warmth in my heart, a tangible awareness of the divine Presence. I knew it was happening—spiritual rebirth—something far more profound than doctrines, creeds, rituals, traditions, or ceremonies. As simply as I can put it, it was JESUS!

So much changed. My heart was filled with a peace that passes understanding. I knew I'd found the truth. I knew I was saved. Most importantly, I had an absolute assurance that I had eternal life and heaven was my final destination. The Holy Spirit convicted my heart to immediately stop teaching yoga at all four universities, since it stems from Hinduism, and to shut down my yoga ashram.

I knew I had to make a clean break with past spiritual pursuits. So, I went back to all of my classes that week and told them that un-knowingly I had misled them, and that Jesus is the only way. Many of my yoga students became Christians as well. Soon after that, I joined an interdenominational Christian commune in Central Florida where we had Bible studies and prayer gatherings every night of the week. I knew without a doubt that I had finally found the answer. It truly was like the dawning of a new day.

(*For a more detailed presentation of what it means to be "born again," go to the Addendum.*)

Worshiping in spirit and in truth

After I was born again, I became zealous about reading the Bible in its entirety. That was something I never did as a practicing Catholic. We normally just read the catechism, which contains excerpts from Scripture. However, when I started digging into the whole Word of God, I found a gold mine of revelation that transformed my thinking on many important issues.

As you examine the answers I give to the twenty-five questions that come next, I urge you to take to heart Jesus' famous conversation with "The Woman at the Well." In it, He made the enduring statement:

> *"But the hour is coming, and now is, when the true*
> *worshipers will worship the Father in spirit and truth;*
> *for the Father seeks such to worship Him.*
> *God is a Spirit: and they that worship Him must*
> *worship Him in spirit and in truth."*
> *(John 4:23-24 KJV/A)*

According to this wonderful counsel from the Savior, to qualify as "true worshipers," Christians must worship God two primary ways: "in spirit" and "in truth." But what do those two directives mean?

Worshiping "in spirit"—This requirement first means adoring God from the heart, instead of participating in religious traditions and rituals out of sense of obligation. However, it involves much more. This exceptional spiritual state is only fully possible when a person is born again and receives a "new spirit" infused with God's Spirit (an experience that is also called "regeneration"). That establishes a connection with the Creator that can be achieved no other way. It is the wonderful reality of being truly cleansed by the blood of Jesus and reconciled to God. (See Ezekiel 36:26, Titus 3:5.)

Worshiping "in truth"—This mandate is fulfilled two main ways. We worship "in truth":

- When we seek God with a sincere and honest heart,
- When we discover truth in God's Word and apply it to our lives, conforming our beliefs, our attitudes, our actions, and our approach to God by those clear biblical standards.

In the ensuing pages, we will focus on twenty-five beliefs of the Catholic Church—comparing those doctrines and practices to the treasury of revelation found in the Bible.

If we cling to God's Word above religious beliefs, traditions, and rituals, and take God's directives over our own opinions, it is quite possible that we will emerge as the "true worshipers" that the Father is seeking.

What a wonderful thought!

Two Biblical Promises for You

"However, when He, the Spirit of truth, has come,
He will guide you into all truth."
(John 16:13)

"If you abide in My word, you are My disciples
indeed. And you shall know the truth, and
the truth shall make you free."
(John 8:31-32)

Question 1

Is the Catholic Church the one true church, the Mother-church to which all Protestants should return?

There are twenty-four different expressions of Catholicism, with approximately 1.3 billion adherents worldwide. The Roman Catholic Church (also known as the Latin Church or Western Catholic Church) has the largest membership (about 98.6%). Twenty-three other Catholic Churches make up the Eastern Catholic Church (totaling only about 18 million members). This includes divisions such as, the Armenian Catholic Church, the Coptic Catholic Church, and the Ethiopian Catholic Church). They all have autonomy (described as *sui iuris*—a Latin phrase meaning "of one's own right"), however, they are in submission to the pope, who is also recognized as the Bishop of Rome. Though united in essential areas of dogma and practice, the liturgical rites of these various expressions of Catholicism may differ in some ways.

The word "Catholic" means universal—an implication that the Catholic Church in its entirety is the universal church. The Roman Catholic Church is, in a sense, the hub of the wheel; it is the Roman rite or the Roman tradition out of which the other spokes extend.[1]

The exclusive claims of Catholicism

Numerous times through the centuries, in council meetings and by means of official papal documents, the belief has been reaffirmed that the Catholic Church claims to be the one true church. The Fourth Lateran Council of the Catholic Church held in 1215 A.D. released the declaration: "There is one Universal Church of the faithful, outside of which there is absolutely no salvation."[2]

The Council of Trent, held just over three centuries later (1545-1563 A.D.), was conducted primarily to respond to the growing influence of the Protestant Reformation. It also asserted that the Catholic Church is the "mother and mistress of all churches," and is the "true . . . faith, outside of which no one can be saved."[3]

In an encyclical entitled *Mortalium Animos*, released on January 6, 1928, Pope Pius XI, referring to the Catholic Church and the papacy, insisted, "In this one Church of Christ no man can be or remain who does not accept, recognize and obey the authority and supremacy of Peter and his legitimate successors."[4] He also stated concerning other Christian denominations, "If, as they continually state, they long to be united with Us and ours, why do they not hasten to enter the Church, 'the Mother and mistress of all Christ's faithful'? Let them hear Lactantius crying out: 'The Catholic Church is alone in keeping the true worship. This is the fount of truth, this the house of Faith, this the temple of God: if any man enter not here, or if any man go forth from it, he is a stranger to the hope of life and salvation.'"[5]

A statement released after the Vatican II Council (1962-65) reasserts, "It is through Christ's Catholic Church alone, which is the general means of salvation, that the fullness of the means of salvation can be obtained."[6] However, the same document provided a bridge for wayward Christians to return, instructing, "Catholics must joyfully acknowledge and esteem truly Christian endowments derived from our common heritage, which are to be found among our separated brethren, and they must strive for the re-establishment of unity among all Christians, by making a common effort of purification and renewal."[7]

Catholicism is based on the unchanging premise that there are no other legitimate expressions of true Christianity. Protestant sects and non-denominational Christian groups are apparently considered "separated brethren" who must be "purified" of false beliefs and experience a "renewal" of commitment to the Mother Church. Any reunification must include submission to the pope as the Vicar of Christ and embracing the doctrines and sacraments of the church. There is no middle ground. Although this is the official stance of the

Catholic Church, I recognize that there are many genuine, loving Catholics who are more lenient, more liberal, more acceptant of those who belong to non-Catholic Christian denominations, or non-denominational Christian churches, and I deeply appreciate that graciousness. Regardless, the foundation of Catholic doctrine in this area remains unchanged.

What is the true church?

This idea that the Catholic Church is the only true church was ingrained in me as a child. However, I am now convinced that view is neither theologically, nor logically correct. I am persuaded that the true "church" is not identified by the membership role of any organization, Catholic or otherwise. Just because someone bears a denominational title—"Catholic," "Greek Orthodox," "Baptist," or "Lutheran," etcetera—that does not automatically indicate inclusion in the family of God.

The true "church" is not an organization, but an organism (a living body of believers), bound together by common beliefs and by a common experience of heart. It is comprised of all who have been born again, "made alive" in Christ—having received the indwelling of God's Spirit which results in the "regeneration" of a new spirit that is "created . . . in true righteousness and holiness" (Titus 3:5, Ephesians 2:1; 4:24).

The Professing Church—Catholics make up about half of the 2.6 billion adherents to Christianity worldwide. All of these (Catholic, Protestants, and non-denominational Christians) comprise that group which could be termed the "professing church" (those who "profess" faith in a historical Christ—His divine origin, virgin birth, sinless life, message, death, burial, resurrection, and ascension).

The Possessing Church—In the nucleus of the "professing church," there is a smaller-in-number group that could be termed the "possessing church" (those who not only "profess" faith in a historical Christ, but actually "possess" a personal relationship with Him and a commitment to living a Word-based lifestyle). Believers from many denominations, and those who have no denominational affiliation whatsoever, can be found within this smaller group. The "possessing church" is the true church. Its members are not listed in a manmade directory; they are spiritually discerned, and are "registered in heaven," in the "book of life" (Hebrews 12:23, Philippians 4:3).

Knowing Him, not just knowing about Him

The next few sentences are extremely important. Please underscore them in your mind and heart. It is not enough to just intellectually assent to the historical existence of the Lord Jesus and what He accomplished. True believers not only know *about Him*; they *know Him*—personally. That truth is confirmed in one of the opening lines of Jesus' great intercessory prayer for all New Testament believers to come. He declared:

> *"This is eternal life, that they may know You, the only*
> *true God, and Jesus Christ whom You have sent."*
> *(John 17:3)*

Notice, the Savior did not say, "That they may know *about* You, Father"; He said, "That they may *know* You, the only true God, and Jesus Christ whom You have sent." In another passage, Jesus also declared:

> *"I am the good shepherd; and I know My sheep,*
> *and am known by My own."*
> *(John 10:14)*

All the years I functioned as a Catholic, I was faithful. I loved God. I had a passion to serve God. I thought seriously about becoming a priest or a monk. I trusted in the Gospel and participated in the sacraments, but I did not know Jesus personally. No one ever explained to me how to invite Him into my heart and life. Yet that is the core essence of true Christianity.

Being begotten of the Word of God and born of the Spirit of God work together to bring those who are thirsty into a real relationship with the Everlasting Father. (See James 1:18, John 3:5, and more information in the Addendum.) Receiving "the Word of life" and "the Spirit of life" into our hearts together impart the gift of eternal life (1 John 1:1, Romans 8:2). These are impartations that come from God. They cannot be imparted through a mere organization.

The true church is not built by any program, outreach, or religious effort. "Unless the LORD builds the house, they labor in vain who build it" (Psalms 127:1). Rather, it is bound together by a common experience of heart: a spiritual encounter with the Savior of the world.

Acts 2:47 reveals, "The Lord added to the church daily" those who were saved. The apostles and disciples did not accomplish it by their efforts alone; God did it—supernaturally.

It works the same today.

Question 2

Is the pope the sole Vicar of Christ on earth; did he inherit this status from Peter, and is he infallible in all his decisions and declarations?

All Catholics are taught to revere the pope as the sole Vicar of Christ (God's chief representative on earth). The official stance is that this position is inherited from Peter, who is considered the first pope and the first Bishop of Rome. The Bible passage often used to prove this doctrine of papal succession is Matthew 16:13-19:

> *When Jesus came into the region of Caesarea Philippi, He asked His disciples, saying, "Who do men say that I, the Son of Man, am?"*
> *So they said, "Some say John the Baptist, some Elijah, and others Jeremiah or one of the prophets."*
> *He said to them, "But who do you say that I am?"*
> *Simon Peter answered and said, "You are the Christ, the Son of the living God."*
> *Jesus answered and said to him, "Blessed are you, Simon Bar-Jonah, for flesh and blood has not revealed this to you, but My Father who is in heaven.*
> *And I also say to you that you are Peter, and on this rock I will build My church, and the gates of Hades shall not prevail against it.*
> *And I will give you the keys of the kingdom of heaven, and whatever you bind on earth will be bound in heaven, and whatever you loose on earth will be loosed in heaven."*

In verse 18, Jesus declared that Simon's name would be Peter (the original Greek is *Petros*). That was not the first time Jesus conferred a name with that meaning on Simon. When this fisherman by trade was first introduced to the Son of God, Jesus made a similar announcement. However, instead of the Greek word *Petros* being used, the Aramaic word *Cephas* was chosen for Simon's new name. Here is the passage:

> *One of the two who heard John speak, and followed*
> *Him, was Andrew, Simon Peter's brother.*
> *He first found his own brother Simon, and said to him,*
> *"We have found the Messiah" (which is translated, the*
> *Christ). And he brought him to Jesus.*
> *Now when Jesus looked at him, He said, "You are*
> *Simon the son of Jonah. You shall be called Cephas"*
> *(which is translated, A Stone). (John 1:40-42, See 1*
> *Corinthians 1:12; 3:22; 15:5, Galatians 2:9)*

Both *Petros* (from the Greek) and *Cephas* (from the Aramaic) mean "a rock" or "a stone"—so Catholic theologians explain, according to Jesus' prophetic words, Peter was "the rock" on which the church would be built. Though I embrace a different interpretation, even if this was the Messiah's intended meaning, Jesus never foretold that there would be a continuation of such an office. Nor did He command that there should be a group of church leaders titled cardinals who would wear red (scarlet) vestments as a symbol of their willingness to shed blood, if necessary, in the defense of the Catholic faith. Nor did He instruct that a college of these cardinals, made up of no more than 120 bishops and Vatican officials, would elect candidates to such an influential position by a two-thirds majority.[8] These are all just religious traditions that developed through the centuries.

The voting process utilized in choosing a pope could be compared to the method the early disciples used to try and fill the apostolic position abdicated by Judas Iscariot. They cast lots between two noted disciples, Barsabas and Matthias. (See Acts 1:12-26.) Because the lot fell on Matthias, they included him as one of the twelve apostles. However, we are not told in Scripture this was actually God's will or something He led them to do. They may have just assumed it was. I tend to think the person divinely ordained to replace Judas was someone altogether unexpected, someone who was intent on destroying the church initially. His name was "Saul of Tarsus," later to be known as Paul, the apostle (Acts 9:11). This seems like a far more logical choice, because Paul actually manifested the "signs of an apostle" (2 Corinthians 12:12). Jesus chose the other eleven by Himself; He could certainly choose the twelfth.

I also tend to believe that the "rock" Jesus referenced in this well-known passage was not Peter, but rather, it was the "rock" of divine revelation. Remember when Simon confessed that Jesus was the Messiah, Jesus responded:

> *"Blessed are you, Simon Bar-Jonah, for flesh*
> *and blood has not revealed this to you,*
> *but My Father who is in heaven.*
> *And I also say to you that you are Peter, and on this*
> *rock I will build My church, and the gates*
> *of Hades shall not prevail against it."*
> *(Matthew 16:17-18)*

Look closely at the wording and the construction of the sentence. Jesus did not say, "I've given you this name that means 'a rock,' Peter, because on *you* I will build My church." Instead, it seems more likely that His statement communicated something like the following:

> People have not convinced you of my identity, Peter; My Father in heaven has revealed this to you, and on this rock of divine revelation, I will build My church and will empower them to overcome Hades itself. Those who receive this inspired insight will not be shaken from it.

Whether or not this interpretation is right is inconsequential. It is true that Jesus *could* have meant Peter when He spoke of the foundation "rock" of the church. However, even if He did, He never commanded that such a superior apostolic office be established perpetually.

The infallibility of the pope

There are two expressions of infallibility in Catholicism: ordinary and extraordinary. Ordinary infallibility happens when the bishops throughout the world, along with the pope, agree on certain tenets dealing with faith and morals. Extraordinary infallibility applies to the pope himself. Ecumenical councils are also considered infallible when they make solemn decrees on faith and morals. (The word "ecumenical" means from the whole world.)

Though assumed by many Catholics throughout the history of the church, the infallibility of the pope has never been an established Catholic doctrine until the last 150 years. It was formally declared during the First Vatican Council held in 1869-70 when Pope Pius IX was in office.[9] Strangely, centuries prior, in 1334, Pope John XXII issued a bull titled *Quia Quorundam* in which the concept of papal infallibility was described as a doctrine or work of the devil.[10] So two different popes, whose opinions are supposed to be inspired and authoritative, expressed two very different opinions on this issue.

Many Catholics and non-Catholics are unaware that the Pope is only considered infallible at certain choice times.

There are four criteria for papal infallibility:

1. The pope must be speaking about faith and morals.

2. He cannot introduce a new doctrine and declare it infallible. It must be handed down through tradition and Scripture.

3. He must be speaking officially in his role as the head of the Catholic Church.

4. He must officially declare that what he is teaching is infallible.

That level of indisputable authority occurs only when the pope claims to be speaking *ex cathedra* (which means *from the seat*—an implication that the message is coming *from the papal throne* or more perfectly, *from the seat of Peter).*

This belief is based on a statement Jesus made at the end of His conversation with Peter, promising him the power of "binding" and "loosing." Here is the exact quote:

> *"And I will give you the keys of the kingdom of heaven,*
> *and whatever you bind on earth will be bound in*
> *heaven, and whatever you loose on earth*
> *will be loosed in heaven." (Matthew 16:19)*

These phrases Jesus used were well-known Hebrew idioms in that day, used in the Mishna, the oral tradition of the Jews. To "bind" meant to prohibit certain behaviors and beliefs by indisputable authority; to "loose" meant to allow or establish them by indisputable authority. Did Jesus give this authority exclusively to Peter, to be passed down to his successors? Absolutely not! The same promise with the same wording was made to all the disciples two chapters later:

> *"Assuredly, I say to you, whatever you bind on earth*
> *will be bound in heaven, and whatever you loose*
> *on earth will be loosed in heaven."*
> *(Matthew 18:18)*

The Complete Jewish Bible renders it this way:

> *"Yes! I tell you people that whatever you prohibit on*
> *earth will be prohibited in heaven, and whatever you*
> *permit on earth will be permitted in heaven."*
> *(Matthew 18:18 CJB)*

All believers who fulfill the call to discipleship, who are truly walking with God, who are living a life of sacrifice and abiding in truth, are authorized to declare and establish the biblical, New Covenant standard of truth in this world.

All sincere, yielded, and dedicated sons and daughters of God are "ambassadors of Christ," commissioned to share moral, religious, and spiritual guidelines with all those they influence (2 Corinthians 5:20). You could also describe that responsibility as "binding" and "loosing," just as Jesus did. This is the true meaning of that passage.

The full list of "infallible" statements

Read the subtitle above one more time. Then imagine how long this "full list" might be before you go to the next page. You are probably expecting a lengthy record of hundreds of papal pronouncements spoken over many centuries. Surprise! Only two papal declarations have officially been labeled *ex cathedra*—yes, only two:

- Pope Pius IX claimed infallibility in asserting the doctrine of the Immaculate Conception of Mary in 1854, in his bull titled

"Ineffabilis Deus" ("grandfathered in after the First Vatican Council's declaration of papal infallibility in 1870").

- Pope Pius XII claimed infallibility in proclaiming the doctrine of the Assumption of Mary as an article of faith in the Catholic Church, November 1, 1950.[11]

Both these Marian doctrines are extra-biblical and were never a part of the New Covenant belief system espoused by the early church. (They will be more fully examined later in this book.)

If papal infallibility is true, then these two doctrines are indisputable. They cannot be questioned by any Catholic. However, because they are not supported by Scripture, they absolutely should be questioned—by Catholics and non-Catholics alike—as well as the legitimacy of this extreme claim that popes can speak, at certain times, without error—or, as *ex cathedra* implies, "*from the seat of Peter.*"

Though papal infallibility has been executed only twice, through the centuries, "the Magisterium" has expressed numerous decisions on matters of faith and morals considered infallible, especially during the decision-making process of ecumenical councils.

The word "Magisterium" is from the Latin word *magister* meaning teaching. Within Catholicism, it means three primary, related things:

1. The authority imparted to the Catholic Church to teach the doctrine of Christ,

2. The authorities in the church who together validate and teach those doctrines (the pope—who is the Bishop of Rome—as well as all the other bishops in the church, united together),

3. The authorized teachings themselves.

(More information on the Magisterium is in Appendix #8.)

The meaning of papal titles

Believers outside the Catholic Church would most likely agree unanimously that no single individual should ever be considered the sole Vicar of Christ, the chief representative of the Lord Jesus Christ in this world. The Bible instead insists there is only "One God" and "one mediator between God and men, the man Christ Jesus" (1 Timothy

2:5). Besides, it is possible that the early church had plurality of leadership. Paul visited Jerusalem and perceived that "James, Cephas, and John" (all three) were "pillars" in the church, and normally, pillars in a building are of equal height (Galatians 2:9).

The Bible clearly reveals that God ordains apostles, prophets, pastors, teachers, and evangelists in the church (the fivefold ministry) to represent Him and to fill various offices of ministerial authority and service. (See Ephesians 4:10-12.) Scripture also confirms the status of bishops and elders (1 Timothy 3:1, 1 Peter 5:1). But the Bible never suggests that there should be a "chief apostle" or "supreme shepherd" at the head of the church other than the Son of God who is called, "the Apostle and High Priest of our confession" (Hebrews 3:1). Jesus is also referred to—ironically, by the apostle Peter—as "the Shepherd and Bishop of our souls" and "the Chief Shepherd" (1 Peter 2:5, 5:4). Jesus alone qualifies for these excellent entitlements, because:

> *He is the head of the body, the church, who is the*
> *beginning, the firstborn from the dead, that in all things*
> *He may have the preeminence.*
> *(Colossians 1:18, See Ephesians 5:23)*

The meaning of the word "pope"

The word "pope" is not found in the Bible. According to the Catholic Encyclopedia, it comes from the "ecclesiastical Latin *papa*," and the "Greek *papas*," and is "a variant of *pappas*, [meaning] father."[12] Is it acceptable for this title to be used for a religious leader? Jesus taught otherwise, instructing His disciples:

> *"Do not call anyone on earth your father; for One is*
> *your Father, He who is in heaven."*
> *(Matthew 23:9)*

In all fairness, though, there seem to be biblical exceptions to this injunction. For instance, Paul described both Titus and Timothy as his "sons in the faith," inferring his position as their spiritual father. (1 Timothy 1:2, Titus 1:4.) He also exhorted the Corinthian church:

> *For though you might have ten thousand instructors in*
> *Christ, yet you do not have many fathers; for in Christ*

> *Jesus I have begotten you through the gospel.*
> *(1 Corinthians 4:15)*

There is no indication, however, that this word was consistently used for Paul in acknowledging his status. He was never referenced as "Father Paul." It was a symbolic, relational description, not an official title. Paul was a spiritual father to Timothy and Titus because apparently, he had brought them into the kingdom, cared about them, and was personally involved in their lives, helping them to become spiritually mature leaders.

So, the title "pope" is probably meant to be a warm, affectionate term—a way of proclaiming that the person occupying this position is the respected patriarchal head of the Catholic "family," not just the leader of an organization. However, Ephesians 3:15 indicates that the "whole family in heaven and earth" is named after the name of Jesus, so He alone should receive this recognition.

Pontifex Maximus

The pope is also referred to as "Pontifex Maximus" (Latin for the greatest priest or chief priest). He is also called "the Supreme Pontiff of the Universal Church." The word "pontiff" was originally used for the members of "the college of priests" in the ancient, religion of the Roman empire. That polytheistic worldview involved the worship of many false gods and goddesses. Such deities are, indisputably, the product of human imagination. Paul revealed that they are demons masquerading as divine beings. (See 1 Corinthians 10:20-22.)[13] Though "Pontifex Maximus" began strictly as a religious title for pagan priests, it was eventually assigned to political leaders of the empire as well, beginning with Augustus.[14]

Regarding the Catholic use of this title, it is logical that it be conferred on a religious leader who presides over nearly half-a-million subordinate priests worldwide. However, biblically and technically, once again, such an exalted status belongs to Jesus alone, for He is "the Great High Priest" (the true and eternal "Pontifex Maximus") according to the following verse:

> *Seeing then that we have a great High Priest who has*
> *passed through the heavens, Jesus the Son of God,*

let us hold fast our confession.
*For we do not have **a High Priest** who cannot*
sympathize with our weaknesses, but was in all points
tempted as we are, yet without sin.
Let us therefore come boldly to the throne of grace,
that we may obtain mercy and find grace
to help in time of need.
(Hebrews 4:14-16)

Two other important points need to be made:

- **Symbolic meaning**—Though the etymological roots of this title are not certain, it has been suggested that the word "pontifex" comes from a combination of the Latin word for "bridge" and the suffix for "maker"—so the title "Pontifex Maximus" means the greatest bridge builder.[15] Once again, this role and this position belong to Jesus alone, for He is the One who built the bridge from time to eternity, from earth to heaven, through His death and resurrection.

- **Overflow from the Old Testament**—The concept of an earthly "high priest" is an overflow from the Old Testament way of doing things, which was certainly right, relevant, and revealed by God for that season, but no longer correct, for the New Covenant has drastically altered the divine order.

Good popes and bad popes

Some popes have been very influential in promoting righteous causes and establishing justice in the world. For instance, Pope John Paul II was a key player in the destabilization of communism in eastern Europe from 1979 to 1989. What an accomplishment that was! But not all popes have exhibited the godly character expected of someone filling such a notable and respected position. Through the centuries, there have even been some very corrupt popes.

You can easily do the research yourself if you want to verify that claim. However, I am not interested in citing specific examples, because corruption can be found in the leadership of many religious organizations. An expose' of immorality, greed, violence, or ungodly behavior would accomplish little or nothing—except in proving that the office of the pope has not always been occupied with saintly individuals who were shining examples of holiness. Instead, some have been erring, sin-prone human beings in need of redemption, just like the rest of us, at certain stages of our earthly journey.

Question 3

Is infant baptism biblical, and is eternal life granted at the moment of sprinkling?

The Bible records Jesus being dedicated to God as an infant. Leviticus 12:1-8 commands that forty days after the birth of a son and eighty days after the birth of a daughter, Jewish parents were to bring their newborn child to the tabernacle (later on, to the temple) to be dedicated to the Lord. That was the time required in the Law of Moses (the Torah) for the cleansing of the mother. One of the Gospel writers mentioned when this took place for the infant Jesus:

> *Now when the days of her purification according to*
> *the law of Moses were completed, they brought Him to*
> *Jerusalem to present Him to the Lord*
> *(as it is written in the law of the Lord, "Every male who*
> *opens the womb shall be called holy to the Lord"),*
> *and to offer a sacrifice according to what is said in the*
> *law of the Lord, "a pair of turtledoves*
> *or two young pigeons."*
> *(Luke 2:22-24)*

This biblical story could be used to support infant dedication (minus animal sacrifices, of course, which were part of the Old Testament ritual, yet have since been phased out). But there is no precedent and no prescribed Scriptural procedure for infant baptism. Jesus, who is our example, was baptized as an adult, at the age of thirty. (See Luke 3:23.) The biblical account is one of the most powerful and moving stories and is found in three of the four Gospels.

> *Then Jesus came from Galilee to John*
> *at the Jordan to be baptized by him.*
> *And John tried to prevent Him, saying, "I need to be*
> *baptized by You, and are You coming to me?"*
> *But Jesus answered and said to him, "Permit it to be so*
> *now, for thus it is fitting for us to fulfill all*
> *righteousness." Then he allowed Him.*
> *When He had been baptized, Jesus came up*
> *immediately from the water; and behold, the heavens*
> *were opened to Him, and He saw the Spirit of God*
> *descending like a dove and alighting upon Him.*
> *And suddenly a voice came from heaven, saying, "This*
> *is My beloved Son, in whom I am well pleased."*
> *(Matthew 3:13-17)*

Now fast-forward about three-and-a-half years. Right before closing out His ministry on the earth and ascending into heaven from the Mount of Olives, Jesus commanded His followers to make baptism a required part of a true conversion experience:

> *"Go therefore and make disciples of all the nations,*
> *baptizing them in the name of the Father and of the*
> *Son and of the Holy Spirit, teaching them to observe all*
> *things that I have commanded you; and lo, I am with*
> *you always, even to the end of the age." Amen.*
> *(Matthew 28:19-20)*

He is also recorded saying:

> *"He who believes and is baptized will be saved."*
> *(Mark 16:16)*

On the day of Pentecost, after the power of the Holy Spirit fell in the upper room, Peter preached the first sermon of the New Testament era. He then finished his message by presenting the following mandate with its associated promises:

> *"Repent, and let every one of you be baptized in the*
> *name of Jesus Christ for the remission of sins; and you*
> *shall receive the gift of the Holy Spirit. For the promise*
> *is to you and to your children, and to all who are afar*

off, as many as the Lord our God will call."
(Acts 2:38-39)[16]

Even though Peter indicated the promise was for our children, he never implied that baptism should be administered to infants. Both of my children were baptized at a young age, but only after they expressed a sincere desire to acknowledge Jesus as Lord of their lives.

Another important book of Acts example involves the apostle, Philip. After he finished sharing the Gospel with the Ethiopian eunuch, that government official responded, "See, here is water. What hinders me from being baptized?" Then Philip said, "If you believe with all your heart, you may." The eunuch replied, "I believe that Jesus Christ is the Son of God." Clearly, a spiritual kind of informed consent was necessary then and should still be expected now. Philip would have withheld baptism from the eunuch if he did not truly, deeply, and thoroughly believe. (See Acts 8:26-39.) It should be withheld from infants also. Babies cannot believe with all their heart.

In these examples, it is clear baptism was only administered to individuals mature enough to sincerely repent, believe the Gospel, and commit to a life of discipleship. A newborn cannot fulfill these directives.

Household baptisms

Supporters of infant baptism often point out that certain individuals in the early church, after their conversion, had their entire households participate with them in baptism. However, the Scripture never even suggests that infants were included or children so young that they could not comprehend the meaning of the rite. For proof, check out this list of the four "household" baptisms recorded in the Bible, reading the passages yourself:

1. Cornelius' household (See Acts 10:1-48).

2. Lydia's household (See Acts 16:11-15).

3. The Philippian jailer's household (Acts 16:16-34).

4. Stephanas's household (1 Corinthians 16:15).

One thing is undeniable—the Bible does not promote the practice of sprinkling during the rite of baptism. The very word "baptism" is descriptive of full immersion. That was the way it was administered to the Lord Jesus Christ Himself and all who became part of the church in the beginning.

The Jewish followers of the Lord understood this, because baptism in the New Testament was an overflow of the ritual *miqvah* bath of the Old Testament era, which was required of priests before ministering to God in the temple, as well as other purposes. To this day, for a *miqvah* to be "kosher" and the purification process to be effective, observant Jews insist that full immersion is necessary.[17] The same is true for the New Covenant practice of water baptism. Even if we are Gentiles, we want to be "kosher," right?

Contracting the disease of sin

The phrase "original sin," first used by Augustine, is a traditional way of describing the "origin of sin in the human race" and the passing on of a sinful nature. It was Adam's transgression in the beginning (partaking of the tree of the knowledge of good and evil) that brought a sinful status and a sinful state on all mankind. A corrupt nature, prone to rebellion, and guiltiness before God, has been transferred to all of Adam's offspring because of the fall, as well as a condition of spiritual death. The Catholic Catechism explains it this way: "original sin is called 'sin' only in an analogical sense: it is a sin 'contracted' and not 'committed'—a state and not an act" (CCC 404).

Original sin has been a controversial and debated doctrine among theologians of various Christian denominations for centuries. Without resorting to the use of that terminology, the fact that human beings are brought into this world with a fallen nature is verified by the following scriptures:

> *Behold, I was brought forth in iniquity, and in sin*
> *my mother conceived me.*
> *(Psalms 51:5)*

> *Therefore, just as through one man sin entered the*
> *world, and death through sin, and thus death spread to*
> *all men, because all sinned.*
> *(Romans 5:12)*

> *Therefore, as through one man's offense judgment came*
> *to all men, resulting in condemnation, even so through*
> *one Man's righteous act the free gift came to all*
> *men, resulting in justification of life.*
> *For as by one man's disobedience many were made*
> *sinners, so also by one Man's obedience*
> *many will be made righteous.*
> *(Romans 5:18-19)*

It is a mystery how the transfer of this sin-nature takes place. Are the souls of babies created perfect by God, simultaneous with conception, but then contaminated because of sinful influences they encounter and sinful choices they make? Or are souls created along with bodies during the reproduction process, a combination of the soul of the mother and father, thus inheriting a fallen state all the way from Adam? Is this fallen nature unaffected by spiritual rebirth and in need of being constantly subdued even after a person makes the willful decision to serve God? There are many opinions offered, but the fact of the matter is simple: a battle rages within every human being. Listen to Paul's words that reveal the cry of his heart:

> *For the good that I will to do, I do not do;*
> *but the evil I will not to do, that I practice.*
> *Now if I do what I will not to do, it is no longer*
> *I who do it, but sin that dwells in me.*
> *I find then a law, that evil is present with me,*
> *the one who wills to do good.*
> *For I delight in the law of God according*
> *to the inward man.*
> *But I see another law in my members, warring against*
> *the law of my mind, and bringing me into captivity to*
> *the law of sin which is in my members.*
> *O wretched man that I am! Who will deliver*
> *me from this body of death?*
> *I thank God—through Jesus Christ our Lord! So then,*
> *with the mind I myself serve the law of God,*
> *but with the flesh the law of sin.*
> *(Romans 7:19-25)*

Notice in this passage, Paul does not say the problem is in his soul, but in his flesh. James also indicated an ongoing battle with the lower nature when he exhorted:

> *Let no one say when he is tempted, "I am tempted by*
> *God"; for God cannot be tempted by evil,*
> *nor does He Himself tempt anyone.*
> *But each one is tempted when he is*
> *drawn away by his own desires and enticed.*
> *Then, when desire has conceived, it gives*
> *birth to sin; and sin, when it is*
> *full-grown, brings forth death.*
> *(James 1:13-15)*

Does baptism remove "original sin"?

The Catholic Church teaches that during infant baptism "original sin" is removed, regeneration takes place, the indwelling of the Holy Spirit occurs, placement in the body of Christ happens, and the gift of eternal life is granted. During that ritual, the baptized infant becomes a child of the Almighty God. This doctrinal stance is verified by the following three quotes from a Catholic website:

> "Even if nothing else was said in Scripture implying infant baptism, we could conclude it to be necessary just from this simple fact: babies need to have original sin removed from their souls."[18]

> "The Catholic understanding is that baptism is a sign that effects what it symbolizes, bringing about several things. One of these effects is regeneration— God's very life comes into the person, taking away the guilt of original sin and infusing sanctifying grace into the soul, making the person a new creation."[19]

> "When we are baptized—when we are born again, when we are born of the Spirit—we are in Christ. Infants need to be baptized, just like anyone else, so that they can be "in Christ," so that they can put on Christ,

so that they can become children of God, so that they can become members of the body of Christ, so that they can be granted eternal life."[20]

The Catholic Catechism also offers the serious admonition:

"The Church and the parents would deny a child the priceless grace of becoming a child of God were they not to confer baptism shortly after birth."[21]

If that last quote is true, trying to dissuade others from this practice of infant baptism would be a grievous and terrible offence, robbing innocent, helpless newborn babies of magnificent blessings from God. However, if this doctrine is false, promoting it is just as serious a transgression, because doing so grants false hope that can lock its victims inside the walls of religious deception for their entire lives. So, this is not a trifling matter. For one view to be right, the other must automatically be terribly wrong.

The biblical perspective on baptism

There is no scriptural proof, nor any scriptural precedent, for the astounding claims the previous Catholic quotes make concerning the efficacy of infant baptism. If this concept is true, Catholic children should be some of the godliest in the world, and that certainly is not the case. I and many of my childhood friends are living proof. Just ask the nuns who taught us in grade school. A conscious awareness of surrender to Jesus' Lordship is necessary for regeneration to take place, as the following verse conveys:

But as many as received Him, to them He gave the right to become children of God, to those who believe in His name: who were born, not of blood, nor of the will of the flesh, nor of the will of man, but of God.
(John 1:12-13)

An infant cannot consciously "receive" Jesus as his or her Savior. An infant cannot consciously "believe" in His precious and powerful name. Therefore, an infant, through sprinkling, cannot be "born again" (regenerated). Catholics who believe this is a correct interpretation of biblical truth usually have a genuine, sincere desire to include babies in God's redemptive plan, to protect them, and to impart the best that can be provided to them spiritually—I acknowledge that. However, sincerity is not always proof of veracity. Most likely, we have all been completely wrong about certain religious concepts we sincerely held at various stages of our journey.

Far too often, the tragic result of believing in infant baptism is this: Catholic infants who were never regenerated at baptism grow up to be Catholic adults who assume they have already obtained this salvation experience, so they do not seek after it. So, established church tradition, instead of enriching them, ends up robbing them of the beauty of this life-transforming encounter with the Lord Jesus Christ.

Regeneration

The word "regeneration" only appears twice in the Bible. It is so translated from the Greek word *paliggenesea* (pronounced pal-ing-ghen-es-ee'-ah). One time, it refers to the spiritual rebirth of those who repent and believe; the other instance, it refers to the complete, supernatural transformation of this fallen world and a return to Eden-like, paradise conditions. (See Matthew 19:28.) Here is the passage that describes the "regeneration" of people who become recipients of God's grace:

> *But when the kindness and the love of God*
> *our Savior toward man appeared,*
> *not by works of righteousness which we have done,*
> *but according to His mercy He saved us,*
> *through **the washing of regeneration***
> *and renewing of the Holy Spirit,*
> *whom He poured out on us abundantly*
> *through Jesus Christ our Savior,*
> *that having been justified by His grace we should*
> *become heirs according to the hope of eternal life.*
> *(Titus 3:4-7)*

Does this sound like a spiritual happening taking place in infants or adults? Read this passage again carefully and I believe you will agree, it must be referencing adults, for the following two reasons:

- Regeneration is described coming to those who are capable of attempting religious "works of righteousness" to obtain salvation.
- Regeneration comes to those requiring "mercy" from God because of a sinful past.

Believing that this happens during infant baptism grants a false sense of security to Catholic parents concerning their children. Quite possibly, it could also prevent Catholic adults, many of whom are genuine in their love for God, from receiving the wondrous things the Father desires to impart. Let me restate and reemphasize the dilemma: those who have been sprinkled as infants will most likely assume they already possess certain benefits of the Gospel that only come when a person is truly born again. In the process, unfortunately, James 4:2 is fulfilled: "You do not have because you do not ask."

I participated in all the sacraments of the church growing up (except matrimony, holy orders, and extreme unction, of course), yet I never experienced spiritual rebirth (regeneration) until I consciously, as a nineteen-year-old seeker of truth, repented of my sin and invited Jesus to live in my heart and be Lord of my life. What a transformation I received spiritually as a result, something I am very passionate about sharing with others. My motive is not to "prove I am right" religiously, but rather, to open the door compassionately so that others can experience this incredible spiritual impartation.

Wasn't John the Baptist filled with God's Spirit as an infant?

One reason for the belief that dedicated infants can be filled with the Holy Spirit is what the angel of the Lord said to Zacharias about his soon-to-be-born son, later known as John the Baptist:

> *But the angel said to him, "Do not be afraid, Zacharias,*
> *for your prayer is heard; and your wife Elizabeth will*
> *bear you a son, and you shall call his name John.*
> *And you will have joy and gladness,*
> *and many will rejoice at his birth.*
> *For he will be great in the sight of the Lord, and*
> *shall drink neither wine nor strong drink.*
> ***He will also be filled with the Holy Spirit,***

> *even from his mother's womb.*
> *And he will turn many of the children*
> *of Israel to the Lord their God."*
> *(Luke 1:13-16)*

The assumption is this: if John the Baptist was filled with the Holy Spirit while still an infant, any other child, once dedicated to God, can also be filled with the Holy Spirit. But the Bible never offers such an expectation spiritually. It is just a hypothetical idea based on an isolated event in Scripture that cannot be applied as a general rule for all infants consecrated to God.

Other scriptures that are misinterpreted

One of the main Bible passages, often misinterpreted concerning baptism, is from the conversation Jesus had with Nicodemus. I quoted more of it in the Introduction. Just three verses will be our focus now:

> *Jesus answered, "Most assuredly, I say to you,*
> *unless one is born of water and the Spirit,*
> *he cannot enter the kingdom of God.*
> *That which is born of the flesh is flesh, and*
> *that which is born of the Spirit is spirit.*
> *Do not marvel that I said to you,*
> *'You must be born again.'" (John 3:5-7)*

Quite often, both Catholics and Protestants think that the word "water" in this statement refers to water baptism, so many assume that water baptism and being born of the Spirit happen simultaneously. I believe it means something altogether different. First, Jesus insisted that human beings must be "born of water and the Spirit," then He followed up with the statement, "That which is born of flesh is flesh, and that which is born of Spirit is spirit." So, it can be logically deduced that being "born of water" is the same as being "born of the flesh." It is a reference to the breaking of the water during childbirth when the amniotic sac breaks, and the amniotic fluid pours out.

In other words, Jesus was saying that all those aspiring to heavenly citizenship must pass through two stages to inherit eternal life. First, we must be born into this world as human beings ("born of the water"), to face the trials and tests that are here, to learn the lessons that can only be learned by passing through this fallen world. Second, we must be "born of the Spirit," which is necessary for redemption and restoration to take place, and for the gift of eternal life to be granted. Neither stage can be bypassed on the journey to becoming fully manifested, resurrected, glorified sons and daughters of God—destined to be "heirs of God and joint heirs with Christ" forever (Romans 8:17).

You see, only by deserving judgment can we ever know the mercy of God. Only by making errors can we know the great value of being embraced by His forgiveness. Only by going through pain can we experience the healing that flows from the compassionate heart of Jesus. So, to see God more completely, we must pass through this fallen world that is so opposite to Him in so many ways. Not only do we see Him in greater measure, if we yield to His influence, we also become more like Him—which is truly a lifelong journey. Therefore, to enter the kingdom of God, we must first be "born of the water" (born as human beings in fleshly forms). Then we must be "born of the Spirit," (receiving the regeneration of a new spirit infused with God's Spirit).

What about children who die as infants?

One of the most troubling questions that both Catholic and non-Catholic theologians have wrestled with for centuries is the issue of where infants and little children go if they die. This is certainly a legitimate concern. The doctrine associating salvation with infant baptism grants a comforting assurance of eternal well-being for the children of Catholic families. But what about infants or young children who die without being baptized in the church? What is their eternal destination? To provide an answer to this probing question, the concept of Limbo was proposed among Catholics, probably during the Middle Ages. However, it has never been formally adopted by the church. (See Question #22 for elaboration.)

Actually, we know very little about the afterlife of infants or young children who die at an early age. The primary Scripture passage on which many base their hope is Mark 10:13-15:

> *Then they brought little children to Him, that He might
> touch them; but the disciples rebuked
> those who brought them.*

*But when Jesus saw it, He was greatly displeased and
said to them, "Let the little children come to Me, and do
not forbid them; for of such is the kingdom of God.
Assuredly, I say to you, whoever does not receive the
kingdom of God as a little child will
by no means enter it."*

There are two other parallel passages highlighting this key event in the life of Jesus: Matthew 19:13-15 and Luke 18:15-17. In Matthew and Mark's version of the story, the Scripture states that the people brought "children" to the Lord, so translated from the Greek word *paidion* (pronounced pahee-dee'-on). Luke's version is different, though, using the Greek word *brephos* (pronounced bref'-os), which is properly translated "infants":

*"Then they also brought infants to Him that
He might touch them."
(Luke 18:15)*

The entire three-verse passage is often used as proof of the Catholic concept that infants can be granted the born-again experience through baptism, at which point they are ushered into God's kingdom. However, that interpretation stretches what Jesus said beyond His intended meaning to accommodate a theological stance.

The Savior of mankind never alluded to infant baptism in this passage. However, these often-quoted words of the Messiah do imply that God will somehow mercifully treat those who die in their early years and most likely usher them into His kingdom, when their souls leave their bodies. Also, He made no stipulation concerning the belief system, race, religion, nationality, or culture those children belong to; instead, it seems to be an all-inclusive statement. Therefore, the real meaning of Jesus' words remains a great mystery. Such a view cannot be proposed with absolute assurance, but it seems plausible.

The Bible teaches that Jesus descended into the lower parts of the earth immediately after his death on the cross, to preach the Gospel to the dead. He did that apparently to give Old Testament saints, who had trusted in insufficient animal sacrifices, an opportunity to accept His substitutionary death as their means of salvation, opening the door to Paradise to them. (See Ephesians 4:9, 1 Peter 3:18-20; 4:6.) If He offered such an opportunity to adults in the afterlife, He could certainly do the same for infants and children who die before they understand these important biblical concepts. (Traditionally, this point of maturity is called "the age of accountability"—a concept not clearly defined in Scripture, but implied—See Deuteronomy 1:39.)

The Bible does not go into detail concerning these things, but we do know that God is just, gentle, loving, and compassionate, so whatever the process may be, we can trust that the Everlasting Father will never treat little ones unfairly or unjustly. Yes, in this area of doctrine, we must simply trust.

The circumcision argument

Catholic theologians also propose the following argument concerning infant baptism: that according to Paul's writings, baptism has replaced circumcision and that circumcision was normally administered when a child was eight days old. So, it logically follows that baptism should also be administered to infants. Just as male Jewish children are not old enough to understand or acknowledge the symbolism of the circumcision ritual to which they are subjected (an act that acknowledges their inherited covenant relationship with the God of Abraham), so newborn Christian children do not have to comprehend what is happening to them for baptism to be effective and right. Please consider the following two responses:

Circumcision in the Old Testament—God explicitly commanded that Israelite sons be circumcised on the eighth day (Genesis 17:10-13). But nowhere in the Bible (Old or New Testaments) does God explicitly command the baptizing of infants. This practice is based solely on symbolism and doctrinal assumptions.

Circumcision in the New Testament—Circumcision in this era, though still practiced literally, is representative of a higher spiritual reality. The Complete Jewish Bible of Romans 2:28-29 insists that "the real Jew is not merely Jewish outwardly: true circumcision is not only natural, external, and physical. On the contrary, the real Jew is one inwardly; and true circumcision is of the heart, spiritual not literal; so that his praise comes not from other people but from God." Physical circumcision by itself was and is insufficient to signify the establishing of a covenant relationship with God. Even in ancient times, it was not really efficacious unless the Israelite who was circumcised physically (in his flesh) was also circumcised spiritually (in his heart).

Here is the passage of Scripture some Catholics use to try and prove the connection between circumcision and baptism (as translated in the New Catholic Bible). Speaking to believers in Jesus, Paul insisted:

> *In him also you were circumcised, not with a physical*
> *circumcision but with a spiritual stripping away of the*
> *old nature with the circumcision of Christ.*
> *When you were buried with him in baptism, you were*
> *also raised with him through faith in the power of*
> *God who raised him from the dead.*
> *(Colossians 2:11-12 NCB)*

You may want to read those two verses again, slowly and carefully. Although the thoughts run together, clearly, Paul is not equating baptism with circumcision. Verse eleven shares that when we are "in Christ" (under His Lordship, the position we assume when we are born again) that we are "circumcised with the circumcision made without hands." In other words, God cuts away from our hearts the dominance of carnality and worldliness. We are not entirely free from the lower nature, but we are graced to throw off its control. When verse twelve adds that we are also "buried with Him in baptism," it is not a continuation of the same comparison. It is similar. It is connected; however, it is a different analogy.

- **Circumcision** is an emblem of the cutting away of the curse of a sinful nature and the influence of a fallen world.
- **Baptism** is an emblem, a sacred ceremony, representing the idea that those who are crucified with Christ are buried with Him (dying to self and to this world). Then, just as Jesus rose from the dead, they rise out of this death to self (symbolized by the waters of baptism) to "newness of life"—a new heart, a new beginning, a new life—spiritually resurrected (Romans 6:4).

Let it be emphasized: in both these areas, the substance is far more important than the shadow. The thing symbolized is far more important that the symbol by which it is represented. What baptism represents is far more important than baptism itself. The supernatural transcends and supersedes the natural.

Baptism is a wonderful, God-ordained ritual, but what it represents is far more wonderful. Countless millions of people have been baptized in various Christian denominations, as infants or adults, by sprinkling or immersion. Many such persons have participated in the ritual but never experienced the reality of what was being symbolized. They were never truly buried with Christ (dying to self and to the world); and they were never resurrected with Him (living an overcoming life of victory over sin and oneness with the Father). Thus, they are Christians in name only and baptism was nothing more than an empty ritual. That is a tragedy when it happens—to be so close, yet so far away.

In circumcision and baptism, is parental faith sufficient?

In an article about "Infant Baptism" on a Catholic website, you can find the following explanation about the parental role:

> "The faith of the parents sufficed when it came to circumcising a child. Do we not see that principle in the New Testament as well? Jesus saw the faith of the friends of the paralytic and healed the paralytic in Matthew 9:2. When people cannot have faith, the faith of family or friends suffices. So it is with infant baptism. The faith of the parents sanctifies the children, as Paul says in 1 Cor. 7:14. This is just as much a New Testament concept as it is an Old Testament concept."[22]

Responding to this assertion is dependent on unveiling the meaning of one of the key scriptures mentioned:

> *For the unbelieving husband is sanctified by the wife,*
> *and the unbelieving wife is sanctified by the husband;*
> *otherwise your children would be unclean,*
> *but now they are holy.*
> *(1 Corinthians 7:14)*

The word "sanctified" means two primary things:

1. Cleansed from the defilement of evil,

2. Set apart for God's purposes.

It would be very easy to take Paul's statement beyond its intended meaning. Just because someone is sincerely devoted to God, his or her unconverted spouse (guilty of ungodly behavior) is not automatically saved eternally (fully "cleansed from the defilement of evil"). Of course not! They are sanctified only in the sense that they are dedicated to God by the intercession of the godly partner in the marriage. In a sense, God is legally released, or possibly, prayerfully persuaded, to deal with that person more profoundly. That unsaved spouse possesses a definite advantage spiritually, whether he or she recognizes it or not.

So it is for the children of a devoted parent. God honors the parent's commitment by pouring out a greater measure of grace on the children, to protect them and to guide them, helping them to make the right choices in life. Are they automatically saved? No, they must make the decision on their own to serve God. They are "holy" only in a qualified sense, having been dedicated to God by their parents.

Inanimate things are considered holy if they are dedicated to the Creator. Some examples include: a parcel of ground (Exodus 3:5), the Sabbath (Exodus 20:8), the place where the ark of the covenant was located (Exodus 26:33), and the garments of the priests (Exodus 28:2). Describing these things as "holy" does not mean they are holy by nature, but holy by association or assignment. Parcels of ground, days of the week, storage space under a tent in the wilderness, and clothing to be worn in religious rituals can only be holy by association with God or assignment by God to a sacred purpose.

In a similar fashion, children are "holy" because of association with at least one parent who is actively living a holy life or because they have been prayerfully assigned by their parents or a parent to the purposes of God. Upon reaching an age of being able to understand the difference between good and evil, they must then make the quality decision themselves to serve God to receive from Him the gift of being holy by nature. (See Ephesians 4:22-24.) This pattern, supported by Scripture, is logical and sensible.

As already quoted, in Acts 2:38-39, Peter presented an unequivocal mandate to those who heard him preach his Pentecost message:

*"Repent, and let every one of you be baptized in the
name of Jesus Christ for the remission of sins; and you
shall receive the gift of the Holy Spirit."*

Then he followed up with the statement:

*"For the promise is to you and to your children, and to
all who are afar off, as many as the Lord
our God will call."*

Does that mean "the gift of the Holy Spirit" is automatically given to the children of those who received Peter's admonition? No, it simply means that such a promise will be available to them as they mature in life, if they choose to repent and be baptized.

A final thought on baptism

Peter was also the Bible writer who compared baptism to the flood in Noah's day. Here is the passage making that comparison, speaking of those—

*Who formerly were disobedient, when once the Divine
longsuffering waited in the days of Noah, while the ark
was being prepared, in which a few, that is,
eight souls, were saved through water.
There is also an antitype which now saves us—baptism
(not the removal of the filth of the flesh, but the answer
of a good conscience toward God),
through the resurrection of Jesus Christ.
(1 Peter 3:20-21)*

Being "baptized in water" did not cleanse the world permanently. It soon became corrupt again. It will take a baptism of fire at the end of this age for the process to be fully effective. (See 2 Peter 3:10-12.) Similarly, water baptism, even for an adult, is not sufficient by itself.

Those who desire to truly be dedicated to God should seek Him also for the "baptism with the Holy Spirit and fire" (Matthew 3:11). Water does not have the power to change a person's character, but the "consuming fire" of God's supernatural presence does (Hebrews 12:29). Water baptism does not take away "the filth of the flesh"—for an infant or an adult. Subduing the fallen nature requires impartations from God that are far more powerful. If done properly, though, water baptism is a worshipful indication that someone is attempting to have "a good conscience toward God."

A few months after my conversion, I was baptized in water. It was a very blessed and sacred moment, and the presence of God was present in a very special way, because I understood with my heart what this God-ordained ritual of the church meant. I knew that as I was immersed in the water, I was making a conscious, prayerful decision to be buried with Christ: dead to self, dead to sin, dead to the world, and resurrected in Jesus. I intended to serve Him the rest of my days in newness of life. It was a powerful time of connecting with the heavenly Father in an unforgettable, life-changing, and devoted way.

I pray, if you have never been baptized with the conscious awareness of its profound meaning, that this blessed event will happen soon in your life.

Question 4

Is the concept of an exclusive, ministerial priesthood still part of God's plan?

Before I offer Scriptural responses to the title-question of this chapter, let me first say unequivocally that I have a very deep admiration for those men who have sincerely chosen the sacrificial life of the priesthood. Great love for God, devotion to spirituality, commitment to service, and compassion for others are normally the kind of strong motivations behind such a lifelong decision. Also, there are some priests who have championed social justice and pro-life causes who truly fit in the "hero column" of my memory banks. Now, having revealed my heart in this matter, let's proceed together into the more technical and theological responses to this ancient religious tradition.

The Catechism Stance

The Catholic catechism teaches that there are two divisions of the priesthood: the "common priesthood" (normal Catholics) and the "ministerial priesthood" (clergy).[23] However, I have found that this distinction is not common knowledge, nor is it the actual, functional mindset of most Catholics.

In the Old Testament, the word "priest" is translated from the Hebrew *kohen*, which in essence means one who draws near to God. It speaks of a person authorized to minister in sacred matters who acts as a mediator between people and God. So, the priests of that era were called to draw near to God in worshipful devotion, and then, to represent Him to the Israelite people, officiating in religious observances.

An exclusive priesthood was God's design for that era. God told Moses to anoint his brother, Aaron, as the high priest, and Aaron's sons as priests. That family line served as priests in the tabernacle of Moses, and later, in the temple of Solomon, off and on, for about 1,600 years until Jesus came. The Levites (one of the twelve tribes of Israel) also served in a kind of subordinate priestly capacity, serving fellow Israelites in religious matters. (See Exodus 30:30, Leviticus 21:10, Numbers 3:1-12, Deuteronomy 18:1-8, Jeremiah 33:21.)

However, such a distinction was a "a shadow of good things to come, and not the very image of the things" (Hebrews 10:1). In other words, that system was not God's permanent plan; it was symbolic of something better that He intended to do in the future.

The New Testament era

This concept of an exclusive priesthood was abolished in the New Testament era, a truth plainly revealed in Scripture. Since the coming of the Holy Spirit on Pentecost, every true, born-again believer is called to fill the role of a priest, verified by the following declaration from Peter's epistle, presented to the entire church:

> *If indeed you have tasted that the Lord is gracious.*
> *Coming to Him as to a living stone, rejected indeed by*
> *men, but chosen by God and precious,*
> *you also, as living stones, are being built up a spiritual*
> *house, a holy priesthood, to offer up spiritual sacrifices*
> *acceptable to God through Jesus Christ.*
> *(1 Peter 2:3-5)*

First, this passage describes all of God's people as a "spiritual house" constructed out of "living stones." True born-again believers out of all denominations make up this corporate "temple of the living God," His dwelling place worldwide (2 Corinthians 6:16, See Ephesians 2:19-22). Each believer is also described as an individual "temple" in which the Holy Spirit dwells. (1 Corinthians 3:16-17; 6:19-20.)

Second, this passage describes all of God's people as a "holy priesthood"—a priesthood determined, not by natural birth, but by spiritual rebirth—a priesthood cleansed and made holy, not by the blood of animals, but by the blood of Jesus Christ.

Third, this passage encourages God's people to offer up "spiritual sacrifices" to God. That includes sacrifices of righteousness, sacrifices of thanksgiving, sacrifices of joy, and sacrifices of praise. (See Psalms 4:5; 116:17; 27:6; Hebrews 13:15.) True believers are not only called to *offer* "spiritual sacrifices," they are called to *become* sacrifices to God. Read the following exhortation, presented to the entire church:

> *I beseech you therefore, brethren, by the mercies of God,*
> *that you present your bodies a living sacrifice, holy,*
> *acceptable to God, which is your*
> *reasonable service.*
> *And do not be conformed to this world, but be*
> *transformed by the renewing of your mind, that you*
> *may prove what is that good and acceptable*
> *and perfect will of God.*
> *(Romans 12:1-2)*

What an amazing shift took place after Jesus ascended to heaven! In the Old Testament era, Israelites came prayerfully to the temple, to the priests, for their help in offering sacrifices to God. In this New Testament era, for those who are born again, the ancient methods of approaching God have been lifted to a much higher spiritual reality:

- We are no longer required to go to the temple to offer up worship; we are the temple.
- We are no longer required to go through mediatorial priests to be reconciled to God; we are the priests.
- We are no longer required to bring animal sacrifices to God; we trust in the supreme sacrifice, the crucified Savior, and then in worshipful devotion, we also become "living sacrifices," offered on an altar to Him (Romans 12:1).

Long before this radical paradigm shift took place, God declared prophetically, "Behold, I will do a new thing." (Isaiah 43:19). This "new thing" is a wonderful thing!

Candidates for the priesthood

Jesus launched His earthly ministry in the synagogue at Nazareth by quoting the Messianic prophecy recorded in Isaiah 61:1-2:

*"The Spirit of the Lord GOD is upon Me, because the
LORD has anointed Me to preach good tidings to the
poor; He has sent Me to heal the brokenhearted, to
proclaim liberty to the captives, and the opening of
the prison to those who are bound; to proclaim
the acceptable year of the LORD."*
(See Luke 4:16-19.)

Even though the Messiah spoke only this brief excerpt from the
original prophetic passage, that chapter continues with a more detailed
description of what He would be sent to accomplish:

*To console those who mourn in Zion, to give them
beauty for ashes, the oil of joy for mourning, the
garment of praise for the spirit of heaviness; that they
may be called trees of righteousness, the planting
of the LORD, that He may be glorified.*
(Isaiah 61:3)

Then the prophecy develops three verses later to reveal the new
identity granted to those who would ultimately receive the wondrous,
life-changing ministry of the Messiah in this New Covenant era:

*But you shall be named the priests of the Lord; men
shall call you the ministers of our God.*
(Isaiah 61:6 MEV)

This is an all-inclusive statement. Go back to the first two verses.
All those who receive the "good tidings" of the Gospel, all those
whose broken hearts are healed by the love of Jesus, all those who are
liberated from spiritual captivity and brought out of the prison of the
fallen nature, all those who mourn over their sins and receive God's
comfort, all those who are given "beauty for ashes" (the beauty of a
relationship with God in exchange for the ashes of past defeats in life)
are given the status of being "priests of the Lord." How can this be?

Because such blessed individuals have a story of salvation and redemption to share. They have a testimony—a faith-building witness
that what God has done for them, He will do for others. They are God's
authorized representatives, sent forth into this world to reveal His
name, proclaim His Word, share His grace, and spend the rest of their

lives praising Him. That's what priests do, and that is the God-given role of all those who are born again.

Even in Old Testament times, God promised the entire nation of Israel that if they would observe and obey His commandments, they would be a "kingdom of priests" (Exodus 19:5-6). It was God's deep desire then that all His people fill a priestly role; it is still His deep desire in this present era.

Entering the holy of holies

Under the Old Covenant, only the high priest could enter the holy of holies in the tabernacle of Moses. The ark of the covenant was in that sacred space and the glory cloud of God's presence rested on the top of the ark, which was also called the mercy seat. That was God's representative throne on earth. However, when Jesus died on the cross, the separating veil between the holy place and the holy of holies was "torn in two from top to bottom" (Mark 15:38). That could have been God's intense way of declaring symbolically that the way had been made for all His people to experience His personal presence. A beloved Bible passage validates this interpretation:

> *Therefore, brethren, having boldness to enter*
> *the Holiest by the blood of Jesus,*
> *by a new and living way which He consecrated*
> *for us, through the veil, that is, His flesh.*
> *(Hebrews 10:19-20)*

Think of the profound implications of these two verses. If all true believers can now "enter the Holiest by the blood of Jesus," why would we need the mediation of a priest? It is also true that during the Old Testament era, the high priest could only enter the holy of holies one time a year—on Yom Kippur, the Day of Atonement.

Amazingly, all born-again believers now "have access by one Spirit to the Father"—not just one day of the year, but every moment of every hour of every day (Ephesians 2:18). This is a wonderful truth! But to fully enjoy its reality, those who truly love God and desire spiritual intimacy with Him must break free from established religious traditions that would pull us all back to the old order. The writer of Hebrews indicated that will take "boldness" on our part.

Addressing priests with the title of "Father"

Traditionally, the way to address a priest is with the title, "Father." One admirable thing about Catholics is the respect they normally show for ministry leaders and abiding by this custom is certainly a sign of that. However, as I already shared under Question #2, Jesus taught something much different, instructing His disciples:

> *"Do not call anyone on earth your father; for One is*
> *your Father, He who is in heaven." (Matthew 23:9)*

As far as we know, none of the leaders in the early church were ever addressed this way, not even the most prominent apostles. You never read about Father Timothy, Father Titus, or Father Barnabas. Yes, there are degrees of gifts, callings, and abilities distributed throughout the body of Christ, but we are all equally lost without the redemptive price that Jesus paid and equally saved by that blood.

At times, titles are legitimately tied to specific God-ordained roles in the church (pastor, bishop, apostle, deacon, etc.), however, we must be careful to only use titles according to God's directives. As an inter-denominational minister of the Gospel, I even feel uneasy when people use the title "Reverend" in addressing me. Why? Because the only time that the word "reverend" appears in Scripture, it refers to God:

> *He sent redemption unto his people: he hath*
> *commanded his covenant for ever:*
> *holy and **reverend** is his name.*
> *(Psalms 111:9 KJV)*

The ground is level at the cross. We should just consider ourselves brothers and sisters in the body of Christ and reverence our heavenly Father above all.

Give this truth time to cure

Little things often grab my attention symbolically and add to the treasure chest of metaphors and analogies that I use in my teaching. Here is one that fits right now. During the last five decades of ministry, I have assisted several times in the construction of church buildings. I have helped in just about every aspect of the process, including laying the foundation.

Have you ever watched concrete being poured into a form to provide a strong, solid base for the building being erected? It starts off as a thick, viscous liquid that fills up every corner. Then it must be smoothed out on the top before it hardens or sets. Usually, it takes about forty-eight hours to fully cure. Only then can the rest of the building be erected securely.

In like manner, before you go much further in this book, I encourage you to give this truth about the priesthood time to "cure" in your heart, because it is so foundational to everything else that I share in the ensuing chapters. If the foundation of our faith is going to be stable and strong, it is imperative that we understand all true believers are priests of God—period. All who are born again have access into God's presence, to minister to Him in a priestly capacity. All who have been cleansed from their sins are called to represent God as priestly ambassadors, expressing His love to a fallen world.

It's time that all believers see themselves in this blessed God-given role and break free from religious traditions that deny this right to all but a select few. There was no exclusive group who claimed the status of being "priests" in the early church, and if we are going to replicate authentic New Testament Christianity in this hour, there will no exclusive group within the body of Christ claiming the priesthood status now. So, let us rejoice exceedingly, as the apostles John and Peter did, to declare the following scriptures to every fellow believer in Christ:

> *But you are a chosen generation, **a royal priesthood**,*
> *a holy nation, His own special people, that you may*
> *proclaim the praises of Him who called you out of*
> *darkness into His marvelous light. (1 Peter 2:9)*

> *To Him who loved us and washed us from our sins in*
> *His own blood, and has made us kings and **priests***
> *to His God and Father, to Him be glory*
> *and dominion forever and ever. Amen.*
> *(Revelation 1:5-6)*

> *Blessed and holy is he who has part in the first*
> *resurrection. Over such the second death has no power,*

> *but they shall be **priests of God and of Christ**, and shall*
> *reign with Him a thousand years.*
> *(Revelation 20:6)*

By this last passage, it is apparent that Christians are not only priests of God during this earthly sojourn; they will fill this role for eternity—living forever in the presence of the everlasting Father and worshipfully serving Him in the New Creation. If all true believers will be priests in eternity to come, then all true believers should be recognized as priests during this earthly sojourn through time.

I hope the concrete of this infinite truth sets perfectly in your heart before we proceed. While it is fresh, smooth it over in your mind and your heart. We are building a sacred spiritual structure to enshrine the timeless truths of God's Word. By the end of this book, I believe the final edifice will be a spectacular, doctrinal cathedral raised up for the glory of the Infinite One.

Question 5

Is ecclesiastical clothing for priests, nuns, monks, and other church leaders scriptural?

There is no record scripturally that the leadership in the early church wore ecclesiastical garments to indicate their ministry calling or level of authority in the church. They wore ordinary clothing. They were common people that God used in an uncommon way, but they never sought to identify themselves as clergy by wearing distinctive religious apparel. As is often the case, this practice was carried over from the Old Covenant era, when there *was* an exclusive priesthood who were commanded by God to wear clothing that identified them with their office. God, like a Master Tailor, even gave them specific designs for the unique apparel they were instructed to wear.

All of that changed with the entrance of the New Covenant.

The tradition of religious clothing being assigned to Christian church leaders became more pronounced in the fourth century as Christianity evolved. Then about seven hundred years later, in 1215, during the Fourth Lateran Council, it was made mandatory for all Catholic clergy to wear distinctive dress.[24]

There are two designated types: clerical clothing for ordinary dress and liturgical clothing for sacred ceremonies. These dress policies were intended to make the Catholic leadership easier to recognize on the street and elsewhere; nevertheless, this custom was never a directive from God. There is absolutely no passage in the New Testament that makes this a religious requirement.

The tension between two motivations

Some who wear ecclesiastical garments may do so with a kind of spiritual pride. However, there are many humble-hearted, sincere religious leaders, in both Catholic and Protestant denominations, who wear clerical garments with a different mindset altogether. Conforming to such a religious trend can be a selfless, even courageous act, because those who do so realize that wearing the "uniform" of the clergy subjects them to closer scrutiny by the public. To an even greater degree, they feel the pressure to be exemplary in their behavior—in words, actions, and reactions—because the legitimacy of the Bible hinges on it, at least, in many people's minds. So, no blanket statement about this practice fits all persons and circumstances.

Even though religious garments were required for priests in Jesus' day, He rebuked the religious leaders in Israel, because apparently— for some of them—the practice was feeding their egotism and pride, reinforcing within them a sense of spiritual superiority. Here is one passage that reveals Jesus' stance:

*Then Jesus spoke to the multitudes and
to His disciples, saying:
"The scribes and the Pharisees sit in Moses' seat.
Therefore whatever they tell you to observe, that
observe and do, but do not do according to their
works; for they say, and do not do.
For they bind heavy burdens, hard to bear, and lay
them on men's shoulders; but they themselves will not
move them with one of their fingers.
But all their works they do to be seen by men. They
make their phylacteries broad and enlarge
the borders of their garments.
They love the best places at feasts,
the best seats in the synagogues,
greetings in the marketplaces, and
to be called by men, 'Rabbi, Rabbi.'"
(Matthew 23:1-7)*

Jesus gave an even more stern warning concerning the scribes, who were teachers of the Torah and who made copies of God's Word:

*"Beware of the scribes, **who desire to go around in long***
***robes,** love greetings in the marketplaces, the best seats*
in the synagogues, and the best places at feasts,
who devour widows' houses, and for a pretense make
long prayers. These will receive greater condemnation."
(Luke 20:46-47)

Of course, these were not sincere, devoted servants of God. Quite the contrary, they were hypocritical religious leaders, taking advantage of their position of authority among the people of God for self-gain and self-promotion. Consequently, and quite ironically, though the Lord Jesus was the One who originally gave the design for distinctive priestly dress during the Old Testament era—when He walked the earth, this practice was not viewed by Him in a positive light.

Removing the distinction

Even if clerical garments are worn with humility and the motivation is purely a sense of responsibility, there is one negative aspect to this practice that should be considered. Ecclesiastical clothing serves as a reinforcement in the minds of churchgoers that there is a distinct difference between the "ministry" (those who are qualified for positions of authority in the body of Christ) and the "laity" (those who are not). The word "laity" means common people, and it comes from the Greek *laikos*, meaning "of the people." However, that word, or similar terms like lay minister, layman, or lay person, are not found in the Bible. No such divisions were promoted in the early church.

Admittedly, there are levels of authority in the leadership of the body of Christ (such as, apostles, prophets, bishops, evangelists, teachers, pastors, and deacons). However, all believers are called to be ministers, to one degree or another.

As mentioned in the last chapter, all who receive "beauty for ashes" and "the garments of praise for the spirit of heaviness" are granted this ministry status. Isaiah prophesied concerning all New Covenant people of God to come, saying:

*But you shall be named **the priests of the LORD**;*
*men shall call you **the ministers of our God**.*
(Isaiah 61:6)

Peter also included all believers in his exhortation:

> *As each one has received a gift,* **minister** *it to one*
> *another, as good stewards of the manifold grace of God.*
> *(1 Peter 4:10)*

These two scriptures should lead us to a firm conclusion—that all Christians, regardless of their status, are just "common people" upon whom God has poured out "uncommon grace" and we are all called to minister that grace to others. All true Christians are priests of God. So, if unique garments should be worn by those who qualify for the priesthood, all professing believers in Jesus should adorn themselves in this manner. It is somewhat ironic that one of the greatest believers in the early church, Paul the apostle, described his style of dress in a quite self-defacing way:

> *To the present hour we both hunger and thirst, and we*
> *are poorly clothed, and beaten, and homeless.*
> *(1 Corinthians 4:11)*

Poorly clothed? Did Paul even care about that? I doubt it seriously. Because ecclesiastical garments weren't even a consideration in his mind. Of course, they were following the teachings of the One who said, "Don't worry about your life—what you will eat or drink; or about your body—what you will wear" (Luke 12:22 CJB).

Isn't it amazing that the Son of God Himself did not wear any distinctive clerical clothing, yet He was "the apostle and high priest of our profession of faith," walking among us! (Hebrews 3:1 NCB) If it was not important for Him, why should it be important for any of those who claim to represent Him? If the King of kings did not wear a mitre during His earthly sojourn, why should the pope? If Jesus did not adorn Himself with a zucchetto, a biretta, or a galero (various kinds of ministerial head wear), why would any church leader think that such religious regalia has any importance whatsoever?

The greater glory and beauty of spiritual clothing

In the second book of the Bible, we read of very specific designs being given for priestly garments—and how God indicated it was "for glory and for beauty." However, that was only for those few Israelites who were chosen for that elite ministry position (Exodus 28:2, 40). The spiritual attire, worn by all New Covenant sons and daughters of God, is even more glorious and more beautiful and includes "garments of praise," "garments of salvation," and "robes of righteousness" (Isaiah 61:3, 10). Other scriptures tell us to "put on" the following just as we would "put on" clothing:

- "Put on tender mercies, kindness, humility, meekness, long-suffering" (Colossians 3:12).
- "Put on the new man who is renewed in knowledge" (the re-born spiritual nature) (Colossians 3:10).
- "Put on the Lord Jesus Christ" (His nature, His mindset, His attributes) (Romans 13:14).
- "Above all these, clothe yourselves with love, which binds everything together perfectly" (Colossians 3:14 CJB).

Yes, these are the most exceptional articles of clothing that any believer in Jesus could wear, the royal wardrobe of the sons and daughters of the King of kings.

Ultimately, all of God's family will "put on immortality" in the eternal state. The resurrected, glorified people of God are depicted in Scripture wearing radiant, white, celestial garments (representing righteousness) that will be our adornment for all eternity (1 Corinthians 15:54, See Revelation 3:5, 18; 4:4; 7:9; 19:8, 14, 2 Corinthians 5:1-5).

Based on that prophetic foresight, we should ask ourselves this final question: If all believers will be clothed the same spectacular way in the eternal state to come, why should there be any differentiation now? We should either all wear clerical clothing or all wear common clothing—one or the other. Of course, the logical conclusion is definitely the latter.

Question 6

Does the Bible require celibacy for priests, nuns, monks, and other church leaders?

L et me begin by stating once again that I have a profound respect for the priests, nuns, monks, and other Catholic leaders who have taken vows of celibacy because of their sincere commitment to God and His work. What an excessive, uncommon amount of devotion it takes for anyone to make such a selfless, sacrificial choice! If you happen to be a Catholic leader walking this path, I admire you.

I fully relate to the passion for God that constrains a person to choose this self-denying lifestyle, having embraced a similar decision myself for a lengthy period. During the season of my life when I was exploring Eastern religions, I lived what could be described as a celibate, monastic life, pursuing various spiritual disciplines about fourteen hours a day. Then, after being born again, I made a covenant with God that I would not even consider marriage until He clearly spoke to me if or when I should marry and who I should marry. Dating and marriage were not in the picture at all. Instead, I totally devoted myself to seeking God, studying His Word, traveling evangelistically, and sharing the Gospel in the U.S. and overseas. I simply loved Jesus with all my heart and wanted to be as useful to Him as possible. So, the single life seemed like the best choice.

Eventually, at the age of thirty-nine, God spoke to me very clearly that it was time to marry, and He showed me who was to be my spouse (my dear wife, Elizabeth). When it is God's timing, it is wonderful. (I often encourage young, unmarried people with the truism, "God reserves the best for those who leave the choice to Him.") Prior to marriage, I never took an actual "vow of celibacy"; I just prayerfully flowed with the grace and the will of God through that season of my life and obeyed what He spoke to my heart. I believe this is the way such a serious and sacred choice should be made—on an individual basis, prayerfully, under the guidance of the Holy Spirit, and only for the season that God dictates.

The demand for celibacy

There are differences in doctrine between Roman Catholicism (the Latin Rite or Western Rite) and the Eastern Rites. In the latter, "there have always been some restrictions on marriage and ordination. Although married men may become priests, unmarried priests may not marry; and married priests, if widowed, may not remarry. Moreover, there is an ancient Eastern discipline of choosing bishops from the ranks of the celibate monks, so their bishops are all unmarried."[25]

The tradition in the Western or Latin-Rite Church has been for priests as well as bishops to take vows of celibacy, a rule that has been firmly in place since the early Middle Ages.

Catholic theologians claim that the church's demand for priests, nuns, monks, and other church leaders to be celibate is based on the witness of Scripture, such as the following:

- **Jesus' example**—He was unmarried and lived His life totally committed to the ministry calling that rested upon Him. So, those who aspire to a ministry calling should follow His example. The Son of God did make the strong statement, "As the Father has sent Me, I also send you" (John 20:21).

- **Jesus' command**—In Luke 14:33, Jesus insisted, "Whoever of you does not forsake all that he has cannot be My disciple," and "forsaking all" would logically include marriage.

Also, when discussing the sensitive issue of marriage and divorce, Jesus shocked His followers with the following statement:

> *"For there are eunuchs who were born thus from their mother's womb, and there are eunuchs who were made*

> *eunuchs by men, and there are eunuchs who have made*
> *themselves eunuchs for the kingdom of heaven's sake.*
> *He who is able to accept it, let him accept it."*
> *(Matthew 19:12)*

In ancient times especially, a eunuch was literally a castrated man used primarily by rulers in the Mideast and Asia as a harem guard or a palace official. Jesus used that as a metaphorical comparison for three kinds of individuals:

1. Those who are simply not motivated by a desire for sexual expression in their lives or who are born with abnormal sexual organs ("born thus from their mother's womb"),

2. Those who are forced by others into accepting the lifestyle of a eunuch for one reason or another, including the extreme of castration,

3. Those who impose restrictions on themselves regarding sexual expression in their lives to fully devote themselves to God and the advance of His kingdom.

If believers feel called to follow this self-denying path, it could be the Lord's leading. The apostle Paul—who apparently lived a celibate life—offered his point of view concerning marriage, sexuality, and celibacy in the following passage:

> *Now concerning the things of which you wrote to me:*
> *It is good for a man not to touch a woman.*
> *Nevertheless, because of sexual immorality, let each*
> *man have his own wife, and let each*
> *woman have her own husband.*
> *Let the husband render to his wife the affection due her,*
> *and likewise also the wife to her husband.*
> *The wife does not have authority over her own body,*
> *but the husband does. And likewise the husband does*
> *not have authority over his own body, but the wife does.*
> *Do not deprive one another except with consent for*
> *a time, that you may give yourselves to fasting and*
> *prayer; and come together again so that Satan does not*
> *tempt you because of your lack of self-control.*
> *But I say this as a concession,*

not as a commandment.
For I wish that all men were even as I myself.
But each one has his own gift from God,
one in this manner and another in that.
But I say to the unmarried and to the widows:
It is good for them if they remain even as I am;
but if they cannot exercise self-control,
let them marry. For it is better to
marry than to burn with passion.
(1 Corinthians 7:1-9)

Further on, in the same chapter, Paul elaborated on his reasons for suggesting such an extreme discipleship commitment:

But I want you to be without care. He who is
unmarried cares for the things of the Lord—
how he may please the Lord.
But he who is married cares about the things of the
world—how he may please his wife.
There is a difference between a wife and a virgin.
The unmarried woman cares about the things of the
Lord, that she may be holy both in body and in spirit.
But she who is married cares about the things of the
world—how she may please her husband.
And this I say for your own profit, not that I may put a
leash on you, but for what is proper, and that you may
serve the Lord without distraction.
(1 Corinthians 7:32-35, See verses 36-40)

So, Paul urged, not just leaders, but all believers, if they are able—and if they are so gifted by God—to accept a state of singleness for the purpose of serving God "without distraction." However, he never made that a mandatory apostolic decree. Neither did he, nor any other Bible writer, suggest ministry leaders should take a "vow of celibacy." Quite possibly, part of the allure toward this austere measure of religious devotion stems from an obscure passage in Isaiah's writings:

Do not let the son of the foreigner who has joined
himself to the LORD speak, saying, "The LORD has
utterly separated me from His people"; nor let the

eunuch say, "Here I am, a dry tree."
For thus says the LORD: "To the eunuchs who
keep My Sabbaths, and choose what
pleases Me, and hold fast My covenant,
Even to them I will give in My house and within My
walls a place and a name better than that of sons and
daughters; I will give them an everlasting name
that shall not be cut off."
(Isaiah 56:3-5)

According to this passage, God promised an exceptional, eternal reward for those who impose this spiritual discipline upon themselves. However, He did not hinge this promise to a mandate for all who occupy ministerial positions of authority in the church. In fact, quite the opposite is the case, as we will soon see.

The irony of Peter's situation

How ironic it is that Peter is considered "the first pope" by most Catholics, yet he was married! There's plenty of proof. Matthew 8:14 reveals that Jesus prayed for "Peter's wife's mother" when she had a fever, and she was healed. Also, Paul, in his letter to the Corinthians, mentioned that Peter, who was also named Cephas, and the other apostles were married. Then he asked the pointed question:

Do we have no right to take along a believing wife,
as do also the other apostles,
the brothers of the Lord, and Cephas?
(1 Corinthians 9:5)

If the very one considered by Catholics to be the original apostolic head of the church did not fulfill this sacred charge, then how, why, and when did such a demanding and challenging tradition creep into the church? Consider the following historical data:

"The first written mandate requiring priests to be chaste came in AD 304. Canon 33 of the Council of Elvira stated that all "bishops, presbyters, and deacons and all other clerics" were to "abstain completely from their wives and not to have children." A short time later, in 325, the Council of Nicea, convened by Constantine, rejected a ban on priests marrying requested by Spanish clerics . . . The Church was a thousand years old before it definitively took a stand in favor of celibacy in the twelfth century at the Second Lateran Council held in 1139, when a rule was approved forbidding priests to marry. In 1563, the Council of Trent reaffirmed the tradition of celibacy."[26]

Mandatory celibacy has been a controversial doctrine ever since it was initiated, and it is still a hotly contested issue among Catholic people worldwide, as well as an exclusively male priesthood. Technically, the idea is proposed that "the Catholic Church forbids no one to marry. No one is required to take a vow of celibacy; those who do, do so voluntarily. They 'renounce marriage' (Matthew 19:12); no one forbids it to them. The Church simply elects candidates for the priesthood (or, in the Eastern rites, for the episcopacy) from among those who voluntarily renounce marriage."[27] However, those aspiring to be priests in the Roman Catholic tradition realize that position will not be granted to them unless they "voluntarily" accept celibacy. So, if the issue is honestly assessed, it is a required status.

It is somewhat shocking to many Catholics to find out that at least seven popes were married men, eleven popes were the sons of prior popes or other clergy, and six popes in office after 1139 A.D. were known to have illegitimate children.[28] So, the Catholic Church has not been consistent in promoting this protocol, neither have the leaders of the church been exemplary in their conduct.

What the Bible teaches on this controversial subject

Paul instructed in at least two epistles that anyone filling the role of a bishop, a deacon, or an elder in the church should be "the husband of one wife," not celibate. (See 1 Timothy 3:2-12, Titus 1:6.) How could that biblical mandate ever fit in the mold of present-day, established Catholic doctrine and tradition?

Although some may have this "gift" of singleness to concentrate on ministry, originally it was not, and never should be, a requirement for all those filling visible, ministerial roles in the church. Neither should anyone be compelled to make a "vow" that could be broken later if a decision was made to marry. Ecclesiastes 5:5 warns:

Better not to vow than to vow and not pay.

The most serious commentary that could possibly be brought up on this subject concerns Paul's prophetic warning in one of his letters to his protégé Timothy, who was a pastor:

Now the Spirit expressly says that in latter times
some will depart from the faith, giving heed to
deceiving spirits and doctrines of demons,
speaking lies in hypocrisy, having their own
conscience seared with a hot iron,
forbidding to marry, *and commanding to abstain*
from foods which God created to be received with
thanksgiving by those who believe and know the truth.
(1 Timothy 4:1-3)

"Deceiving spirits"? "Doctrines of demons"? That's very intense wording, isn't it? However, it's not just my view; it's an indisputable revelation from God—inspired by the Holy Spirit who authored this epistle through Paul. Therefore, this dire warning makes any final stance on this issue all-the-more important. It is easy to see from the study of biblical prophecies that we are already in the "last days," so this passage definitely relates to our era.

Is celibacy wrong? No! There are times when God may lead devoted followers that direction. Is mandating celibacy wrong? Yes! Because by making this a religious regulation, the church is usurping God's position of authority in the lives of those who desire to serve Him with all their hearts. He may lead some to live single lives, yet He may lead others to marry. It is up to God, not an organization.

Mandating celibacy also tends to set many God-loving individuals up for serious moral failure, because they are not able to handle the loneliness of a single life or the temptations that come as a result. Is marriage a cure-all for potential immorality? No, of course not! However, in many cases, it is a much healthier choice—mentally, emotionally, and spiritually—enabling devoted believers to be stronger in maintaining a pure heart and a righteous example in positions of leadership. In the final analysis, those who say "I do" are not inferior to those who say "I won't"—if the choice made is an act of worshipful submission to the will of God.

Question 7

The Sacrament of Confession: Is it necessary for penitent persons to confess their sins to a priest?

A s we enter the next three chapters dedicated to the sacrament of Reconciliation (which includes Confession, Absolution, and Penance), once again, I must first express my profound respect for the priests who spend countless hours in a confessional listening to broken-hearted, sorrowful, repentant people confessing their sins. How overwhelming and challenging that task must be, both mentally and emotionally! What patience and compassion must be in the hearts of those priests who consistently and conscientiously carry out such a duty for their parishioners! If you happen to be a priest who has prayerfully shouldered this burden, may God pour out His mercy and grace on your life in return for the mercy and grace you have sought to extend to others.

Second, I want to also express my deep respect for Catholics who are willing to humble themselves in confessing their sins to a priest. Being transparent to that degree normally requires a sincere desire to be right with God and possess a clean heart. Such strong motivations are to be praised whenever and wherever they are found.

The definition of sin

To properly examine the various aspects of this tradition, we must first establish the definition of sin, especially from the unique stance offered in Catholicism. Two primary words translated "sin" in the Bible are the Old Testament, Hebrew word *chattah* (pronounced khat-taw-aw') and the New Testament, Greek word *hamartia* (pronounced ham-ar-tee'-ah). Both these words mean "missing the road" or "missing the mark."

Missing the road—The "missed road" is the one that carries pilgrims through this wilderness world to their heavenly destiny. It is described many ways in Scripture, such as: "the way of truth," "the way of peace," "the way of holiness," and "the way of the Lord" (Psalms 119:30, Luke 1:79, Isaiah 35:8 KJV, Proverbs 10:29). Sin is what lures troubled individuals off this holy path, convincing them to forge their own way through the menacing jungle of a treacherous world where deception, danger and death are always hiding in the shadows.

Missing the mark—The "missed mark" is like the bull's eye of a spiritual target. The aim is total perfection in all that we think, say, or do. Anything outside of that "bull's eye" is sin. Not only are there sins of commission (wrong thoughts, words, or actions); there are also sins of omission (failing to think, say or do the things that we should).

No wonder the Bible says, "All have sinned, and fall short of the glory of God" (Romans 3:23). Only God is perfect. Human error is inevitable and inescapable. So, we might as well admit it: we have all missed the road and missed the mark many times in life. We are all in desperate need of a Savior. So, let us pray for one another, help one another, and uphold one another on this challenging journey.

The two categories of sin in Catholicism

According to Catholic teaching, sins are divided into two primary categories: mortal sins and venial sins. Mortal sins (also called "cardinal sins") are serious or grave transgressions. The concept of "mortal sins" is based especially on this passage of Scripture:

> *If anyone sees a brother commit a sin that does not*
> *lead to death, he should intercede for him, and God*
> *will grant him life—provided that the sin is not deadly.*
> *There is a sin that leads to death, and I do not*
> *say that you should pray about it.*
> *All wrongdoing is sinful, but not all sins are deadly.*
> *(1 John 5:16-17 NCB)*

According to Catholic theology, for a transgression to be labeled a "mortal sin," the following three conditions must be met:

1. It must be a grave issue.

2. It must be committed with full knowledge or awareness that the sinful action is a grave offense.

3. It must be committed intentionally and deliberately; it must be a premeditated act.

One Catholic source explains, "Mortal means death; they are sins that cause death to the soul. Mortal sins completely sever one's relationship with God and the sacrament of Penance and Reconciliation (commonly called Confession) is necessary to restore this relationship."[29]

Another source offers: "Mortal sins cannot be done 'accidentally.' A person who commits a mortal sin is one who knows that their sin is wrong, but still deliberately commits the sin anyway. This means that mortal sins are 'premeditated' by the sinner and thus are truly a rejection of God's law and love."[30]

Yet another Catholic source claims breaking any of "The Ten Commandments," would normally constitute a mortal sin, as well as any of the grievous transgressions listed in the following passages of Scripture:[31]

Now the works of the flesh are evident, which are:
adultery, fornication, uncleanness, lewdness,
idolatry, sorcery, hatred, contentions, jealousies,
outbursts of wrath, selfish ambitions, dissensions,
heresies, envy, murders, drunkenness, revelries, and the
like; of which I tell you beforehand, just as I also told
you in time past, that those who practice such things
will not inherit the kingdom of God.
(Galatians 5:19-21)

Do you not know that the unrighteous will not
inherit the kingdom of God? Do not be deceived.
Neither fornicators, nor idolaters, nor adulterers,
nor homosexuals, nor sodomites, nor thieves,
nor covetous, nor drunkards, nor revilers,

> *nor extortioners will inherit the kingdom of God.*
> *(1 Corinthians 6:9-10)*

Venial sins "usually involve a less serious action and are committed with less self-awareness of wrongdoing. While a venial sin weakens the sinner's union with God, it is not a deliberate turning away from Him and so does not wholly block the inflow of sanctifying grace."[32]

Venial sins are "an illness of the soul rather than its supernatural death."[33] Though a Catholic understandably would not be as distressed over this lesser kind of sin, the recommendation is still "to go to confession from time to time with venial sins to unburden your soul."[34]

Biblically, all sins cause death to the soul. Only one sin was committed in the beginning—partaking of the tree of the knowledge of good and evil—and it caused Adam and Eve to die spiritually and they began dying physically. It also passed death on to all their offspring, verified by the following passage:

> *Therefore, just as through one man sin entered the*
> *world, and death through sin, and thus death*
> *spread to all men, because all sinned.*
> *(Romans 5:12)*

The Bible does indicate degrees of sin (see John 19:11), however, all sin has a death-dealing effect. To reduce some sins to a "venial" status could result in a person feeling less pressured to overcome them. The following distinctions are not found in Scripture:

> "Venial sin does not deprive the sinner of sanctifying grace, friendship with God, charity, and consequently, eternal happiness." (CCC 1863)

> "To die in mortal sin without repenting and accepting God's merciful love means remaining separated from him forever by our own free choice." (CCC 1033)[35]

The following quote from Ezekiel is all-inclusive: "The soul that sins, it shall die" (Ezekiel 18:4 MKJV). All sin must be dealt with through repentance, and all sin must be cleansed—to be in fellowship with God and to be ready for heaven.

The fourth sacrament

Reconciliation is the fourth of seven sacraments. *(See Appendix #5 for the full list.)* The Council of Trent affirmed that the two main purposes of the Catholic priesthood are: number one, to forgive sin, and number two, to administer the sacrament of the Eucharist. So, the subject matter of this chapter is high on the list of important issues.

The Catholic Encyclopedia states that Reconciliation "is called a 'sacrament' not simply a function or ceremony, because it is an outward sign instituted by Christ to impart grace to the soul."[36]

This sacrament is also described as "the 'tribunal of penance,' because it is a judicial process in which the penitent is at once the accuser, the person accused, and the witness, while the priest pronounces judgment and sentence."[37] So, each time a priest hears a confession, it is like a separate court case being heard.

The availability of reconciliation with God does not extend outside of the Catholic faith, for "no unbaptized person, however deep and sincere his sorrow, can be validly absolved . . . one must first be a member of the Church before he can submit himself and his sins to the judicial process of sacramental Penance."[38] So this is a serious issue. If Catholic doctrine is right, no one can be forgiven of sin unless he or she participates in this traditional approach.

The history of and practice of confession

During the first centuries of Christianity, confession was something performed publicly. Because of the humiliation and shame involved, it usually happened only once, and often, toward the end of a person's life.

It was not until the seventh century that it transitioned into private confession to a priest.[39] Other sources offer an even later date. The present rules regarding this important facet of the Catholic faith were established at the Vatican II Council (1962-65).

Now, in the twenty-first century, Catholics are encouraged to go to Confession at least once a year, especially prior to Easter and the obligation of receiving Communion during that season (from Easter to Pentecost) (CCC 1457). Participation in this sacrament is required to receive Absolution (forgiveness of sins: release from both guiltiness and punishment).

All grave sins must be confessed and if a participant intentionally and knowledgably withholds mentioning a mortal sin, that act of confession and subsequent absolution are both invalidated. Also, another mortal sin of sacrilege is committed that must be confessed.[40] Catholics who willingly choose to hide their grave sins this way are comparable to a car stuck in a muddy ditch with the wheels spinning and going nowhere.

The three primary reasons for this sacrament

The idea that confession to a priest is necessary to be reconciled to God is based on three primary beliefs (concepts that are examined under Questions #4 and #8):

1. The belief that in the New Testament era, there is still an exclusive, mediatorial priesthood,

2. The belief that priests have been authorized by God to be the source of forgiveness being granted to His people,

3. The belief that this is a legacy passed on from the early disciples.

The five-step process of Confession

When a Catholic goes to Confession, five steps are taken:

1. **Greeting the priest**—Upon entering the confessional, penitent persons make the sign of the cross and greet the attending priest by saying:

    "Bless me, Father, for I have sinned. It's been [number of days/months/years] since my last confession."

2. **Listing sins**—Confessors then list their sins (mortal and venial). The priest (also called the "confessor") may converse with penitent persons to help jog their memory, help them confess satisfactorily, or instruct them how to overcome certain areas of weakness. A final statement made by one confessing covers all transgressions still unconfessed, "I am sorry for these and all my sins."

3. **Praying the Act of Contrition**—After confessing all their sins, penitent persons end by praying "The Act of Contrition," worded as follows:

> "My God, I am sorry for my sins with all my heart. In choosing to do wrong and failing to do good, I have sinned against You whom I should love above all things. I firmly intend, with Your help, to do penance, to sin no more, and to avoid whatever leads me to sin. Our Savior Jesus Christ suffered and died for us. In his name, my God, have mercy."[41]

4. **Absolution**—The priest then pronounces absolution over those who confess their sins (to be discussed at greater length in the next chapter). This is the statement he makes:

> "God, the Father of mercies, through the death and the resurrection of His Son has reconciled the world to Himself and sent the Holy Spirit among us for the forgiveness of sins; through the ministry of the Church may God give you pardon and peace, and I absolve you from your sins in the name of the Father, and of the Son and of the Holy Spirit."[42]

> As absolution is granted, the priest makes the sign of the cross over the penitent person who responds by saying, "Amen." The priest then gives the exhortation, "Give thanks to the Lord, for He is good." The confessor responds, "His mercy endures forever." The priest may pray a prayer before dismissal, then he may make the comforting declaration, "Your sins are forgiven. Go in peace." The penitent person responds, "Thanks be to God, and thank you, Father," then leaves the confessional and performs the prescribed penance. (Closing statements may vary.)

5. **Penance**—At the close of the confessional time, the priest assigns a certain penance to those who have confessed their sins that is normally performed before leaving the sanctuary. It is often comprised of memorized approved prayers repeated a certain number of times. It can also involve such things as

"fasting, or the giving of alms, or acts of mortification, or a way of the Cross, or a rosary. All of these are to 'make up' for the sin, and to prove that the sorrow was sincere."[43] When reparation is needed, penance may involve returning stolen goods, restoring the reputation of someone slandered, or payment of compensation for injuries.

Functioning in the "presence" and "person" of Jesus

It needs to be understood, by non-Catholics especially, that Catholic priests are not attempting to usurp God's position as the source of all forgiveness. Their mindset is instead to fill the role of administrators of His forgiveness—not masters of forgiveness, but servants of forgiveness. God does the forgiving; the priest is used as "God's instrument of forgiveness."[44] In other words, he merely facilitates the process.

I believe this privilege and responsibility of helping others obtain forgiveness is much broader than what Catholic doctrine allows. Because all born-again believers are priests, they all have the power to share God's forgiveness with those who need it. We tell others about the availability of forgiveness through Jesus ("the word of reconciliation"). Then, we pray for the Father to restore them to fellowship with Himself ("the ministry of reconciliation") (2 Corinthians 5:18-19).

The Corinthian church was a prime example of how this works. A man was guilty of a serious incestuous sin in that congregation (sexual relations with his father's wife). In his first letter to the Corinthians, Paul was very stern in dealing with such blatant disregard for God's laws, warning that "a little leaven leavens the whole lump" (1 Corinthians 5:6). Thankfully, the man repented, and in his second letter to the Corinthians, Paul communicated the following key statements:

> *Now whom you forgive anything, I also forgive. For if*
> *indeed I have forgiven anything, I have forgiven that*
> *one for your sakes in the presence of Christ.*
> *(2 Corinthians 2:10)*

The Greek word *prosopon* is translated "presence" in the New King James Version but rendered "person" in the King James Version. Either translation can be correct and different Catholic versions of the Bible use both. In essence, Paul was declaring that even as the Corinthian believers forgave the man in his stead (as if the apostle were present in person there himself), so he forgave the man in Jesus' stead (as if the Lord were present in person there Himself)—reconciling him back to a status of righteousness.

This passage is often used by Catholics to support their point of view regarding the sacrament of Reconciliation. They insist that Paul was functioning as a priest and forgiveness came through him to the repentant person. Therefore, that situation helped to establish a precedent, that forgiveness must flow to ordinary believers through authorized, ordained spiritual leaders.

I believe that passage proves exactly the opposite, that the Corinthians believers ministered love and forgiveness to the remorseful man as the Lord's representatives themselves. Paul didn't have to be in the equation. The members of the Corinthian church could have reconciled the man without the apostle Paul's involvement. They, too, could minister in Christ's stead (in the "presence" of Christ and the "person" of Christ, becoming His hands extended and His heart expressed). Besides, it is normally required in Catholicism that the priest be physically present to administer confession.[45] Evidently, Paul was a long distance away.

Confess your faults to one another

Here is an important passage of Scripture, which ironically has been used to support both points of view:

> *Is anyone among you sick? Let him call for the elders of*
> *the church, and let them pray over him, anointing him*
> *with oil in the name of the Lord. And the prayer of faith*
> *will save the sick, and the Lord will raise him up.*
> *And if he has committed sins, he will be forgiven.*
> *Confess your trespasses to one another, and pray for one*
> *another, that you may be healed. The effective, fervent*
> *prayer of a righteous man avails much.*
> *(James 5:14-16)*

Some Catholic theologians insist these three verses are inseparably interwoven. First, James instructs the believers who are sick to call the elders of the church (Greek—*presbuteros*: presbyters), which Catholics interpret as being priests (verse 14). However, it was probably a term referring to any recognized, respected ministry leaders in the church at that time (because there were no designated priests).

Then James declares that when they (according to Catholics / the priests) pray the prayer of faith, sick persons will be both healed and forgiven (verse 15). The very next verse urges believers to confess their trespasses to one another. However, it is commonly assumed among Catholics that this is a reference to the "elders" mentioned in verse 14, and therefore, a reassurance that lay people should confess their sins to a priest. I differ with that interpretation. Take all of verse 16 as a single thought, complete within itself:

> *Confess your trespasses to one another, and pray for one another, that you may be healed. The effective, fervent prayer of a righteous man avails much.*

This verse is not urging believers to confess only to "elders"; it is advising that any righteous believers can effectively pray forgiveness and healing into the hearts and lives of other believers. Confessing "to one another," and praying "for one another," according to this verse, is a two-way street. Righteous believers are encouraged to confess to other righteous believers the areas in which they need prayer, in order to be healed spiritually, mentally, emotionally, and even physically.

The Catholic view is a one-way street. If that was James' intended meaning, he probably would have written, "Confess your trespasses to the elders (the *presbuteros*—the priests) and get them to pray for you to be healed and forgiven." Instead, he said, "Confess . . . to one another."

Can you imagine a Catholic person, after Confession, saying to the officiating priest, "Now, Father, confess your sins to me and I will give you absolution"? I don't think that would ever be received well, yet that is literally what this passage conveys. One of the most clear and wonderful verses urging all of us to go to God directly is the following:

> *If we confess our sins, He is faithful and just to forgive us our sins and to cleanse us from all unrighteousness.*
> *(1 John 1:9)*

Once again, if that verse had been written supportive of the Catholic point of view, it probably would have been worded a much different way, such as:

> If we confess our sins to ordained and authorized priests, God is faithful and just to forgive us our sins and to cleanse us from all unrighteousness.

During the Old Testament era, a mediatorial priesthood *was* necessary. Israelites had to enlist the help of the priests to properly offer their sacrifices on the altar at the tabernacle of Moses, and later, at the Temple of Solomon.

In this New Testament era, things have changed dramatically. Making it compulsory to have the assistance of a priest in this present age is a glaring example of reverting to the Old Testament way of doing things—a grievous tendency that caused Paul to lament to the Galatian church, "I am afraid for you, lest I have labored for you in vain" (Galatians 4:11).

The surprising pandemic solution

The closing thought to this chapter is truly an important one. During the recent COVID-19 pandemic, the pope released a statement that Catholics could go to God directly for forgiveness and Confession would not be required, because the churches were closed.[46] Pause and think deeply about that for a moment.

The conclusion is radical and obvious. If Catholics could go to God directly for forgiveness during that two-year-long period, why has that not always been the case, and why can't that arrangement be established indefinitely into the future? Even when the priesthood was functioning during the Old Testament era, God presented the following invitation to the nation of Israel:

> *"If My people who are called by My name will humble themselves, and pray and seek My face, and turn from their wicked ways, then I will hear from heaven, and will forgive their sin and heal their land."*
> *(2 Chronicles 7:14)*

I believe this is still God's passionate plea to all those who desire to be reconciled, an invitation that can now be received personally, without the aid of a mediatorial priest. Some of the most comforting promises from God are found in the following verses:

> *"Come now, and let us reason together," says the LORD,*
> *"though your sins are like scarlet they shall be as white*
> *as snow; thought they are red like crimson*
> *they shall be as wool."*
> *(Isaiah 1:18)*

> *The sacrifices of God are a broken spirit, a broken and*
> *a contrite heart—these, O God, You will not despise.*
> *(Psalms 51:17)*

> *Bless the LORD, O my soul, and forget not all His*
> *benefits: who forgives all your iniquities, who*
> *heals all your diseases.*
> *(Psalms 103:2-3)*

> *For as the heavens are high above the earth, so*
> *great is His mery toward those who fear Him,*
> *As far as the east is from the west, so far has*
> *He removed our transgressions from us.*
> *(Psalms 103:11-12)*

Question 8

What is Absolution, and is it available only through priests?

To absolve means to pardon, forgive, or release. After Confession, the priest absolves the penitent Catholic of his or her sins. According to the official Catholic stance, only a priest can do this, and the person asking for forgiveness must be in the priest's presence, not on the phone or some other communication device. As quoted in the previous chapter, the following is an example of a priestly proclamation of absolution:

> "God, the Father of mercies, through the death and the resurrection of his Son has reconciled the world to himself and sent the Holy Spirit among us for the forgiveness of sins; through the ministry of the Church may God give you pardon and peace, and I absolve you from your sins in the name of the Father, and of the Son and of the Holy Spirit."[47]

It is taught that absolution not only removes the guiltiness of a penitent Catholic, but also, the eternal punishment in hell that would have been the result of mortal sins. However, the penitent person may still be subject to an undetermined amount of time in Purgatory for certain transgressions, even though he or she has been forgiven. How can this be the case since true forgiveness from God wipes out both the sin and the resulting judgment? Consider a very revelatory passage of Scripture that upholds this view:

> *If anyone sins, we have an Advocate with the Father,*
> *Jesus Christ the righteous. And He Himself is the*
> *propitiation for our sins, and not for ours only*
> *but also for the whole world.*
> *(1 John 2:1-2)*

The word "advocate" can mean a defense attorney. Indisputably, a good defense attorney does his utmost to prove his client innocent, even if he or she is guilty. Jesus does that and much more. We were all guilty as charged, but His blood proves our innocence in the sight of heaven.

The word "propitiation" means satisfaction for the demands of justice. Jesus did that, too. He took the judgment that should have fallen on us, tasting death for every person. So why should any additional purgatorial judgment be necessary? To believe that we can qualify more perfectly for a heavenly inheritance by some prolonged period of suffering or purging in Purgatory is to deny the full power of the cross and victory of the empty tomb.

(The related concepts of Purgatory and Indulgences will be more thoroughly addressed under Questions #21-22.)

The post-resurrection commission to disciples

After Jesus rose from the dead, He appeared ten biblically recorded times to His disciples (twelve times, according to Catholic tradition). During one visitation, He breathed on them, then made a stunning proclamation:

> *"Receive the Holy Spirit. If you forgive the sins of*
> *anyone, they are forgiven them. If you retain the sins*
> *of anyone, they are retained."*
> *(John 20:23)*

This passage is often used to try and substantiate the Catholic claim that remitting sins is an exclusive right of ordained priests. However, Jesus did not tell these upper room disciples, "You are now My New Covenant priests, and no repentant persons can be forgiven unless they go through you or those you install in an exclusive priesthood after you." Furthermore, Jesus did not say, "*When* you forgive." Rather,

He said, "*If* you forgive"—implying that it may happen randomly and would not always be a required arrangement.

The apostles (minus Thomas) were probably not the only ones present when Jesus made this declaration. Most likely, less notable disciples were part of that group also (120 were in the upper room just prior to the day of Pentecost—Acts 1:15). So, could it be that this was not just a directive for the primary leadership of the church? Mary and the other women who followed Jesus were in the upper room at times, too, so if this was a commission into a priesthood calling (according to the Catholic mindset), were even women included? (See Acts 1:14.) Of course, there is no way of knowing any of these things for certain, so conclusions cannot be fully reached, one way or the other.

Just prior to sharing these instructions about imparting forgiveness, Jesus breathed on all those disciples present and said, "Receive the Holy Spirit." The connection between these two things is vital. It implies that all who are filled with the Holy Spirit are simultaneously empowered to share forgiveness with others—either by communicating promises from God's Word or by praying with those who are seeking to be forgiven. Of course, no believer should ever do this indiscriminately but be discerning, sharing forgiveness only with those who are sincere, and withholding it from those whose hearts are not inclined toward God, those who would only make mockery of the process. (See Acts 2, 10:44-48, 19:1-7.) Being selective this way is a satisfactory fulfillment of Jesus' command to either "forgive" or "retain" sins.

Let me reemphasize, Jesus never said this was the standard way it had to happen. He never said believers had to be involved in another person receiving forgiveness from God. However, it can be very helpful. Those who already have a relationship with God tend to have strong faith that can override a guilty person's sense of unworthiness, fear of rejection, tendency toward self-condemnation, and internal battles with unbelief.

I know this kind of arrangement helped me immensely. The man who led me to the Lord had strong faith that Jesus was the only way, while I had very little. He knew that Jesus was the Savior, while I was not convinced. He had confidence in the promises of God, while I was wondering if the Bible was even true. He fully believed I could be born again, while I was unsure if such an experience was truly available. So, his faith was powerful in overriding my unbelief. He persisted this way because he knew I had a genuine desire for God. So, he prayed God's forgiveness over my life—and God transformed me dramatically. If I had been a mocker, he would have said bluntly, "I can't pray forgiveness for you, because you are not sincere," and my sin would have been "retained." I believe this is the intended meaning of this passage.

Two extreme examples

There are two extreme examples of "forgiving" and "retaining" sins in the New Testament. The first martyr of the church, Stephen, forgave those who stoned him saying, "Lord, do not charge them with this sin" (Acts 7:60). Strangely, in that case, as it was with Jesus on the cross, those prayed for were not repentant and not asking for forgiveness, yet the love of God in Stephen overruled those negatives (so there are exceptions to the rules I just shared).

Paul did quite the opposite, praying the Lord would retain the sin of someone who had persecuted his ministry. He complained, "Alexander the coppersmith did me much harm. May the Lord repay him according to his works" (2 Timothy 4 :14). So, there is no iron-clad biblical example or rule concerning how we should act and react in this area of spirituality.

Conclusions about Reconciliation

Exercising the power to absolve sins is considered by Catholics to be a major aspect of the "binding and loosing" authority that Jesus initially presented, along with the "keys to the kingdom of heaven," to Peter, then through Peter, to the rest of the disciples and the entire church. (See Matthew 16:16-19: 18:18.)

In other words, priests, who have supposedly inherited their position from the original disciples, have the "keys" to open the door of salvation and the door of eternal life to those submit themselves to the discipline of the confessional.

What should our response be to such bold claims? After studying the related scriptures, it is clear that the power to impart forgiveness of sins does not rest exclusively with Catholic clergy. All believers are priests by New Covenant standards (see 1 Peter 2:5; 2:9), therefore, all true believers have inherited the authority to bind and loose, a privilege and responsibility given to the entire New Testament church in Matthew 18:18. Since this binding and loosing power is spiritually linked to the keys of the kingdom of heaven in Matthew 16:19, those keys also pass to all believers, keys that enable them to open the door to eternal life to those who do not yet know Jesus.

This sacrament called Reconciliation (involving Confession, Absolution, and Penance) is simply a church tradition; it is not a biblical one. It serves to bring people under religious bondage, because participants fear, if they do not remain Catholic, and if they do not go through a priest, they cannot be properly forgiven.

If the thief on the cross could appeal personally to the crucified Savior, saying "Remember me when you come into your Kingdom," then the rest of us can cry out to Him directly, no matter how messed up our lives may be. We can also expect the same kind of acceptance Jesus gave that remorseful criminal when He pledged:

> *"Assuredly, I say to you, today you*
> *will be with Me in Paradise."*
> *(Luke 23:42-43)*

That condemned person was not required to go through an earthly mediator; he met the compassionate Son of God Himself. Though most likely he was deeply depressed, fearful, troubled, guilt-ridden, desperate, and broken, Jesus healed his soul and gave him eternal hope in the midst of overwhelming despair. No one else was involved: just the dying thief and the Great High Priest. All he needed to do was sincerely repent and believe.

That is all the rest of us need to do.

Question 9

What is the purpose of Penance, and is it a requirement biblically?

Catholics who participate in the sacrament of Reconciliation (Confession, Absolution, and Penance) are usually very sincere about their faith. To enter the small confines of a confessional, then kneel and remorsefully admit detailed information about personal failures to another human being requires deep humility, strong convictions, and a genuine longing to conform to God's standards. To possess that level of sensitivity to the conscience is certainly commendable in a world that, especially in these modern times, pridefully refuses to follow any religious rules. But is this tradition necessary?

We have already examined Confession and Absolution. Now, the concept of Penance needs to be assessed. For the sake of non-Catholics reading this book, I will explain the process. After Catholics confess their sins, the officiating priest first gives absolution (explained in the previous chapter), then he prescribes a certain "penance" that must be performed. Although some critics interpret it otherwise, Penance is not an attempt to "earn" forgiveness, because absolution has already been given. Penance comes afterward. Then what is it for?

Here's a very simple explanation:

> "Doing penance after Confession is about making those first few steps in a new direction . . . God's transforming love doesn't leave me in my sin; its goal is to transform me now. The grace of the sacrament works

by changing my heart. And if my heart is truly changed, then I need to begin to live differently as well. So after Confession, I take those first few "baby steps" in a new direction by doing my penance, fully and faithfully. Not because by doing these things I mistakenly imagine that I'm "earning" God's love and forgiveness. No, we love, because God has loved us first." (See 1 John 4:19)[48]

So Penance is a way of restoring priorities, getting on the right track, and expressing a renewed love for God by making a religious commitment. The usual penitential assignment from the priest, designed to kickstart this journey toward improved spirituality, is a combination of memorized prayers, like reciting the "Our Father" ten times, the "Hail Mary" ten times, and the "Glory Be" prayer five times. *(The exact wording of these prayers is shared in Appendix #2.)* The Catholic Catechism goes deeper in its explanation:

> "Many sins wrong our neighbor. One must do what is possible in order to repair the harm (e.g., return stolen goods, restore the reputation of someone slandered, pay compensation for injuries). Simple justice requires as much. But sin also injures and weakens the sinner himself, as well as his relationships with God and neighbor. Absolution takes away sin, but it does not remedy all the disorders sin has caused. Raised up from sin, the sinner must still recover his full spiritual health by doing something more to make amends for the sin: he must 'make satisfaction for' or 'expiate' his sins. This satisfaction is also called 'penance.'" (CCC 1459)

The last part of this quote reveals the full purpose of this third step in the sacrament of Reconciliation. The definition for the word "expiate" is::

> "Atonement for some wrong-doing. It implies an attempt to undo the wrong that one has done, by suffering a penalty, by performing some penance, or by making reparation or redress. (Etym. Latin ex-, fully + piare, to propitiate: expiare, to atone for fully.)"[49]

Other Catholic writers shine an even brighter light on this subject, such as the following explanation:

> "The priest assigns this penance as partial satisfaction for the sins that were confessed and remitted...Sacramental satisfaction is the penitential work imposed by a confessor in the confessional in order to make up for the injury done to God and atone for the temporal punishment due to sin already forgiven."[50]

According to this perspective, even though confessed sins have been forgiven, they may still incur temporal (temporary) punishments (which Catholics believe could be either in this life or in Purgatory). So, atonement must be made to escape such an outcome. Fulfilling the penance assigned by the priest has the power to remove that punishment, either partially or completely. So, even though the "Penance" is not an attempt to "earn" forgiveness, it could be seen as an attempt to "earn" deliverance from the consequences of sin.

To "atone" means to make amends, so the penitent person is attempting, by religious works, to "make amends" for the transgressions committed and avoid the resulting judgments and/or negative outcomes. Practical acts of honesty and integrity are commendable, like returning stolen goods, or attempting to undo the bad effects of a lie. Any truly remorseful person should do these things without a priest dictating specific behavior. I am in full agreement with making amends in any way possible. However, I cannot comprehend how repeating two or three sets of memorized prayers could possibly aid in accomplishing such a lofty goal. Ironically, during His "Sermon on the Mount," right before sharing "The Lord's Prayer," Jesus cautioned against this very practice:

> *"When you pray, do not use vain repetitions as the*
> *heathen do. For they think that they will be*
> *heard for their many words.*
> *Therefore do not be like them. For your Father*
> *knows the things you have need*
> *of before you ask Him."*
> *(Matthew 6:7-8)*

Yet the very thing Jesus warned against is exactly what has happened, sanctioned by centuries of established church tradition. Why would ten "Our Fathers" (repeated far too often in a mantra-like, mechanical, and nearly mindless way) be more effective than praying the "Our Father" just one time, slowly, in deep sincerity, from the depth of the heart? Of course, the latter is far better.

(For a more thorough treatment of the concept of repetitious prayers, see Appendix #3. For an inspiring teaching on a creative use of "The Lord's Prayer," see Appendix #4.)

Penance on steroids

Some Catholics carry the idea of penance beyond the confessional and the altar. It can involve numerous expressions of self-discipline, self-denial, or even self-punishment, to somehow reach this impossible-to-reach goal of satisfactorily atoning for sin. Though certainly not promoted by the church, some desperate individuals have gone as far as acts of self-torture. For instance, in the 11th century, Peter Damian, a Catholic Benedictine monk, taught that "spirituality should manifest itself in physical discipline; he admonished those who sought to follow Christ to practice self-flagellation for the duration of the time it takes one to recite forty Psalms."[51] That sounds quite painful, doesn't it? Painfully unnecessary as well.

Though the vast majority of Catholics would never entertain the thought of implementing such a masochistic practice, it does graphically illustrate an important point: sometimes people get so desperate to free their minds of guilt, they will carry self-mortification to an extreme God does not expect or demand, just to try and feel free from sin and worthy of His love.

Martin Luther, at one time a sincere, God-fearing, Catholic monk, confided that he went through "such anguish as no pen can describe."[52] He frankly admitted, "When I was a monk, I wearied myself greatly for almost fifteen years with the daily sacrifice, tortured myself with fastings, vigils, prayers, and other very rigorous works. I earnestly thought to acquire righteousness by my works."[53]

In 1510 Martin Luther went to Rome where he was appalled by the corruption he witnessed among some of the priests and church leaders. However, he was so eager to feel free from his sins that he "climbed the Scala Sancta ("The Holy Stairs"), supposedly the same stairs Jesus ascended when He appeared before Pilate."[54] Though the historical data was debatable and unproveable, church authorities insisted the steps were authentic, that they had been carried from Jerusalem to Rome, and the priests claimed God would pour out His mercy and forgiveness on all who climbed the stairs on their knees. "Luther did so, repeating the Lord's Prayer, kissing each step, and seeking peace with God. But when he reached the top step, he looked back and thought, 'Who knows whether this is true?' He felt no closer to God."[55] So it is with all the empty, feeble efforts we make to achieve righteousness in the sight of God through our own religious efforts.

The concept of doing penance to expiate, to atone for sin, when taken to an extreme, robs the cross of its power and the glory from the holy One who was crucified there. That is so important, it needs to be said again—and please read it slowly, letting every word sink in:

The concept of doing penance to expiate, to atone for sin, when taken to an extreme, robs the cross of its power and the glory from the holy One who was crucified there. You may want to worshipfully say "Amen" right now. If you do, you are well on your way to true freedom in Christ. Remember, Jesus is referred to as the "propitiation for our sins"—and as already explained, that means, satisfaction for the demands of justice (1 John 4:10). How can we add anything to that?

The powerful concept of justification

The word "justified" means to be legally acquitted of all guilt and reckoned righteous in the sight of God—just as if the sin was never committed.

Though complementary attitudes like authenticity and humility significantly enhance any prayerful approach to God, the main biblical requirement for remorseful persons to be justified is faith. Paul's epistle to the Romans emphasizes this truth with bold and blunt passages like the following:

> *Therefore we conclude that a man is justified by faith*
> *apart from the deeds of the law.*
> *(Romans 3:28)*

*Therefore, having been justified by faith, we have peace
with God through our Lord Jesus Christ.*
(Romans 5:1)

This very concept of justification by faith was the biblical truth that finally liberated Martin Luther from the internal torment that racked his soul. He wrote:

> "Night and day I pondered until I saw the connection between the justice of God and the statement that 'the just shall live by his faith.' Then I grasped that the justice of God is that righteousness by which through grace and sheer mercy God justifies us through faith. Thereupon I felt myself to be reborn and to have gone through open doors into Paradise. The whole of Scripture took on new meaning and whereas before the justice of God had filled me with hate, now it became to me inexpressibly sweet in greater love. This passage of Paul became to me a gate of heaven."[56]

I believe at that moment of inspired insight Luther was truly born again. Something similar could happen for you as well—if that kind of precious encounter with the Lord has not yet been a part of your spiritual journey. *(In the Addendum, I share awesome truths about this wonderful, spiritual rebirth.)*

Revelation 1:5 declares that Jesus washes us from our sins "in His own blood." Faith in that purchase price justifies us before God. The seven-word statement originally spoken by the prophet Habakkuk and quoted by Paul in Romans 1:17, changed the world forever—"The just shall live by his faith."

We "live"—we come alive in a supernatural sense—when we dare to believe in the sufficiency of what Jesus accomplished through His death, burial, resurrection, and ascension. At that point, we are no longer dead in our sins; we are "alive" in Christ.

*For the wages of sin is death, but the gift of God is
eternal life in Christ Jesus our Lord.*
(Romans 6:24)

Yes, eternal life is a gift. A gift is not something you earn; a gift is something given as an expression of love and something you receive with gratitude and thanksgiving. No one can become good enough to obtain this or any other gift from God, even if we spend decades involved in the deepest acts of penance possible. "Without faith it is impossible to please" the Father, so when we receive by faith the wonderful things He has provided, it pleases Him greatly (Hebrews 11:6).

Reasons for self-mortification

If penance is not necessary to "atone" for our sins, why does the Bible teach the need for us to be "crucified with Christ"? (Galatians 2:20) Why does the Bible tell us to "put to death" our "members which are on the earth" (our lower nature)? (Colossians 3:5). Why should we fast, participate in prayer vigils, or deny ourselves in any way? The following list gives the ten main biblical reasons for self-mortification and self-denial:

1. To keep the flesh under control (See 1 Corinthians 9:27, Galatians 5:24.),

2. To keep from re-crucifying the Son of God by our actions and attitudes and bringing shame to His name (Hebrews 6:4-6),

3. To keep the death-dealing, soul-destructive effects of sin from being reintroduced in our lives (1 Peter 2:11),

4. To be clean before God, that He might use us more effectively (John 15:5),

5. To more perfectly fulfill the will of God (Romans 12:1-2),

6. To be more effective and fruitful in prayer (James 5:16),

7. To have greater peace and joy in our lives (Isaiah 57:21),

8. To express our love, gratitude, and worship more sufficiently toward the Father (Psalms 140:13, John 14:15),

9. To become a better witness of the truth to others (Titus 1:5-7).

10. To walk in deeper intimacy with God (James 4:8-10)

The last scripture above is probably the most helpful in discerning the truth and reaching a conclusion. It needs to be quoted entirely.

Draw near to God and He will draw near to you.
Cleanse your hands, you sinners; and purify your
hearts, you double-minded. Lament and mourn and
weep! Let your laughter be turned to
mourning and your joy to gloom.
Humble yourselves in the sight of the Lord,
and He will lift you up.

A true lover of God will do these things, however, this penitential approach is not an end in itself; it is a means to an end. The final outcome should be the spiritually healthy state of happiness, holiness, and wholeness in Him.

Taking up the cross

In the Catholic Catechism, the admonition is given, "Taking up one's cross each day and following Jesus is the surest way of penance."[57] That assertion misses the mark. Penance is not the reason we take up a cross to follow Jesus. That's not what the symbol conveys.

A cross is a complete death to self for the purpose of impacting the world around us with the love of God and salvation truth. It's not about penance. It's not about our own personal failures being atoned for, our own personal needs being met, or somehow avoiding time in Purgatory because of our past sins.

Bearing a cross is about sharing the burden of lost humanity. It's about denying ourselves so that we can more effectively help the helpless, reach the unreached, and give hope to the hopeless, just as Jesus, the firstborn Son of God did. Very simply put, it's about loving God back for the great love He has poured out on us.

Penance or repentance?

So, what's the difference between penance and repentance? The following is a helpful comparison between the two concepts:

"According to dictionary definitions, the primary meaning of penance is the deeds done out of penitence, which also focuses more on the external actions than does repentance which refers to the true, interior sorrow for one's hurtful words or actions."[58]

The following two definitions explain these closely related terms in even greater simplicity:

- **Repentance** is an attitude, a change of mind, godly sorrow, and remorse over sin or wrongdoing.
- **Penance** is an action resulting from repentance, an attempt to make amends for sin or wrongdoing.

There are a few biblical passages in which something similar to "penance" is commanded, though that word is not used. For instance, God revealed through the prophet Ezekiel:

> *If the wicked restores the pledge, gives back what he has*
> *stolen, and walks in the statutes of life*
> *without committing iniquity, he shall*
> *surely live; he shall not die.*
> *(Ezekiel 33:15)*

One of the most powerful revelations in this area is found in the wisdom of Proverbs 16:6:

> *In mercy and truth atonement is provided for iniquity;*
> *and by the fear of the LORD one departs from evil.*

When we repent, God provides the mercy and truth that together cover the iniquity of our past, but our "penance" should be to gratefully and worshipfully respond to God's goodness by fearing Him and leaving behind those things that once corrupted us.

When Jesus came to earth to launch the New Testament era, He taught the need of making amends (which could also be interpreted as a performance of "penance"). However, in this passage, He placed that action before, not after repentance:

> *"Therefore if you bring your gift to the altar, and there*
> *remember that your brother has something against you,*
> *leave your gift there before the altar, and go your way.*
> *First be reconciled to your brother, and then come and*
> *offer your gift." (Matthew 5:23-24)*

So, it is true, there are times when remorse for sin or for wrong-doing is insufficient by itself; there must be an attempt to compensate in some way for damages done or relationships breached. Of course, that's not always possible, but when it is, God expects it.

John the Baptist, the forerunner of the Messiah, had a primary message that Jesus later repeated, "Repent, for the kingdom of heaven is at hand" (Matthew 4:17). During his ministry, he gave a stinging rebuke to certain religious leaders who were apparently living hypocritical lives:

> *"Brood of vipers! Who warned you to flee from the*
> *wrath to come? Therefore bear fruits*
> *worthy of repentance."*
> *(Luke 3:7-8)*

After administering a "baptism of repentance" to those persons who flocked to his Jordan River preaching site, John explained in greater detail what kind of actions should be evidenced in the lives of those who claimed to be repenting (Acts 19:4):

> *"And even now the ax is laid to the root of the trees.*
> *Therefore every tree which does not bear good fruit is*
> *cut down and thrown into the fire."*
> *So the people asked him, saying,*
> *"What shall we do then?" He answered and said to*
> *them, "He who has two tunics, let him give to him who*
> *has none; and he who has food, let him do likewise."*
> *Then tax collectors also came to be baptized, and said*
> *to him, "Teacher, what shall we do?"*
> *And he said to them, "Collect no more*
> *than what is appointed for you."*
> *Likewise the soldiers asked him, saying, "And what shall*
> *we do?" So he said to them, "Do not intimidate anyone*
> *or accuse falsely, and be content with your wages."*
> *(Luke 3:9-14)*

John never implied that these "fruits worthy of repentance" were necessary for people to somehow escape a lengthier sentence in Purgatory. These acts of righteousness, performed externally, were simply proof that true repentance had taken place internally. On the highest level, they are part of living of life of adoration toward God.

Paul, the apostle, fused the two concepts together while he was explaining his conversion to King Agrippa. Concerning the visitation he received from the Lord Jesus, he said:

> *"Therefore, King Agrippa, I was not*
> *disobedient to the heavenly vision,*
> *but declared first to those in Damascus and in*
> *Jerusalem, and throughout all the region of Judea, and*
> *then to the Gentiles, that they should repent, turn to*
> *God, and do works befitting repentance."*
> *(Acts 26:19-20)*

One primary biblical example of a repentant individual who sought to make amends for a former wicked lifestyle is found in Luke 19. Zacchaeus was a "chief tax collector and he was rich" (Luke 19:2). When Jesus called Zacchaeus to be His disciple, he responded by saying, "Look, Lord, I give half of my goods to the poor; and if I have taken anything from anyone by false accusation, I restore fourfold." Jesus responded by saying, "Today salvation has come to this house" (Luke 19:8-9).

Of course, it was faith in Jesus as the Messiah that saved Zacchaeus, not religious works. The penitential deeds he promised to do were the outgrowth of His faith, the evidence of his faith, and the proof of his sincere heart toward God. Most importantly, the actions Zacchaeus executed had relevance; they were true reparation for damage that had been done. Repeated prayers are an insufficient substitute for that.

The Douay-Rheims Version of Scripture

Maybe part of the misunderstanding has resulted from what used to be the main Bible of choice for Catholics: the Douay-Rheims Version of Scripture (1899 American Edition). Sixty-six times the word "penance" appears in that translation.

Usually, it is found where the words "repentance" or "repent" appear in other translations of the Bible, such as the following verse that identifies Jesus' dominant message at the start of His ministry.

The New King James Version of Matthew 4:17 says:

> *From that time Jesus began to preach and to say,*
> *"**Repent**, for the kingdom of heaven is at hand."*

The Douay-Rheims Version says:

> *From that time Jesus began to preach, and to say: **Do**
> **penance**, for the kingdom of heaven is at hand. (DRA)*

The Greek word translated "repent" in the NKJV and "do penance" in the DRA is *metanoeo* (pronounced met-an-o-eh'-o), normally translated "repent" (thirty-four times in the KJV). It cannot mean both things. No other major translations of the Bible substitute the word "penance" for the word "repent" in this and other related passages. Maybe that's because:

> "The purpose of the version [the Douay-Rheims Version], both the text and notes, was to uphold Catholic tradition in the face of the Protestant Reformation which up until the time of its publication had dominated Elizabethan religion and academic debate. As such it was an effort by English Catholics to support the Counter-Reformation."[59]

The newer, more modern New Catholic Bible, published in 2007, only uses the word "penance" three times. Twice it is found in the commentary, not the Bible itself. Only once does it appear in the actual text, in one of the books that is not accepted in the Protestant Canon. Ironically, that passage talks about the insufficiency of penance if a person's lifestyle does not change. Here is the exact quote:

> *If someone bathes after touching a corpse and then*
> *touches it again, what has been gained by washing?*
> *So it is with the one who fasts for his sins and then*
> *goes out and commits them again. Who will listen to*
> *his prayer? **And what has he gained by his penance?***
> *(Wisdom of Ben Sira 34:30-31)*

Thankfully, in all other passages, this newer Catholic translation reverts back to the intended meaning of the Greek word *metanoia* (pronounced met-an-oy'-ah) translating it repent, and the Greek word *metanoeo* (pronounced met-an-o-eh'-o), translating it repentance.

Finding the proper balance

Truth is usually found in the middle of two extremes. A person claiming to be a Christian can swing too far to the left, rejecting the concept of penance altogether, confessing God's promises of forgiveness, yet hypocritically continuing in a very carnal lifestyle. Or a believer who falls into error can be so overwhelmed by grief, so imprisoned by self-condemnation, that he or she is driven to repeatedly implement excessive spiritual disciplines in a desperate effort to try and somehow reclaim God's love and fellowship. The first approach is devoid of true repentance and sincere devotion and is an insult to the grace of God; the second approach is devoid of faith-filled confidence in the Father-heart of God and frustrates His grace (See Jude 1:4, Galatians 2:21.) There is a " middle ground "—a pleasant place where you make positive progress spiritually, pursuing God with passion, yet all the while maintaining the joy of the Lord and faith in His Word. God wants you to be balanced.

The necessity of reconciliation with the church

Finally, the Catholic Catechism stipulates that reconciliation with God is not possible unless a person is also reconciled to the church. Of course, that does not mean just any church; it means the Catholic Church that most Catholic believers refer to as "the Mother Church"— the "Mother" of all the breakaway Protestant Christian sects. The full quote from the Catholic Catechism is as follows:

> "The words bind and loose mean: whomever you exclude from your communion, will be excluded from communion with God; whomever you receive anew into your communion, God will welcome back into his. Reconciliation with the Church is inseparable from reconciliation with God." (CCC 1445)[60]

Taken literally, this statement means that no one can truly be forgiven and saved unless he or she becomes a Catholic, returning to the fold. It strongly indicates that non-Catholics who love Jesus, who consider themselves genuine Christians, who have received the Savior into their hearts, who have been born again, if denied Communion in the Catholic Church, would also be denied communion with God.

That's a very unacceptable assertion. It slams the door of forgiveness shut to millions of Bible-believing Christians who are outside of Catholicism. To raise such a standard indicts one group or the other. There is no middle ground. It pushes all of us to a religious precipice. If it is true, non-Catholics who reject this belief are guilty of grave apostasy. If it is false, Catholics who promote this idea have fallen into serious heresy. So, resolving this issue is of the utmost importance—for all of us. Thankfully, that Catechism clause is not true. It is a misrepresentation of true Christianity. Jesus promised, "The one who comes to Me I will by no means cast out" (John 6:37). Approaching Him on your own with repentance and faith is sufficient to be forgiven.

Here are the main five takeaway points you need to remember:

1. Confessing your sins to a priest is unnecessary. Just go to God directly.

2. Repeating a few memorized prayers to fulfill penance and complete the sacrament of Reconciliation is relatively futile and empty. Seek God sincerely. Pray from your heart.

3. Whenever possible, make right any wrongs you have done that have damaged others, but you do not need a priest or church leader to give you specific directions on how to do that. Follow your conscience and the direction of the Holy Spirit.

4. Draw near to God, especially after times of failure in your life. Pursue Him consistently by any biblical means of sacrifice that you feel impassioned to implement (fasting, benevolence toward the needy, times of seclusion, a more discipline prayer life, serving others with humility, etc.).

5. Reconciliation with the Catholic Church is not necessary to obtain reconciliation with God. However, you should pursue reconciliation with believers and non-believers, whenever possible.

Are you unsure if you are truly forgiven? Surrender your heart and life to Jesus now. He is "a friend of sinners" (Luke 7:34). He will forgive you. "He delights in mercy" (Micah 7:18). It's very simple.

Question 10

Is the Catholic method of canonizing saints scripturally correct, or do all true believers bear this title?

For a little over a millennium, the Catholic Church has formally acknowledged thousands of individuals who exhibited deeper-than-normal devotion to the Lord and greater-than-normal evidence of spirituality, to confer on them the blessed and notable status of "sainthood."

> "The official process for declaring someone a saint is called canonization. Prior to the year 1234, the Church did not have a formal process as such. Usually, martyrs and those recognized as holy were declared saints by the Church at the time of their deaths."[61]

This practice has evolved in significant ways. (Those who are interested in pursuing a very detailed historical account should read the article accessible at the link mentioned in this endnote.)[62]

In the present evaluation process, two levels of spirituality must be evidenced before the third and final status of "sainthood" is conferred:

> "Once a candidate is declared to have lived life with heroic virtue, he may be declared Venerable The next step is beatification. A martyr may be beatified and declared "Blessed" by virtue of martyrdom itself. Otherwise, the candidate must be credited with a miracle.

In verifying the miracle, the Church looks at whether God truly performed a miracle and whether the miracle was in response to the intercession of the candidate saint. Once beatified, the candidate saint may be venerated but with restriction to a city, diocese, region, or religious family. Accordingly, the Pope would authorize a special prayer, Mass, or proper Divine Office honoring the Blessed. After beatification, another miracle is needed for canonization and the formal declaration of sainthood."[63]

"As with the beatification, the ceremonies of canonization normally take place in Rome at St. Peter's basilica within a Pontifical Mass. Inserted between the penitential rite and the Gloria, this simple ceremony is marked by great solemnity."[64]

Veneration, beatification, canonization—this three-step process of selecting and affirming candidates for sainthood (including the requirement of two post-mortem miracles) was never practiced in the early church and cannot be found anywhere in the Bible. It is merely a church tradition that emerged long after the original disciples began preaching the pure Gospel of the kingdom of God.

The starting point

Here's some deeper details about how this tradition began:

"In 993, St. Ulrich of Augsburg was the first saint to be formally canonized, by Pope John XV. By the 12th century, the church officially centralized the process, putting the pope himself in charge of commissions that investigated and documented potential saints' lives. And in 1243, Pope Gregory IX asserted that only a pope had the authority to declare someone a saint. A version of that canonization process is still in place. Recent popes are known for canonizing in large numbers: John Paul II canonized 482 saints – more than the 300 or so canonizations in the previous 600 years. And Francis' first canonization included 813 people – the "Martyrs of Otranto" – who were beheaded by Ottoman soldiers in 1480 after refusing to convert to Islam."[65]

Since the beginning of this practice, over 10,000 saints have been recognized by the Catholic Church. However, Catholic authorities themselves admit, "The precise number . . . will always be debatable. Early Christian communities venerated hundreds of saints, but historical research by 17th- and 18th-century Catholic scholars determined that very few of these saints' stories were backed by solid historical evidence. Lives of such well-known figures as St. George, St. Valentine, and St. Christopher were based either on a legend that often predated Christianity or were entirely made up."[66]

Many saints have been assigned feast days by the church during which their lives and their devotion to God are formally celebrated. Some have large groups of followers who revere them in special ways. Some religious orders are even named after honored saints, often, the founders of the orders themselves.

It is also a normal practice for every Catholic, during the ritual of Confirmation, to take the name of a saint who then becomes that person's patron saint, with whom he or she expects to enjoy a special lifelong relationship. (When I was confirmed, I took the name Christopher and prayed to him for several years, until the church announced that he was probably no more than a fictitious figure, and all my petitions went up in smoke.)

The strange office of "the devil's advocate"

Have you ever heard someone referred to as "the devil's advocate"? The dictionary defines such a person as an individual "who expresses a contentious opinion in order to provoke debate or test the strength of the opposing arguments."[67]

The real meaning of that title goes much deeper. Unknown to most people, it originated in Catholicism, and was associated with the investigative process of confirming someone to sainthood. Here's the back story:

"In 1587, Pope Sixtus V established the position of advocatus diaboli, or 'devil's advocate,' as part of the process of beatification or canonization — aka becoming a saint. The devil's advocate was the church's skeptic, picking apart stories of reported 'miracles' and more to argue against someone's sainthood. The advocate had to be present for any part of the sainthood process to be considered valid. However, the title was primarily a popular moniker — the position's official designation was the 'promoter of the faith,' or promotor fidei."[68]

What an interesting tidbit of Catholic trivia, right!?!? However, it's not trivial at all. More than just intriguing historical information, it will be used in a more profound application further into this chapter.

The true, biblical standard

Now we arrive at the intersection of creed and controversy. Just like your parents taught you, please look both ways before attempting to cross the street. According to the Bible, every true follower of Jesus is considered a "saint," not just those who achieve an exceptional, above-normal state of dedication and holiness in their walk with God. Also, there is no requirement biblically that miracles result from the intercession of such "sainted" persons before or after they die for them to rightfully bear exalted title. Having made those assertions, now, let's prove they are correct by going to the only reputable source: the Bible. Consider the following Scripture passages that indicate all the members of early churches were considered saints:

Paul, an apostle of Christ Jesus by the will of God, and Timothy our brother, to the saints and faithful brothers in Christ at Colossae: Grace to you and peace from God our Father.
(Colossians 1:1-2)

To the church of God that is in Corinth, to those sanctified in Christ Jesus, called to be saints together with all those who in every place call upon the name of

our Lord Jesus Christ, both their Lord and ours.
(1 Corinthians 1:2)

None of the believers in either of these churches had to have the approval of church authorities for "sainthood" to be applied to them. They automatically obtained that status by devoting themselves to the Lord Jesus. This status is the inheritance of all true believers— both those on earth and those in heaven. Certainly, those who live worshipful, devoted, godly lives are fulfilling this calling more than others, but sainthood is a common birthright. Yes, true salvation equals sainthood.

Of course, we have an adversary in the arena with us. The devil is called "the accuser of the brethren." Moreover, his demonic underlings have been infected with his nature and purpose. Certainly, they all hurl accusations toward the people of God to somehow prove their unworthiness (Revelation 12:10, See Job 1:6-22).

Negative, self-demeaning thoughts fester in our own minds as well. Often, we participate in this satanically-inspired smear campaign, and we become our own worst enemies—in a sense, we become the "devil's advocate"—berating ourselves, condemning ourselves, and disqualifying ourselves. If that happens, wonderful promises from the Bible can bring hope, restoration, and wholeness—like the following:

For You, Lord, are good, and ready to forgive, and
abundant in mercy to all those who call upon You.
(Psalms 86:5)

"But this is the covenant that I will make . . . their
iniquity, and their sin I will remember no more."
(Jeremiah 31:31, 34)

If God chooses to forget the negatives of your past, once you repent and commit your life to Him, you need to forget them, too— then confess the promise of Colossians 1:12 (ESV):

Giving thanks to the Father, who has qualified you to
share in the inheritance of the saints in light.

Did that powerful verse grab your attention? Yes, you read it correctly—if the Lord Jesus Christ lives in your heart, you are *qualified* to be a saint, because God Himself has qualified you for this holy status—by virtue of your relationship with Him. I have read articles written by Catholics who insist this title—"the saints in light"—is a reference to those who have already entered the bliss of heaven and that we share in their inheritance by asking for their intercession. However, I offer that believers in Jesus are called to live "in the light," right here, right now. The following verse from John's first epistle proves that stance:

> But if we walk in the light as He is in the light, we have
> fellowship with one another, and the blood of Jesus
> Christ His Son cleanses us from all sin.
> *(1 John 1:7)*

If we "walk in the light," we are assuming the role of the "saints in light." We do that by abiding in the light of God's truth and the light of God's love. (See Psalms 119:130, 1 John 2:9-10.) So how does God "qualify" His people to fill such a notable position? You are about to discover the way this miraculous process takes place.

Saints of the Old Covenant

We need to understand that this title rested on God's people of the Old Covenant long before the full price of redemption was paid on Golgotha. Here are three scriptures that describe in saintly terms all Israelites who were sincere in serving the God of Abraham:

> As for the saints who are on the earth, "They are the
> excellent ones, in whom is all my delight."
> *(Psalms 16:3)*

> Oh, fear the LORD, you His saints!
> There is no want to those who fear Him.
> *(Psalms 34:9)*

> Oh, love the LORD, all you His saints!
> For the LORD preserves the faithful.
> *(Psalms 31:23)*

All these passages were exhortations to Israelites to walk in sincere commitment to Yahweh, the God of their fathers. So, we can easily conclude, if God's Old Covenant people were named "saints" when atonement could only be claimed through the blood of sacrificial animals, how much more should that be an imparted status now that the blood of Jesus, our Savior, has been shed in our behalf!

The New Covenant process of making saints

As already mentioned, Paul often addressed all saved persons in various local churches as saints. Here's another obvious reference:

> *Paul, an apostle of Jesus Christ by the will of God, to*
> *the saints who are in Ephesus, and faithful in*
> *Christ Jesus. (Ephesians 1:1)*

All the Ephesian believers are included in this greeting because they were all considered "saints"—as simple as that. They were not in heaven yet; they were still on the earth. But if they were all considered saints, how and when was that status imparted to them? Defining the term will help us understand. The word "saint" simply means one who has been sanctified. This powerful, biblical term has a triune meaning.

1. Cleansed from the defilement of sin,

2. Made holy by God,

3. Set apart by God to fulfill His purposes.

Every true follower of Jesus is "sanctified" by the following seven spiritual influences (you may want to look up the scriptures):

1. The truth (John 17:19),

2. The name of Jesus (1 Corinthians 6:11),

3. The body of Jesus (Hebrews 10:10),

4. The blood of Jesus (Hebrews 13:12),

5. Faith (Acts 26:18),

6. The Spirit of God (1 Corinthians 6:11),

7. God, the Father (Jude 1:1).

These influences all work together to "sanctify" those who come to the Lord. Linking these complementary influences in a logical order, the process of sanctification takes place similar to the following description (each word in the list just given is in quotation marks): Upon hearing the "truth," repentant sinners call on "the name of Jesus" for salvation; then they set their "faith" on the "body" and "blood" of the Lord (His death on the cross), believing that they can be cleansed from sin through His substitutionary sacrifice. The "Spirit of God" then enters their hearts. At that moment, they are born again, made holy, and brought into oneness with "the Father."

The very moment Jesus enters the heart of a truly repentant sinner, that person is "sanctified" (cleansed from sin, made holy, and set apart for God's purposes). Immediately, the status of being a "saint" is conferred, not by a papal decree, but by God Himself—even if the newly saved person, just prior to that transformational encounter, was walking in deep darkness. But then, a radical transformation—a major identity shift—takes place supernaturally. You were a "sinner"; but then, you become a "saint." Praise God!

So, this saintly calling resides within all true believers: those who are freshly committed to God and those who have walked with Him for decades. However, like the oak tree hidden in the heart of the acorn, this new identity may be "hidden" in the hearts of new believers who still struggle with issues, character flaws, and weaknesses. But if those persons are sincere, and like seed, are buried with Christ, dying to the world, this inward potential is awakened (germinated), and it begins to grow until it becomes a manifested reality. Saintliness is truly a lifelong journey for all who believe.

God intends to assist us in achieving this status

God has made a strong commitment to assist those who turn to Him in this process, but He also expects us to do our part. This dual responsibility is reflected in a powerful passage: Leviticus 20:7-8. First, God commands His people:

> "*Sanctify yourselves therefore, and be ye holy: for I am the LORD your God.*" (KJV)

Then He gives the promise:

> "*And you shall keep My statutes, and perform them: I am the LORD who sanctifies you.*" (NKJV)

In other words, the Father commands those who come to Him to do everything within their power to live a holy and consecrated life (to sanctify themselves). At the same time, He promises His assistance and empowerment, which He readily gives, to sanctify them. Admittedly, our efforts would be futile without His help.

The divine title found in this passage ("the Lord who sanctifies you") in the Hebrew is Yahweh-M'Kaddesh. This is God's self-declared name and role in our lives. He wants to help us obtain a state of holiness and saintliness before Him. We don't have to talk Him into it. Jesus is even called "the King of saints" in Revelation 15:3 (KJV), which is His way of saying all who are under His authority are fashioned into His saintly image. That is God's purpose in His people, and it should be our mindset as well. You can claim the prayer of 1 Thessalonians 5:23-24 as if the Holy Spirit is praying it over you right now:

> *Now may the God of peace Himself sanctify you*
> *completely; and may your whole spirit, soul, and body*
> *be preserved blameless at the coming*
> *of our Lord Jesus Christ.*
> *He who calls you is faithful, who also will do it.*

Please speak that last line out loud: "He who calls you is faithful, who also will do it." God will help you, with all His resources, to arrive at this mark of "the prize of the high calling of God in Christ Jesus" (Philippians 3:14). Don't wait for a committee in Rome to enter your name into a list of prospects. Seize your God-given inheritance!

The error of calling yourself a sinner

Catholics often say a prayer called the "Hail Mary" which ends with this appeal:

> "Pray for us sinners now and at the hour of our death."

We will be examining the idea of praying to Mary and to the departed saints later, in two separate chapters, but a different issue needs to be addressed now. Whether petitioners repeating this prayer realize it or not, referring to themselves repeatedly as "sinners" is actually an admission that they are *not* saved, that they are *not* right with

God. True believers are not "sinners"; they are "saints." Confessing they are still sinners is the same as confessing that they are still lost.

This practice could easily be compared to someone standing up in an Alcoholics Anonymous meeting, and even though he or she has been clean for years, declaring in the present tense, "I *am* an alcoholic." I disagree with that approach. What a negative and harmful self-assessment, imprisoning someone in the prison of the past! The reformed individual (if he or she has been born again) should instead insist, "I *was* an alcoholic, but now I am a new person in Christ."

As the well-known revivalist, Leonard Ravenhill, often insisted —"If you claim being a saved sinner, that's like saying you are a married bachelor, or an honest thief. You're either saved or you're a sinner."[69] The angel told Joseph that Mary, his espoused wife, would have a son named Jesus who would "save His people from their sins" (Matthew 1:21). Notice the angel said "from" their sins, not "in" their sins.

If you look through the Bible at the scriptures that identify the present condition and future destiny of "sinners," I am sure you will conclude as I have, we do not want to identify with that group. Just four verses should be enough for me to prove my point:

> *Evil pursues sinners, but to the righteous,*
> *good shall be repaid.*
> *(Proverbs 13:21)*

> *The destruction of transgressors and of sinners shall be*
> *together, and those who forsake the*
> *LORD shall be consumed.*
> *(Isaiah 1:28)*

> *May sinners be consumed from the earth, and the*
> *wicked be no more. Bless the LORD,*
> *O my soul! Praise the LORD!*
> *(Psalms 104:35)*

> *Therefore the ungodly shall not stand in the judgment,*
> *or sinners in the congregation of the righteous.*
> *(Psalms 1:5)*

Convinced? I hope so. If you have surrendered your life to the Lord Jesus, I encourage you never to describe yourself as a "sinner" again. If you do, be sure to put it in the past tense. Only once did Paul describe himself this way, but he made it very clear that he was referring to his former self. (See 1 Timothy 1:12-15.) Once you give your heart to Jesus, you may still make mistakes, but once you go to the Lord and repent, He restores you to a status of righteousness.

You may protest, "But we sin every day!" Technically, that may be true, because the Bible makes it clear that "all unrighteousness is sin" and the very "thought of foolishness is sin" (1 John 5:17, Proverbs 24:9 KJV). As I wrote in Question #7, anything short of perfection in all our thoughts, attitudes, and actions is sin. The Bible even teaches sins of omission, that if we know to do good and do not do it, that becomes "sin" for us (James 4:17). So, how can we escape this awful dilemma?!?!

Here's the answer: a "sinner," whether he is religious or not, is someone whose dominant mindset is to indulge in practices described as sinful in the Bible. Saints may falter from time to time, but their dominant mindset is rather to be pleasing to God, to surrender to Jesus in all things, and to renew that commitment daily.

The worshipful response

Once God sanctifies your heart, you are holy in his sight. No wonder certain Hebrew and Greek words translated "saint" are also translated "holy." For instance, the Hebrew word *qadosh* is translated twelve times into the word "saints" but a total of 100 times into the word "holy." The Greek word *hagios* is rendered sixty-two times as "saints" but 162 times as "holy" (KJV). When you repent of your sins and invite Jesus to be Lord of your life, you become a new person. From that point, it is your responsibility to:

> *Put off, concerning your former conduct, the*
> *old man which grows corrupt*
> *according to the deceitful lusts,*
> *and be renewed in the spirit of your mind,*
> *and that you put on the new man which was created*
> *according to God, in true righteousness and holiness.*
> *(Ephesians 4:22-24)*

Did you get that? The born-again part of a person—the "inner man"—the new spirit God places in His people the moment they give their hearts to the Lord, is created righteous and holy (Ephesians 3:16). That means your regenerated spirit is infused with God's righteousness and God's holiness.

So, the "new man" is already holy, but to align with your new identity, you make daily decisions to pursue holiness: cleansing your temple of bad habits, refraining from corruptive media, abstaining from coarse language, showing kindness instead of anger, patience instead of irritation, compassion instead of selfishness, forgiveness instead of bitterness, withdrawing from sinful relationships, overcoming addictions—all these and more are part of measuring up to a "holy" standard. It is our responsibility to do so, for God has commanded:

> *"Be holy, for I am holy."*
> *(1 Peter 1:16)*

However, our primary motive for pursuing this goal should not be an attempt to earn a status of righteousness and holiness (for the blood of Jesus bought that for us). Rather, our primary motive should be a response of worship: gratefully applying holy standards to our lives because of three motivations: gratitude for grace, a longing for greater intimacy with God, and a desire to properly represent Him in this world. Let the following verse penetrate your heart:

> *Give unto the LORD the glory due to His name;*
> *worship the LORD in the beauty of holiness.*
> *(Psalms 29:2)*

You see, holiness is first a gift from God to us, but when we respond gratefully to that gift by aligning with God's holy nature, holiness becomes an act of worship that is beautiful in the eyes of the Almighty. That makes our striving for holiness a praise-filled expression of love for God instead of a rut-filled road of rigid, religious requirements.

What does the future hold for the saints?

We are told in the Bible that Jesus is coming back to this world victoriously. One of my favorite passages describing this grand event is Psalms 50:3-5:

*Our God shall come, and shall not keep silent; a fire
shall devour before Him, and it shall be very
tempestuous all around Him.
He shall call to the heavens from above, and to the
earth, that He may judge His people:
"Gather My saints together to Me, those who have
made a covenant with Me by sacrifice."
(Psalms 50:3-5)*

So, all who rise to meet Jesus in the air and are glorified at His coming are referred to as "saints." Then, as the King of kings descends to assume His rightful throne in Jerusalem, we will accompany Him triumphantly. The epistle-writer Jude, believed to be the brother of Jesus, quoted the prophecy of Enoch concerning this grand event:

*"Behold, the Lord comes with ten thousands
of His saints."
(Jude 1:14)*

When this happens, God will establish His kingdom fully on the earth, restoring it to the splendor of an Eden paradise once again. The prophet Daniel tells us what to expect in that soon-to-come, glorious and amazing era:

*Then the kingdom and dominion, and the greatness of
the kingdoms under the whole heaven, shall be given to
the people, **the saints of the Most High**. His kingdom is
an everlasting kingdom, and all dominions shall
serve and obey Him. (Daniel 7:27)*

According to this wonderful verse, when the saints return with the Lord Jesus, they will inherit a restored world from Him, saturated with heavenly glory, and be placed in positions of authority over the nations. (See 1 Corinthians 6:1-3.)

This is not a reference to a few thousand individuals canonized by various popes, or to the members of just one denomination, but all those who have ever surrendered their hearts and lives to the King of saints (Yahweh-M'Kaddesh) from the beginning of time.

Praise God for such a spectacular destiny!

"Now I know what a saint is!"

Let me end this important chapter with an unforgettable story that I read many years ago. It really sums up my thoughts concerning the calling, the nature, and the true identity of those who bear this wonderful title.

> It was an early morning service in a majestic cathedral surrounded by a grove of maple trees. A young boy was walking with his parents down the center aisle of the church, staring at the impressive, multicolored, stained glass windows in the walls. The sun was just beginning to rise over the treetops. As the first rays of the dawn struck the windows, they illuminated the images of various revered persons in the history of the church. Suddenly, the little boy grabbed his mother's hand and excitedly blurted out, "Mommy! Mommy! Now I know what a saint is!" She looked at her little boy with wonder as he explained, "It's someone the light shines through!"

Yes, I agree, a real saint is simply someone the light shines through, someone who has been illuminated by the light of God's Word and the light of God's Spirit and who shines that light daily into a very dark world. It could be the cleaning lady at the business where you work, the nurse who checked you in at the hospital, or the man who scrubbed your vehicle at the local car wash.

If you have received Jesus as Lord of your life, you are included in this blessed family of saints as well.

Question 11

Can the saints in heaven be petitioned to pray in our behalf?

Catholics believe that canonized saints in heaven can be prayerfully petitioned and that one of their primary occupations is interceding for believers who are still on the earth. This heaven-to-earth connection is an integral part of a concept called "the communion of the saints," as referred to in the Apostles' Creed.

(See Appendix #1 for the wording of the Apostles' Creed.)

In the past, some Catholics (now honored as saints) believed so wholeheartedly in this doctrine, that even while they were yet living, they voiced the desire to ultimately fill this role for the benefit of other believers. Here's two examples:

> St. Dominic (1170-1221) said, "Do not weep, for I shall be more useful to you after my death and I shall help you then more effectively than during my life." (CCC 956)

> St. Theresa of Lisieux (1873-1897) said, "I want to spend my heaven in doing good on earth." (CCC 956)

Certainly, this mindset is compassionate and commendable, but is it even possible? Can the saints in heaven help believers on earth after their demise? Can they fill a mediatorial role for those who connect with them in prayer? Could they even process the millions of petitions that might potentially "ascend" to them in a single day?

Altering the terminology

When non-Catholics question the legitimacy of this practice, some Catholics may try to adjust the explanation of the doctrine by explaining that they do not actually pray *to* the saints; rather, they petition the saints to pray in their behalf. However, according to the following quote, that's not a valid clarification:

> "The traditional language of the Church has always been that Catholics pray to the saints, and with good reason—prayer is simply a form of communication. Prayer is simply a request for help. Older usage in English reflects this: We've all heard lines from, say, Shakespeare, in which one person says to another "Pray thee . . . " (or "Prithee," a contraction of "Pray thee") and then makes a request. That's all we're doing when we pray to saints . . . So why the confusion, among both non-Catholics and some Catholics, about what prayer to the saints really means? It arises because both groups confuse prayer with worship. True worship (as opposed to veneration or honor) does indeed belong to God alone, and we should never worship man or any other creature, but only God."[70]

That should clear up some misconceptions about this practice, especially among non-Catholics, right? Not really. It is true in older versions of the Bible, like the King James or the American Standard, you do find the word "pray" used as a petition or a plea to fellow human beings (like Abram saying to Lot, "Separate thyself, I pray thee, from me" Genesis 13:9 KJV). However, newer translations do not use the word "pray" in this manner, but more modern words like "please."

Also, if you check all the occurrences of the word "prayer" (114 times in the New King James Version), you'll find that word *always* refers to petitioning God Himself. Therefore, the quote I just shared concerning the possible meaning of the words "pray" and "prayer" are most likely not even applicable to this discussion.

The bottom line is this: there is no passage in the Bible where an Israelite in the Old Testament or a follower of Jesus in the New Testament "prayed" to anyone but the true and living God, unless they were guilty of idolatry. If you are unsure of this claim, do a search from Genesis to Revelation yourself, entering the words "pray" and "prayer." I guarantee you will not find one example of that happening. Surely, if it was a legitimate biblical practice—and if it was powerful in its implementation—there would be an abundance of incidences throughout Scripture. However, you will not find one.

Revelation from the book of Revelation

There are two primary passages in the book of the Revelation that Catholics tend to cite as proof the saints in heaven can be petitioned in prayer. The apostle John, in the vision he received from God, was allowed to visit the throne room of the Almighty:

> *And I looked, and behold, in the midst of the throne*
> *and of the four living creatures, and in the midst of*
> *the elders, stood a Lamb as though it had been slain,*
> *having seven horns and seven eyes, which are the seven*
> *Spirits of God sent out into all the earth.*
> *Then He came and took the scroll out of the*
> *right hand of Him who sat on the throne.*
> *Now when He had taken the scroll, the four living*
> *creatures and the twenty-four elders fell down before*
> *the Lamb, each having a harp, and golden bowls full of*
> *incense, which are the prayers of the saints.*
> *(Revelation 5:6-8)*

Then three chapters later, when the seventh seal is opened, we find a continuation of this theme:

> *When He opened the seventh seal, there was*
> *silence in heaven for about half an hour.*
> *And I saw the seven angels who stand before God,*
> *and to them were given seven trumpets.*
> *Then another angel, having a golden censer, came and*
> *stood at the altar. He was given much incense, that he*
> *should offer it with the prayers of all the saints upon the*
> *golden altar which was before the throne.*
> *And the smoke of the incense, with the prayers of the*
> *saints, ascended before God from the angel's hand.*

*Then the angel took the censer, filled it with fire from
the altar, and threw it to the earth. And there were
noises, thunderings, lightnings, and an earthquake.*
(Revelation 8:1-5)

The big question is this: do these references to "saints" mean saints on the earth praying or saints in heaven praying, or both? The word "saint" (or "saints") appears 97 times in the entire Bible. The vast majority are references to God's people on the earth, in both the Old and New Testaments. A few times this term refers to God's people who have gone on to a heavenly existence. So, the "prayers of *all* the saints," as indicated in these verses, must be referring to both the saints on earth and the saints in heaven (Revelation 5:8, 8:3-4, emphasis by author).

From the Catholic perspective, however, the "saints" in this vision are the heavenly saints who have been canonized by the church and who pray to the Father in behalf of God's people on earth (an unacceptable view biblically). In deciphering the true meaning of this passage, we should ponder the following five points:

1. The "prayers of the saints," represented as golden bowls of incense, are presented to God from three different sources: the twenty-four elders, the four living creatures (probably cherubim), and the angel who appeared to John. We are never instructed in the Bible to pray to the elders, the cherubim, or any angel, yet they are the ones who made the final connection with the Almighty. So why should we pray to the heavenly saints and not these others? Of course, I am not suggesting that we do this. We are specifically warned in Colossians 2:18 against giving too much reverence to angels.

2. We do not know the actual identity of the twenty-four elders. Some have conjectured that they represent the heads of the twelve tribes of Israel from the Old Testament along with the twelve apostles from the New Testament—but this is only speculation. Besides, John was one of the twelve apostles, and he was the one having the vision. Did he see himself as one of the twenty-four. There were also twenty-four courses of priests that served in the Temple of Solomon—so there

could possibly be a connection there. No one knows for sure. Therefore, no definite doctrine can be established from this vision because the interpretation of this one aspect of the vision is so debatable.

3. The "prayers of the saints" that rise like incense before God are not individually examined by the twenty-four elders or the angel. Both present these prayers to God corporately, like thousands of names on a lengthy petition. Besides, this passage does not seem to relate to individual problems or challenges in the saints' lives that prayerfully require God's attention. It's about a final global resolution. Apparently, these united prayers concern one specific request—that God would execute final judgments on the excess of evil in the earth and restore this world to a paradise state by the second coming of the Messiah. Haven't we all prayed about that, petitioning the Lord, "Your kingdom come, Your will be done, on earth, as it is in heaven"? Surely, the elders, the cherubim, and the angels are all passionate about seeing this happen, too.

4. Finally, John's vision is metaphorical and symbolical, so any analysis of its content involves subjective conclusions based on personal opinions. Normally, major biblical doctrines of the Christian faith are never established by parables, metaphors, or symbolic images. These are primarily used by the Holy Spirit to enhance and to illustrate doctrines plainly revealed in other places in Scripture. Praying to the saints in heaven is never encouraged anywhere in the Bible. It has been extrapolated from passages like these with creative interpretations and imagined meanings.

5. Some Catholics may believe that "the golden bowls of incense" in these passages refer only to the prayers of canonized saints already in heaven. If that were the case, they are the ones— exclusively—whose prayers burn with an incense-like aroma before God's throne, and they are the ones representing ordinary believers who are still in the earth. The intercessory prayers of these heavenly saints are then passed along to the

twenty-four elders, the cherubim, and the angel who in turn present them to God. However, it was David in his earthly, fleshly state who cried, "Let my prayer be set before You as incense, the lifting up of my hands as the evening sacrifice" (Psalms 141:2)

If David, during his earthly sojourn, could offer prayers that burned like incense, so can we. Besides, Revelation 8:3 reveals that these golden bowls contain the prayers of "all" the saints, and (as already stated) that would have to include both saints in heaven and saints on earth.

The argument from the book of Job

Another Bible passage often quoted by Catholics to support this concept of heavenly saints praying on the behalf of earthly believers is Job 5:1 (KJV). Eliphaz, the Temanite, critically and skeptically suggested to Job:

> *"Call now, if there be any that will answer thee; and to which of the saints wilt thou turn?"*

However, this verse was not an inspired word from God. It was advice from Eliphaz that God later described as "words without knowledge" (Job 38:2). So, it was not a Spirit-breathed revelation to be enshrined as truth, but rather, a record of someone's faulty religious opinion. Besides, Eliphaz wasn't suggesting that it would work; instead, he was implying to Job that it would be a futile endeavor that would not work.

The story of the rich man and Lazarus

Another passage Catholics often reference to validate this doctrine is the story of the rich man and Lazarus (Luke 16:19-31). When the rich man died, he went to the chamber in *Hades* reserved for the wicked, and being in torment, he looked across an impassable gulf into a peaceful and blessed realm Jesus called "Abraham's bosom." The rich man appealed to Abraham to send Lazarus back to his living relatives to warn them, which Abraham declined to do, saying it would not work, because they would not listen. One Catholic apologist proposes:

"All of this reveals to us that not only can dead saints hear our requests; they also have some measure of power to carry them out on their own (though no doubt by God's power)."[71]

There are seven main reasons this story cannot be used to support the idea that God's people on earth can petition the saints who have gone on to heaven:

1. The rich man was not alive physically in the world when he presented his appeal to Abraham. He was in the chamber of the wicked in *Hades* (the underworld). If any doctrine could be built upon this story, it would be the possibility of the un-righteous in *Hades* (equivalent to *Sheol* in Hebrew), being able to communicate across the impassable gulf during the Old Testament period, not the people of God on earth being able to pray to the saints in heaven. Also, note that the rich man did not talk directly to Lazarus; he was only able to speak to Abraham.

2. The rich man was condemned before God for his earthly beha-vior; he was not a believer seeking to be pleasing to God. Why choose him as an example of someone praying effectively?

3. This subterranean scene related to a time before the resurrection of Jesus. Now that the full redemption price has been paid, the righteous who depart from this world are accepted immediately into the third heaven (the manifest presence of God)—which would probably be a much greater distance from the lower parts of the earth where *Hades* is located. And we have no idea if the inhabitants of *Hades* can peer into the third heaven, which is also called "Paradise." (See 2 Corinthians 12:1-4.) So, the logistics of this story are completely different than what they would be now.

4. The condemned rich man was talking to an Old Testament saint (Abraham), but Abraham never presented the rich man's appeal to God, which is supposed to be the next step of the process of praying to the saints.

5. The rich man's appeal was not answered, but rather rejected, and nothing happened because of the appeal he made. So, the approach was futile.

6. Jesus gave no indication that Abraham could have fulfilled this request even if he attempted to do so.

7. Evidently, the main reason Jesus shared this story was to exhort the rich not to selfishly hoard their riches, but instead, be compassionate toward the poor—and that eternal destinies can be determined by choices like that. If he was being supportive of the doctrine of praying to the saints, He would have surely chosen more suitable characters, situations, locations, and different results.

So, let me repeat the quote from the Catholic apologist I mentioned at the beginning of this discussion and give three short answers:

> All of this reveals to us that not only can dead saints hear our requests; they also have some measure of power to carry them out on their own (though no doubt by God's power).[72]

Does this story prove that dead saints can hear the prayerful requests of living believers? No, it does not! Does this story prove that Abraham had the power to fulfill the rich man's request? No, it does not! Does this story prove that Jesus endorses such a practice? No, it does not!

The logistical hurdle: omniscience and omnipresence

Praying to the saints, or petitioning the saints to pray in our behalf, is not only unbiblical; it is also illogical. There are 1.3 billion Catholics in the world. What if just ten percent of them petitioned Saint Peter in one day to intercede in their behalf? That's 13 million prayers in one day! Do the math. That breaks down to 541,667 thousand prayers every hour and 9,028 prayers every minute. What if you had 9,028 people talking to you at the same time? Could you handle that mental overload? In order to process that many communications intelligently, effectively, simultaneously, peacefully, responsively, and powerfully, Peter (or any other saint being approached by the multitudes) would require the remarkable divine attribute of omniscience.

In a sense, Peter would also need to be personally present with each petitioner to be involved in a meaningful way. Growing up, I "talked" to my patron saint, Christopher, as if he was right there with me. I never considered the possibility of millions of other Catholics requesting his involvement in their issues at the same time. Therefore, to be in thousands of locations in one minute would also demand a second remarkable, divine attribute: omnipresence.

I would dare to say this dual requirement would make it impossible, even for someone in a perfected heavenly state, to respond to the prayers of earthly believers. In my theology, omniscience and omnipresence are attributes that belong to God alone. The whole idea of praying to the saints is neither logically, nor theologically correct.

Is attempting to contact the dead acceptable in the sight of God?

There is another point that needs to be emphasized. Trying to contact the dead is strictly forbidden in the Bible. Just attempting to do so is called an abomination:

> "When you come into the land which the LORD your
> God is giving you, you shall not learn to follow the
> abominations of those nations.
> There shall not be found among you anyone who makes
> his son or his daughter pass through the fire, or one who
> practices witchcraft, or a soothsayer, or one who
> interprets omens, or a sorcerer, or one who conjures
> spells, **or a medium, or a spiritist, or one
> who calls up the dead.**
> For all who do these things are an abomination to the
> LORD, and because of these abominations the LORD
> your God drives them out from before you."
> (Deuteronomy 18:9-12, See Leviticus 19:31; 20:6, 27)

The King James Version of this passage describes the person who participates in this occult practice as "one who consults with familiar spirits" and a "necromancer." The New King James Version instead uses the word "mediums." God's mandate to His people regarding these spiritual practices is unambiguous:

*"Give no regard to **mediums and familiar spirits**; do not seek after them, to be defiled by them: I am the LORD your God."*
(Leviticus 19:31)

*"And the person who turns to **mediums and familiar spirits**, to prostitute himself with them, I will set My face against that person and cut him off from his people."*
(Leviticus 20:6)

These are strong and stern communications from the Most High God that should be heeded by those who claim to love Him. Admittedly, there is a big difference between a medium trying to conjure up the spirits of the dead to receive psychic communications or predictions, and a Catholic believer petitioning departed saints to pray in his or her behalf. However, both involve an attempt to converse with departed spirit-beings in a different spiritual realm. If the former is forbidden, the latter is forbidden also. If necromancy is described as spiritual prostitution in Leviticus 20:6, then praying to the saints fits into the same category. Forgive me if this sounds harsh, but I believe it is true, and for your benefit, I am attempting to convey the unadulterated Word of God.

In debating this issue, Catholic theologians often cite the example of Moses and Elijah appearing to Peter, James, and John on the Mount of Transfiguration. They claim this supernatural event proves the possibility of communication with saints in the celestial world. Such a proposal begs the following three responses:

1. Peter, James, and John were not praying to Moses and Elijah, asking for them to appear or to pray in their behalf when the visitation took place. It happened at the sovereign will of God.

2. Neither Moses nor Elijah petitioned God to do anything for Peter, James, and John, interceding for them in the manner of departed saints.

3. When Peter, James, and John gave too much reverence to Moses and Elijah (offering to make them tabernacles), they disappeared from the vision, and the audible voice of the Father adjusted the worldview of the disciples by saying:

> *"This is my beloved Son, in whom*
> *I am well pleased. Hear Him!"*
> *(See Matthew 17:1-9, Mark 9:2-7, Luke 9:28-36.)*

This last point is probably the strongest. I believe it would benefit us greatly if the Father spoke again audibly to the millions who have given too much credit and too much reverence to supposed canonized saints, even naming numerous cathedrals and churches after them. Isn't this custom similar to the apostles wanting to make Moses and Elijah "tabernacles"? Shouldn't all this attention and glory should be reserved for God alone?

> *For there is one God and one Mediator between God*
> *and men, the Man Christ Jesus.*
> *(1 Timothy 2:5)*

It is true that when Jesus died on the cross there was an earthquake, and a number of burial sites were affected, so that "many bodies of the saints who had fallen asleep were raised and coming out of the tombs after His resurrection they went into the holy city and appeared to many" (Matthew 27:51-53). However, these visitations happened purely at the will of God, not because Israelites were praying specifically to those saints to intervene for them. Such a practice is an attempt to penetrate a realm that God withholds from human beings living in this world.

The reference to Jeremiah in Second Maccabees

Catholics, at times, reference a book that is not contained in the Protestant canon of Scripture concerning this doctrine (2 Maccabees 15:14-17, Douay-Rheims 1899 American Edition). In this passage, a dream is related in which Jeremiah, who is in heaven, is praised as a lover of the Israelite people who prays often for them.

Once again, even if that book was inspired and if that dream was true, it does not prove that any Israelites communicated prayer requests to

Jeremiah or expected to get a personal response from him or personal involvement in presenting their petitions to God. It is possible that the saints in heaven can intercede for those on earth—and I would not be surprised if they do. However, it is not possible for communication to take place between us and them.

God's Word tells us to pray for the saints, not to the saints

There is probably no better way to close this chapter than to quote Paul's exhortation to the Ephesian church:

> *Praying always with all prayer and supplication in the*
> *Spirit, being watchful to this end with all perseverance*
> *and supplication for all the saints.*
> *(Ephesians 6:18)*

This one verse adjusts our focus and shifts it where it needs to be placed: not pursuing prayer *from* departed saints above but praying *for* living saints below.

The icing on the cake

The following passage paints an amazing picture from which we can draw some convincing final conclusions (which will provide the icing on the cake, if you will):

> *Therefore we also, since we are surrounded by so great*
> *a cloud of witnesses, let us lay aside every weight, and*
> *the sin which so easily ensnares us, and let us run with*
> *endurance the race that is set before us,*
> *looking unto Jesus, the author and finisher of our faith,*
> *who for the joy that was set before Him endured the*
> *cross, despising the shame, and has sat down at the*
> *right hand of the throne of God.*
> *(Hebrews 12:1-2)*

This description of a heavenly throng of witnesses surrounding us may be literal, but most likely, it is metaphorical. Regardless, it sums up the chapter that precedes it powerfully (Hebrews, chapter 11). It's as if the writer is saying that all the heroes of the faith in heaven that were listed (Noah, Abraham, Sarah, Moses, and so on) are watching the progress of God's people on earth and cheering us onward. I tend to think it's just figurative speech—but even if it was literal, even if the departed saints can peer into this realm and into our lives, this passage does not encourage us to look to them. It does not say, "Appeal to the cloud of witnesses to intercede in your behalf." Instead, it explains we should always be, "Looking unto Jesus, the author and finisher of our faith."

He is "the Great High Priest" who "ever lives to make intercession" for His people. Furthermore, "the Spirit Himself intercedes for us" (Hebrews 7:25 MKJV, Romans 8:26 NCB).

If that be true, if both the Lord Jesus Christ and the Holy Spirit —omniscient, omnipotent, and omnipresent—are petitioning the Father in our behalf, why would we ever involve ourselves in the questionable pursuit of trying to contact mere saints to intercede for us whose authority, power, and attributes pale in comparison?

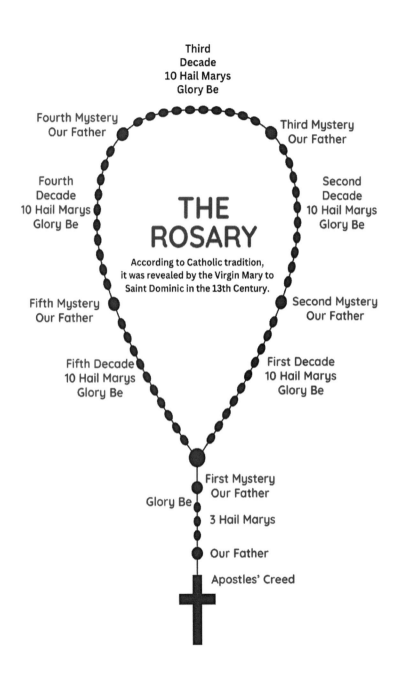

Third
Decade
10 Hail Marys
Glory Be

Fourth Mystery
Our Father

Third Mystery
Our Father

Fourth
Decade
10 Hail Marys
Glory Be

Second
Decade
10 Hail Marys
Glory Be

THE
ROSARY

According to Catholic tradition,
it was revealed by the Virgin Mary to
Saint Dominic in the 13th Century.

Fifth Mystery
Our Father

Second Mystery
Our Father

Fifth Decade
10 Hail Marys
Glory Be

First Decade
10 Hail Marys
Glory Be

First Mystery
Our Father

Glory Be

3 Hail Marys

Our Father

Apostles' Creed

Question 12

What is the rosary; when was it created, and should it be used as an aid to prayer?

The reciting of the rosary is a very sacred religious tradition in the Catholic religion. I understand why many devoted Catholics find solace, peace, and a sense of connection through this prescribed and predictable pattern of prayer. My grandmother prayed the rosary every day—faithfully—and she was a beautiful person, a godly woman, and a faithful believer.

The word "rosary" means a garland of roses. The rose is one of the flowers that symbolizes the Virgin Mary and repeated prayers to her dominate the rosary. The rosary first consists of a crucifix (a cross with the form of the crucified Savior—a reminder of His sacrificial death). The crucifix is attached to a short string of five beads that then connects to a larger, circular string of fifty-four beads, making up a total of fifty-nine. These beads (or knots) are intended to help keep track of the exact sequence of the required prayers so they will be most efficacious.

If you are unfamiliar with the Catholic method of praying the rosary, here is a quick overview of that tradition (as illustrated on opposite page). The worshiper starts by holding the crucifix, and making the sign of the cross. Sometimes, the one praying kisses the cross before reciting the Apostles' Creed. On the first large bead, the "Our Father" is prayed, followed by three "Hail Marys" while moving the fingers across the three smaller beads. Next, while touching the chain, the "Glory Be" is uttered. Then, while gripping the next large bead, the first mystery to be worshipfully pondered is declared, followed by another "Our Father." This begins the reciting of five sets of twelve prayers (called decades). Each of the five decades consists of the "Our Father," followed by ten "Hail Marys," then one "Glory Be."

(The exact wording of the Apostles' Creed and these traditional prayers can be found under Appendixes #1-2.)

Meditating on the Mysteries

Each of the five decades is associated with a biblical mystery that should be pondered while saying that portion of the rosary. There are four sets of five different mysteries that are supposed to be celebrated at designated times. Here is the list:[73]

The Joyful Mysteries (Remembering Jesus' Birth):

These are to be the object of meditation on Mondays and Saturdays, and the Sundays from 1st Sunday of Advent until Lent.

1. The Annunciation to Mary (Luke 1:26–38)

2. The Visitation of Mary (Luke 1:39–56)

3. The Birth of our Lord Jesus Christ (Luke 2:1–21)

4. Presentation of the Child Jesus in the Temple (Luke 2:22–38)

5. The Finding of Our Lord in the Temple (Luke 2:41–52)

The Sorrowful Mysteries (Recalling Jesus' Passion and Death)

These are to be the object of meditation on Tuesdays and Fridays, and the Sundays of Lent.

1. The Agony of Christ in the Garden (Matthew 26:36–56)

2. The Scourging at the Pillar (Matthew 27:26)

3. The Crowning with Thorns (Matthew 27:27–31)

4. The Carrying of the Cross (Matthew 27:32)

5. The Crucifixion of Our Lord on the Cross (Matthew 27:33–56)

The Glorious Mysteries (Celebrating Jesus' Resurrection and His Ascension). These are to be the object of meditation on Wednesdays and Sundays from Easter until Advent.

1. The Resurrection of Our Lord (John 20:1–29)

2. The Ascension of Our Lord (Luke 24:36–53)

3. The Descent of the Holy Spirit upon the Apostles (Acts 2:1–41)

4. The Assumption of the Blessed Virgin Mary into Heaven

5. The Coronation of Our Lady as Queen of Heaven and Earth

(Note: there are no Bible references for the last two mysteries.)

The Luminous Mysteries (The Mysteries of Light)

Pope John Paul II introduced these mysteries in 2002, to be the object of meditation on Thursdays.

1. The Baptism in the Jordan River (Matthew 3:13–16)

2. The Wedding Feast at Cana (John 2:1–11)

3. The Preaching of the Coming Kingdom of God (Mark 1:14–15)

4. The Transfiguration (Matthew 17:1–8)

5. The Institution of the Holy Eucharist (Matthew 26)

Some Catholics, after completing the rosary, add on two more prayers:

> *Hail, Holy Queen, Mother of mercy, our life, our sweetness, and our hope. To thee do we cry, poor banished children of Eve, to thee do we send up our sighs, mourning and weeping in this valley of tears. Turn then, most gracious advocate, thine eyes of mercy toward us; and after this our exile show unto us the blessed fruit of thy womb Jesus, O clement, O loving, O sweet Virgin Mary. Pray for us, O holy Mother of God. That we may be made worthy of the promises of Christ.*

> *O God, whose only-begotten Son, by His life, death, and resurrection, has purchased for us the rewards of eternal salvation; grant we beseech Thee, that meditating upon these mysteries of the most holy Rosary of the Blessed Virgin Mary, we may imitate what they contain and obtain what they promise. Through the same Christ our Lord. Amen.*[74]

Many Catholics also add the Fatima Prayer after each "Glory Be" and before the next "Our Father," It is worded as follows:

> *O My Jesus, forgive us our sins, save us from the fires of hell and lead all souls to heaven, especially those in most need of Thy mercy. Amen.*

Pondering the practice of repetitious prayer

To begin with, I believe that pondering these mysteries is something all believers should do whenever they can, without the use of the rosary (except for the assumption and coronation of Mary—which I believe are erroneous beliefs, to be discussed in upcoming chapters.)

There are both logical and theological reasons why the practice of praying the rosary should be discarded. First, let's approach it with logic. Can you imagine appealing to a fellow human being using a method similar to the rosary. Would you expect a positive response? Or would it be considered silly, futile and even ridiculous?

For instance, if you were a married woman, would you go to your husband, kneel in a certain prescribed position, light a candle, then pull out a string of fifty-nine beads and prayerfully request ten times with every decade, "Please take out the garbage." Then on the single beads, between the decades, would you prayerfully promise in a somewhat monotone voice, "If you do, I will iron your shirts." Then, while clutching the chain between the decades, would you pledge, "If you do, I will fix your breakfast and wash the dishes every day. "

What if this same ritual was necessary to repeat every time you wanted to coerce your husband into responding to you for anything you needed from him? Unnecessary and absurd, right? Yes, absolutely.

So if that would not work, then how should a woman approach

her husband? Simple. She should lovingly and respectfully request of him what is needed, and he should then lovingly and respectfully respond by happily complying with her request, all in one easy flow of communication, not something repeated numerous times for greater impact. It's all an exchange based on mutual love and respect, not coercion, control, repetition, or manipulation.

Real prayer is communication to God in an intelligent, spontaneous, and conversational flow of words that convey heartfelt worship and sincere requests. Beads are not necessary to "log" an exact number of prayers to somehow better convince God (or Mary) to hear and respond—or, if the rosary is being prayed for the sake of gaining indulgences, to grant an earlier release from Purgatory. Prayer is not that mechanical; it is relational.

Other religions such as Baha'i, Buddhism, Hinduism, and Islam use prayer beads, but even though the adherents of those religions are usually very passionate and sincere, their traditions and rituals never have and never will lead people to the true God. In fact, Buddhism doesn't even acknowledge the existence of God.

Please ask this question in your own mind: if wrong belief systems emphasize the practice of using prayer beads, why should those who profess to understand the true plan of salvation stoop to imitate something so fruitless and futile. Jeremiah 10:2-3 says, "Learn not the way of the heathen" . . . "for the customs of the people are vain" (KJV).

(See Appendix #3, "More reflections on the practice of repetitious prayer.")

The history of the rosary

Although different opinions exist, many Catholic historians and popes believe the rosary can be traced to a priest named Dominic who ministered in southern France in the beginning of the 13th century. However, this was over a millennium after Jesus walked the earth. Think of that! For over a thousand years, this practice was non-existent among professing Christians.

Here is the back story. For about 200 years, a heretical doctrine spread across Europe called Albigensianism. The members of that sect taught that only the spiritual is good, and that everything material is bad. So human beings are trapped in something evil, the physical body. The sole way to experience salvation was to be set free from the imprisonment of the flesh. A Spanish priest named Dominic Guzman traveled through France teaching against this heretical concept but was unsuccessful in gaining a following. In 1208, Dominic was praying in a forest, pleading with God to show him what was needed to prevail over the Albigensian heresy and establish the truth.

> "Ancient accounts tell us that, after three days of prayer and fasting, three angels appeared in the sky along with a ball of fire. When they disappeared, the Virgin Mary spoke, telling the priest that he must preach her Psalter in order to succeed in his struggle to overcome the Albigensians."[75]

The Marian Psalter was a prayer discipline used by the Cistercians, a monastic order in France. Larger than the rosary, it was comprised of 150 "Hail Marys" divided up into groups of ten, separated by "Our Fathers."

Supposedly, Mary also revealed to Dominic the mysteries that should be pondered along with this method of repetitious prayer. About five years later, in an effort to take over France, a force of 30,000 Albigensians threatened Dominic who had only 1,500 Catholic fighters on his side. "Confident of their upcoming success, the Albigensians spent the night before the battle celebrating in drunkenness and debauchery. The Catholics, on the other hand, spent their night praying the Rosary; launching a surprise attack, though, the Catholic forces won."[76] Dominic attributed their success to the praying of the rosary. Thus promoted, it because a celebrated practice which has grown in popularity since.

Was the visitation of Mary a real vision? Is the praying of the rosary a legitimate practice? Was Dominic's victory on the battlefield proof of its legitimacy? Does it have a biblical basis? All of these questions need to be answered.

Although I do not address in this book the crucially important subject of the proposed visitations of Mary, I firmly believe that they were not authentic revelations from God. Truly committed Catholics usually hallow these accounts and do not question their legitimacy

(Fatima, Lourdes, etc.). However, just because encounters are supernatural does not automatically mean they are right.

Mohammed claimed to have visitations of the angel Gabriel, the same angel that visited Mary, but the resulting belief system of the Muslim faith denies that Jesus is the Son of God and that He went to the cross to provide redemption for humankind.

Even if benefits seem to result from certain religious practices, that does not mean they are approved by God. Many people tout the supposed benefits of Transcendental Meditation, but TM is a dangerous occult practice that can result in demonic influence in a person's life. Spiritual experiences must align with the Word of God to be acceptable in the sight of God, and that is not the case with the rosary or with the communications Dominic claimed to receive from Mary. The early church never prayed the rosary. None of the Bible writers wrote about it or even remotely implied an endorsement for such a practice. If they didn't, we shouldn't—as simple as that.

One of the main reasons for rejecting the use of the rosary is its core emphasis on petitioning Mary. There are fifty-three "Hail Marys," while there are only six "Our Fathers" and six "Glory Be to God" prayers. Wouldn't you agree that tips the scale of importance excessively to Mary's side? She is more emphasized than God! Should any mere human being, though redeemed, be exalted to such a degree? My immediate response would be, "Absolutely not!"

I know this is very hard for committed Catholics to receive, but I do not think Mary should be petitioned at all. Hopefully, the next four chapters will more fully state and prove that position.

Question 13

Is devotion to Mary biblically appropriate, spiritually helpful, and acceptable to God?

The veneration of Mary, the mother of Jesus, is a major doctrinal pillar in Catholicism. Unquestionably, those who are devoted to the mother of Jesus are usually deeply sincere and intensely reverent.

There are seven fundamental concepts surrounding Mary emphasized in Catholicism that need to occupy our attention in this and the next three chapters: the Annunciation (the angel Gabriel announcing that she would conceive by the Holy Spirit), her status as the mother of God, her Immaculate Conception, her Perpetual Virginity, her Assumption into heaven, her position as Queen of heaven, and the practice of petitioning her in prayer.

The sum of all these beliefs concerning Mary is referred to as Mariology or the Marian dogmas of the Catholic Church. Some are found in the Bible, while others are non-biblical. As already shared in previous chapters, two have been established through papal decrees declared to be infallible (spoken *ex cathedra*).

The Annunciation

Here is the passage out of the Gospel of Luke that describes the visitation Mary received from the angel Gabriel:

> *Now in the sixth month the angel Gabriel was*
> *sent by God to a city of Galilee named Nazareth,*

*to a virgin betrothed to a man whose name
was Joseph, of the house of David.
The virgin's name was Mary.
And having come in, the angel said to her,
"Rejoice, highly favored one, the Lord is with you;
blessed are you among women!"
But when she saw him, she was troubled at his saying,
and considered what manner of greeting this was.
Then the angel said to her, "Do not be afraid, Mary,
for you have found favor with God.
And behold, you will conceive in your womb and bring
forth a Son, and shall call His name JESUS.
He will be great, and will be called the Son of the
Highest; and the Lord God will give Him the
throne of His father David.
And He will reign over the house of Jacob forever,
and of His kingdom there will be no end."
Then Mary said to the angel, "How can this be,
since I do not know a man?"
And the angel answered and said to her, "The Holy
Spirit will come upon you, and the power of the
Highest will overshadow you; therefore, also, that Holy
One who is to be born will be called the Son of God.
Now indeed, Elizabeth your relative has also
conceived a son in her old age; and this is now the sixth
month for her who was called barren.
For with God nothing will be impossible."
Then Mary said, "Behold the maidservant of the Lord!
Let it be to me according to your word."
And the angel departed from her.
(Luke 1:26-38)*

There is no more powerful, inspirational, heartwarming account to be found in the Bible. We can all rejoice over heaven's abundant intervention in the lives of lowly human beings who so desperately needed a Savior. That Mary was chosen for such a holy task is awe-inspiring indeed! She should be deeply respected and revered for filling such a pivotal role.

Mary was identified as being "blessed" among women. To be "blessed" means to be supremely happy, spiritual prosperous, highly favored, and one who possesses qualities of character God considers the highest good. To be chosen to be the mother of the Son of God made Mary "blessed" indeed, but this is not a status unique to her. Numerous scriptures confer a "blessed" status on all of God's chosen people who are devoted to Him (e.g., Genesis 26:29, Psalms 1:1; 32:1-2). She may have been the "blessed" virgin Mary, but all who are saved eternally are called "the blessed of the Father." (See Matthew 25:34.)

Mary is also described as being "highly favored" of God in Luke 1:28, but many individuals in Scripture have also received God's favor (e.g., Job / Job 10:12, Gideon / Judges 6:17, David / Psalms 30:7 and more).

The Greek word that is translated "highly favored" is *charitoo* (pronounced khar-ee-to'-o). This unique word can mean a person who is endued with exceptional honor. It is only found twice in the Bible (once in reference to Mary and once in reference to all God's New Covenant sons and daughters). Concerning the latter, *charitoo* is translated "made accepted" in the following passage:

> *Having predestined us to adoption as sons by Jesus Christ to Himself, according to the good pleasure of His will, to the praise of the glory of His grace, by which He **made us accepted** in the Beloved.*
> *(Ephesians 1:5-6)*

So, Mary was "highly favored" because she was chosen to be the virtuous virgin who would carry Emmanuel (God with us) for nine months and raise Him to maturity. (See Isaiah 7:14, Matthew 1:23.) But all born-again believers are "highly favored" because the Savior of all mankind (Emmanuel) dwells in their hearts forever.

Furthermore, we are "accepted in the Beloved" (Ephesians 1:6). The One being referred to as "the Beloved" in this verse is Jesus. That's the word the Father declared over Him at his baptism ("This is My *beloved* Son"—Matthew 3:17). So, basically this verse is communicating that if we have been born again and we are "in Christ" (under His Headship and Lordship), we are just as beloved of the Father as the firstborn Son.

We are just as accepted in the presence of the Father as He. We are "accepted in the Beloved." What a powerful truth!

Let me reemphasize, Mary was "highly favored" because Jesus, the holy and eternal Son of God, dwelt within her womb for nine months, but true believers are "highly favored" because Jesus dwells within their hearts forever. This permanent indwelling was also poured out on Mary, because evidently, she was "born again" along with all the other disciples when the Holy Spirit came into the upper room on the Day of Pentecost. (See Acts 1:14.) So, she was doubly favored by God.

The mother of God

All believers, Catholic and non-Catholic alike, should be very familiar with the following Scripture passage that describes Elizabeth's reaction when Mary, her cousin, came to visit her:

> *Now Mary arose in those days and went into the hill*
> *country with haste, to a city of Judah,*
> *and entered the house of Zacharias*
> *and greeted Elizabeth.*
> *And it happened, when Elizabeth heard the greeting of*
> *Mary, that the babe leaped in her womb;*
> *and Elizabeth was filled with the Holy Spirit.*
> *Then she spoke out with a loud voice and said,*
> *"Blessed are you among women, and*
> *blessed is the fruit of your womb!*
> *But why is this granted to me, that the*
> *mother of my Lord should come to me?*
> *For indeed, as soon as the voice of your greeting*
> *sounded in my ears, the babe*
> *leaped in my womb for joy.*
> *Blessed is she who believed, for there will be a*
> *fulfillment of those things which were*
> *told her from the Lord."*
> *(Luke 1:39-45)*

Of course, for Elizabeth to call Mary "the mother of my Lord" was not a declaration that Mary was the originator of God, or that she came before God, but rather, that she was that holy woman who supplied an earthly womb where the two natures could merge—that Jesus might be fully man and fully God.

The Greek word translated "Lord" in Elizabeth's statement (verse 43) is *kurios*, which is also translated "God" in the New Testament. So, describing Mary as "the mother of our Lord" or "the mother of God" is basically saying the same thing. Those who believe in the glorious miracle of the incarnation understand that the bestowal of this title only means the "mother" of the Son of God in His incarnate state, not His eternal state. All true Christians should be in full agreement with this wondrous insight.

Mary's response has been titled "The Magnificat." It begins with the following lines:

> *"My soul magnifies the Lord,*
> *And my spirit has rejoiced in God my Savior.*
> *For He has regarded the lowly state of His maidservant;*
> *for behold, henceforth all generations*
> *will call me blessed.*
> *For He who is mighty has done great things*
> *for me, and holy is His name."*
> *(Luke 1:46-49)*

I don't believe Mary said this with the expectation of receiving the kind of excessive veneration that has grown through the centuries. It was a humble and worshipful utterance giving glory to God for what He had done and expressing great gratitude to Him for choosing her. Yes, Mary was "the mother of God" in the limited sense that she was chosen as the sanctified 'incubator' in which His earthly, human body could develop.

So far, in these fundamental areas, all true Christians can be united in faith, both Catholics and non-Catholics. We all believe that Mary received an angelic visitation, that she was "highly favored," and that she was the "mother of God" in His earthly incarnation. However, in the next three chapters we will examine some of the more controversial Marian dogmas that are only discoverable outside of the biblical narrative.

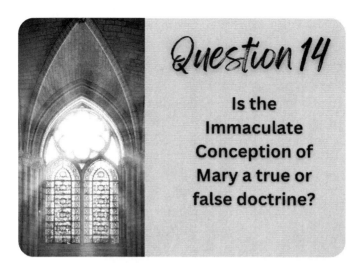

Question 14

Is the Immaculate Conception of Mary a true or false doctrine?

The doctrine of the "Immaculate Conception" introduces the revolutionary idea that Mary was conceived without a transfer of original sin from Adam and Eve.

What is "original sin"? It is an inborn inclination toward evil: a base lower nature, a defiled spiritual condition, a state of separation from God, that is transferred at conception. David lamented this inherited plight, saying:

> *Behold, I was brought forth in iniquity, and in sin my mother conceived me. (Psalms 51:5)*

As mentioned under Question #3, Paul referred to this **hereditary spiritual** condition as "the law of sin" which is in our "members" (Romans 7:23). He also described the consequence of this dilemma:

> *Therefore, just as through one man sin entered the world, and death through sin, and thus death spread to all men, because all sinned."*
> *(Romans 5:12)*

A kind of death-state results from being born into these physical bodies that affects us spiritually, soulishly (mentally and emotionally) and physically. As we age, it causes a continual decline toward physical death, then ultimately, eternal death. Some are more susceptible to the spiritual and soulish aspects than others. To a limited degree, some human beings can rise above this state of spiritual death by yielding to the conscience, exerting will power, and striving to become ethical or religious people—yet even then, they must finally succumb to this fearful stalker when aging takes its toll. Our plight would be hopeless were it not for the answer provided through the incarnation, as revealed in a conclusion Paul reached in his writings:

> *O wretched man that I am! Who will deliver me from*
> *this body of death? I thank God—through*
> *Jesus Christ our Lord!*
> *(Romans 7:24-25)*

Only through a valid salvation experience given by Jesus Christ can this lower nature be effectively conquered, only by being born again and filled with the Spirit of God.

The Bible does not mention anyone ever being exempt from this dilemma. Even the great prophet Elijah "was a man subject to like passions as we are" (James 5:17) Yet it is taught in the Catholic Church that Mary was not included in this inescapable, problematic condition. Such an unconventional idea cannot be found in Scripture, and it was certainly not taught in the early church. It became a major issue of debate among church theologians in the Middle Ages because it was too controversial, and no doctrinal agreement could be reached between the factions.

Surprisingly, it did not gain widespread acceptance until the 19th century when it was adopted as church dogma by Pope Pius IX on December 8, 1854, with the proclamation titled, *Ineffabilis Deus* (an apostolic constitution—the most solemn declaration of church doctrine). It is one of two declarations concerning Mary that were made *ex cathedra* (a communication from the pope considered infallible). The other also concerns her alleged assumption into heaven at the end of her earthly journey (once again, escaping the grips of death).

Surprisingly also, this doctrine of the "Immaculate Conception" had the overwhelming support of the church's hierarchy, although a few, including the Archbishop of Paris, warned that this idea is not stated in the New Testament and could not be deduced from it. Protestants at the time overwhelmingly rejected *Ineffabilis Deus* as an excessive expression of papal power and they rejected the doctrine, declaring it to be without foundation in Scripture. However, a belief being extra-biblical is usually not a matter of major concern for Catholics, because they are required to give equal respect to "Sacred Tradition" and "the Magisterium."

(See Appendix #8 on "The Three Legs of Catholicism").

However, many Catholics are deeply sincere, so they should be motivated by the truth of God's Word more than blind allegiance to church doctrine, church traditions, and church authorities.

It is to such truth-loving, God-loving individuals that I make this appeal—inspect the roots of this doctrine closely and if you agree that it is spurious, discard it, and cling to the Bible. God's Word alone is a lamp unto our feet and a light unto our path.

Question 15

Is it true that Mary is a perpetual virgin, or did she have more children after the Son of God?

A respected Catholic writer explains the passionately defended belief in the perpetual virgin status of Mary, the mother of Jesus, with the following statement:

"The teaching of Mary's perpetual virginity is one of the longest defined dogmas of the Church. It was taught by the earliest Church Fathers, including: Tertullian, St. Athanasius, St. Ambrose, and St. Augustine. And it was officially declared a dogma at the Fifth Ecumenical Council in Constantinople in 553 A.D. That declaration called Mary 'ever-virgin.' A century later, a statement by Pope Martin 1 clarified that 'ever-virgin' meant Mary was a virgin before, during, and after Christ's birth. Of those three aspects of Mary's perpetual virginity, the easiest part to see in Scripture is her virginal conception of Christ. Both Matthew and Luke leave no room for doubt on that (Mt 1:18; Lk 1:34–35, 3:23). That virginal motherhood is the guarantor of both Jesus' divinity and Jesus' humanity. It safeguards the truth that he was both fully God and fully man."[77]

An important part of this statement is absolutely, undeniably true, that Jesus was "fully God and fully man," however, it should be soberly considered that Tertullian died in the 3rd century (220 A.D.),

Athanasius died in the 4th century (373 A.D.), and Augustine died in the 5th century (430 A.D.)—so they were not among the "earliest Church fathers." Quite the contrary, they were centuries removed from the original event. To make such a claim is like saying that Teddy Roosevelt, John F. Kennedy, and Ronald Reagan were among the earliest presidents of the United States.

Although Mary is a shining beacon of virtue, the claim of her "perpetual virginhood" is not in agreement with the biblical narrative. After she conceived of the Holy Spirit and brought forth the Lord Jesus (an amazing fulfillment of prophecy that should fill us with awe), Mary had other children by Joseph, verified often in Scripture.

The following verse clearly indicates that Joseph did not have intimate relations with Mary until after Jesus was born. An angel warned him not to fear taking Mary as his wife, because what was in her womb had been conceived by the Holy Spirit.

> *Then Joseph, being aroused from sleep, did as*
> *the angel of the Lord commanded him and*
> *took to him his wife, and did not know her*
> *till she had brought forth her firstborn Son.*
> *And he called His name JESUS.*
> *(Matthew 1:24-25)*

In this passage, the word "know" is a common biblical description of a man having sexual relations with a woman. This use of this term begins in Scripture with the foreparents of the human race ("And Adam knew Eve his wife; and she conceived" Genesis 4:1, see verse 25). The New Catholic Bible gives an even more clear rendering of what this passage in the Gospel of Matthew was meant to convey:

> *When Joseph rose from sleep, he did what the angel of*
> *the Lord had commanded him. He took Mary into his*
> *home as his wife,* **but he engaged in no marital**
> **relations with her until she gave birth to**
> **a son, whom he named Jesus.**
> *(Matthew 1:24-25 NCB)*

Based on this statement in the first Gospel, we can easily conclude that after Jesus was born, Joseph *did* have conjugal relations with Mary.

Is there any other way of interpreting these words? I don't think so. My conclusion? Simple. Mary was not "ever-virgin."

Did Jesus have brothers and sisters?

There are quite a few passages that mention Jesus having brothers and sisters, such as the following:

> *While He was still talking to the multitudes, behold,*
> *His mother and brothers stood outside,*
> *seeking to speak with Him.*
> *Then one said to Him, "Look, Your mother and Your*
> *brothers are standing outside,*
> *seeking to speak with You."*
> *But He answered and said to the one who told Him,*
> *"Who is My mother and who are My brothers?"*
> *And He stretched out His hand toward His disciples*
> *and said, "Here are My mother and My brothers!*
> *For whoever does the will of My Father in heaven is*
> *My brother and sister and mother."*
> *(Matthew 12:46-50)*

Jesus' brothers are even named in Gospels:

> *"Is this not the carpenter's son? Is not His mother*
> *called Mary? And His brothers James, Joses,*
> *Simon, and Judas?*
> *And His sisters, are they not all with us? Where then*
> *did this Man get all these things?"*
> *So they were offended at Him. But Jesus said to them,*
> *"A prophet is not without honor except in his own*
> *country and in his own house."*
> *Now He did not do many mighty works there*
> *because of their unbelief. (Matthew 13:55-58)*

Other references include Mark 3:32; 6:3, Luke 8:19-21, John 2:12; 7:3-5, Acts 1:4, 1 Corinthians 9:5, Galatians 1:19.

Some Catholic teachers insist that those referred to as Jesus' brothers were really His cousins. However, the Greek word translated "brothers" in Matthew 13:55 is *adelphos* (pronounced ad-el-fos') and that is always the intended meaning. Even when Bible writers addressed fellow believers as spiritual "brethren," the word is *adelphos*. You don't call others in the body of Christ your spiritual cousins; you refer to them as your brothers and sisters. So, whether natural brothers or spiritual brothers are being referenced, *adelphos* is the word of choice. The similar word for "sisters" in the next verse (Matthew 13:56) is *adelphe* (pronounced ad-el-fay').

The word "cousin" only appears once in the King James Version of the New Testament. It is from the Greek word *suggenes* (pronounced soong-ghen-ace') and is a reference to Elizabeth, Mary's cousin, found in Luke 1:36. It can also mean simply a relative. If James, Joses, Simon, and Judas, were his cousins, *suggenes* would have been a more logical word choice.

The other alternative view offered by some Catholics is that Jesus' brothers and sisters were not biological siblings, but step-siblings, children that Joseph had by another spouse before he was wed to Mary. There is no way of proving that, though, because there is no record scripturally or historically of that being the case.

When all these scriptures are taken verbatim, and their meaning weighed out logically and sensibly, it is impossible to believe that Mary possessed the status of being a "perpetual virgin." To embrace that idea, one must overlook very plain evidence in the holy Word of God.

Was this belief spawned by pagan influence?

There exists a strong possibility of pagan influence behind the adoption of the belief of Mary's perpetual virginity. This connection could have been intentional or unintentional, knowledgeable or coincidental. Going back to another Greek word in the New Testament reveals a likely link. The following verse concerns the miraculous nature of Jesus' birth and is often quoted by all professing Christians:

> "Behold, a virgin shall be with child, and shall bring
> forth a son, and they shall call his name Emmanuel,
> which being interpreted is, God with us."
> (Matthew 1:23)

The Greek word translated "virgin" in this verse is *parthenos*. From that word, the related word "Parthenon" was derived. The Parthenon was an impressive, marble temple built between 447 and 432 B.C. on the Acropolis in Athens, Greece, at the peak of the Grecian empire. The Parthenon housed a statue of a female deity in the Greek pantheon referred to adoringly as "Athena Parthenos" (Athena, the virgin goddess). She was haled as the goddess of wisdom.

The Christian Byzantines eventually conquered Greece in the 6th century A.D. and outlawed the pagan worship of the ancient Greek gods. Toward the end of the century, the Parthenon was converted into a Christian church dedicated to the Virgin Mary."[78] So a pagan temple dedicated to a "virgin" goddess was transformed into a Christian cathedral dedicated to the "virgin" Mary. Could there have been an overflow of pagan influence that resulted in overly enhancing Mary's true nature and identity? That's certainly worthy of consideration.

Without question, Mary should be deeply respected for her purity, her obedience to God's calling, her humility, her evident willingness to endure false accusations, her faithfulness to the Almighty, and the awe-inspiring way that God used her to help usher in the New Covenant era. She was a pivotal part of successfully counteracting the evil that invaded this realm through Eve. Yes, all of that is true.

As already mentioned, though, Mary had to be born again and filled with the Holy Spirit in the upper room just like the other disciples to find New Testament salvation and completion in God. She was one of us—an exceptional and exemplary human being, but again, just one of us.

Question 16

Did the Assumption of Mary really take place; is she presently the Queen of heaven, and can believers petition her in prayer?

The doctrine of the Assumption of Mary is surprisingly a very new belief. It was proclaimed by Pope Pius XII on November 1, 1950, in his *Encyclical Munificentissimus Deus*. As with the Immaculate Conception, this Marian dogma was spoken *ex cathedra*, established by a papal decree declared to be infallible. This doctrine makes a clear distinction between the "Ascension" of Jesus and the "Assumption" of Mary, as explained in the following quote:

> "Jesus Christ is the Son of God made man, with both divine and human natures. When he went to heaven, body and soul, at the end of his earthly life, he did so on his own power. Jesus himself was the active agent. Thus, he ascended (active) into heaven. Mary, on the other hand, is of course merely a creature, dependent entirely on the gratuitous grace of God for anything. She could not and did not go to heaven on her own power, but instead was taken there. Thus, she was assumed (passive) into heaven."[79]

Though there is no basis for this belief in Scripture, according to church authorities, it is the logical outcome of Mary's calling, which has linked her inseparably to her Son, both on earth and in heaven. The explanation of this Catholic belief does not posit how, when, or where this miraculous, supernatural transition from Mary's earthly state to her heavenly state was accomplished. Did Mary first die physically? Or was she assumed to heaven without a prior separation of soul and body? Was Mary translated or resurrected? Questions like these have never been sufficiently answered. We know God can do these things, for He has done them in the past. For instance, we have a clear biblical record of the resurrection of saints happening simultaneous with Jesus' resurrection:

> *And Jesus cried out again with a loud voice,*
> *and yielded up His spirit.*
> *Then, behold, the veil of the temple was torn in two*
> *from top to bottom; and the earth quaked,*
> *and the rocks were split,*
> *and the graves were opened; and many bodies of the*
> *saints who had fallen asleep were raised;*
> *and coming out of the graves after His resurrection,*
> *they went into the holy city and appeared to many.*
> *(Matthew 27:51-53)*

We also have clear biblical records of the supernatural translations of both Elijah and Enoch:

> *And it came to pass, as they still went on, and talked,*
> *that, behold, there appeared a chariot of fire, and horses*
> *of fire, and parted them both asunder; and Elijah*
> *went up by a whirlwind into heaven.*
> *(2 Kings 2:11 KJV)*

> *By faith Enoch was translated that he should not see*
> *death; and was not found, because God had translated*
> *him: for before his translation he had this*
> *testimony, that he pleased God.*
> *(Hebrews 11:5 KJV)*

So, we know God can do such wondrous things, because He already has. However, the question remains, "Did God work this incredible miracle for Mary?" If there is no biblical record, how could it ever be emphatically stated as true?

Mary, as Queen of heaven

Embracing the idea that Mary received special treatment in passing from this realm to the next fuels an additional belief that she presently occupies the preeminent role of being the "Queen of heaven."

> "In his 1954 encyclical *Ad caeli reginam* ("To the Queen of Heaven"), [Pope] Pius XII asserts that Mary deserves the title because she is Mother of God, because she is closely associated as the New Eve with Jesus' redemptive work, because of her preeminent perfection and because of her intercessory power."[80]

Mary is revered to this extreme degree because Catholics believe "God has willed her to have an exceptional role in the work of eternal salvation."[81] In 1964, during the Second Vatican Council, Mary was even referred to as the "Queen of the universe," the "Mother of the church" and the "Mediatrix" (confirming her complementary role with the "Mediator," the Lord Jesus Christ). [82]

What a daring proclamation to make, considering the exclusive status the apostle Paul gave to the Son of God when he wrote to Timothy, his pastor-protégé the following words (it is such a convincing passage, I have quoted it in this book several times):

> *For there is one God and one Mediator*
> *between God and men, the Man Christ Jesus,*
> *who gave Himself a ransom for all . . .*
> *(1 Timothy 1:5-6)*

To lift Mary to a nearly-equal, mediatorial status is extremely troubling to me. Some have even dared to name her the Redemptrix or Co-Redemptrix. Thankfully, two popes (Pope Benedict and Pope Francis) both insisted that this title should not be bestowed on Mary, because it could cause confusion concerning her true position, and they were right. Elevating any human being to such a place of divine-like, reverential recognition is totally unacceptable. Isaiah 54:5 declares, "The Lord of hosts . . . your Redeemer . . . is called the God of the whole earth." No one else could ever come near such a glorious status!

Four primary reasons given for Mary's majestic title

In Catholic literature, four primary reasons are usually given for bestowing on Mary the majestic title, "Queen of the universe":

1. The Old Testament pattern of the queen mother:

On a popular Catholic website, the following explanation is given: "In the monarchy of King David, as well as in other ancient kingdoms of the Near East, the mother of the ruling king held an important office in the royal court and played a key part in the process of dynastic succession. In fact, the king's mother ruled as queen, not his wife. The great preeminence of the king's mother may seem odd from our modern Western perspective, in which we think of a queen as being the wife of a king. However, recall that most ancient Near-Eastern kings practiced polygamy. King Solomon had seven hundred wives (1 Kings 11:3)—imagine the chaos in the royal court if all seven hundred were awarded the queenship! But since each king had only one mother, one can see the practical wisdom in bestowing the queenship upon her."[83] (See also 2 Kings 24:12, Jeremiah 13:18-20, 1 Kings 1:16-17, 31, 1 Kings 2:19-20.)

My response: God does not pattern His heavenly government after earthly models. Assigning this royal role to Mary based on the way ancient kings compensated for their polygamous and often immoral lifestyle is not acceptable. Such logic is not a sufficient basis for insisting that this regal title be placed on the mother of Jesus. Moreover, the Scripture confers the honor of ruling and reigning with Jesus Christ on all who have been washed in the precious blood of Jesus, and all who have endured suffering in His name, not just Jesus' earthly mother. (See 2 Timothy 2:12, Revelation 1:5-6; 5:9-10; 20:6.)

2. Mary's influence over Jesus during His incarnation:

At the marriage feast in Cana, those conducting the celebration ran out of wine. Mary asked Jesus to intervene, to which He responded, "Woman, what does your concern have to do with Me? My hour has not yet come." Undeterred, she instructed the servants, "Whatever He says to you, do it" (John 2:4-5). Amazingly, He complied with her wishes and miraculously turned water into wine, and it was described as the best offered to the guests during that feast. That was Jesus' first miracle. So, it logically follows: If Mary was so influential on her Son during His earthly sojourn, isn't it reasonable to believe that she is still influential in the celestial world? That's the assumption many Catholics make and one of the reasons given for her prominent role as an intercessor.

My response: To make the leap from a conversation Mary had with Jesus at the marriage feast at Cana to the status of being enthroned as queen over the universe is much greater than logic allows. If Mary really did occupy such an exalted role, it would be plainly revealed in Scripture, just as it is plainly revealed about the Lord Himself. The following passage makes the claim of Jesus' eternal Lordship undeniable:

> *The LORD has established His throne in heaven,*
> *and His kingdom rules over all.*
> *(Psalms 103:19)*

If this Marian doctrine were true, surely, God would have inserted a declaration in the Bible such as the following:

> The Lord has established His mother's throne in heaven and exalted her as the Mediatrix, Co-redeemer, and Intercessor for all His people.

At least eleven scriptures testify of Jesus being exalted to the right hand of the Father after His ascension, like Romans 8:34:

> *Who is he who condemns? It is Christ who died, and furthermore is also risen, who is even at the right hand of God, who also makes intercession for us.*
> *(See also Mark 16:19, 1 Peter 3:22, Hebrews 10:12)*

If Mary really was the Co-redemptrix that Catholicism claims, should there not be passages of Scripture like the following:

> Who is troubled and oppressed in their souls? Behold, Mary, the Mother of Jesus, has been lifted up to a heavenly position of authority at the right hand of Jesus

and she daily lives to intercede for those who honor
her as the Queen of the universe.

Of course, there are no such passages anywhere in the Old or New Testaments. Assigning this role to Mary requires a drastic bending of certain scriptures to symbolically uphold the dogma. However, that is not how truth is established in the Word of God. Symbols, metaphors, similes, and parables are never used to establish correct biblical doctrine, but to poetically illustrate doctrine that is plainly spoken in other passages of Scripture.

3. The Revelation 12 vision of a "woman clothed with the sun":

First, let's read the passage in the book of the Revelation that Catholic theologians usually assign to Mary:

> *Now a great sign appeared in heaven: a woman clothed
> with the sun, with the moon under her feet, and on her
> head a garland [KJV—a crown] of twelve stars.
> Then being with child, she cried out in labor
> and in pain to give birth.
> And another sign appeared in heaven: behold, a great,
> fiery red dragon having seven heads and ten horns,
> and seven diadems on his heads.
> His tail drew a third of the stars of heaven and threw
> them to the earth. And the dragon stood before the
> woman who was ready to give birth,
> to devour her Child as soon as it was born.
> She bore a male Child who was to rule all nations with
> a rod of iron. And her Child was caught
> up to God and His throne. (Revelation 12:1-5)*

There are varied opinions concerning the correct interpretation of this passage:

Israel—Some insist that "the woman clothed with the sun" is the nation of Israel, the twelve stars are the twelve tribes, and the male Child is the Messiah. That could be true, because Israel is depicted in the role of a wife to Yahweh, the God of Abraham, in other passages. For instance, God pled with Israel in Jeremiah 3:14 saying, "Return, O backsliding children," says the LORD; "for I am married to you."

The redeemed of both covenants—It is also proposed that "the sun-clothed woman" in Revelation 12 spans both covenants, that she represents the wife of God, made up of all Old Covenant saints and all New Covenant saints who ever have been married to Him in a perpetual, covenant relationship. This "bride of Christ," this "wife of the Lamb," will rule and reign with the Lord Jesus Christ eternally. The Scripture testifies that all born again children of God, whose names are in the book of life, are destined to be "kings and priests," reigning with the Son of God forever (See 2 Timothy 2:12, Revelation 1:5-6; 5:9-10; 20:6). Of course, Mary will be one of those persons occupying such an exalted royal position of being co-rulers of the New Creation, but she will not be in a singular preeminent position of authority by herself.

How can the sun-clothed woman be Mary?—The sun-clothed woman cannot be a symbol of Mary by herself, because the end of that chapter indicates that the "woman" has other "offspring" besides the male Child. Here is the continuation of this highly symbolic passage:

> Now when the dragon saw that he had been cast to the
> earth, he persecuted the woman who
> gave birth to the male Child.
> But the woman was given two wings of a great eagle,
> that she might fly into the wilderness to her place,
> where she is nourished for a time and times and
> half a time, from the presence of the serpent.
> So the serpent spewed water out of his mouth like a
> flood after the woman, that he might cause her
> to be carried away by the flood.
> But the earth helped the woman, and the earth opened
> its mouth and swallowed up the flood which the dragon
> had spewed out of his mouth.
> And the dragon was enraged with the woman,
> and he went to make war with the rest of her offspring,
> who keep the commandments of God and have
> the testimony of Jesus Christ.
> (Revelation 12:13-17)

Some who promote the Catholic point of view claim verse seventeen is talking about Mary's spiritual "offspring"—those who were converted through the preaching of the Gospel during the days of the early church. However, the Bible does not teach that explicitly. Besides, if the first "male Child" was a literal, physical son of Mary, the "rest of her offspring" would logically be literal, physical children as well.

Pope Benedict (2005-2013) offered a composite way of looking at this passage, claiming all interpretations are right:

> "In his book Jesus of Nazareth, Volume 2, he [Pope Benedict] writes: 'When the Book of Revelation speaks of the great sign of a Woman appearing in heaven, she is understood to represent all Israel, indeed, the whole Church . . . On the basis of the 'corporate personality' model—in keeping with biblical thought—the early Church had no difficulty recognizing in the Woman, on the one hand, Mary herself and, on the other hand, transcending time, the Church, bride and mother, in which the mystery of Mary spreads out into history'" [Benedict XVI, Jesus of Nazareth 2:222].

On another occasion, Pope Benedict said:

> "This Woman represents Mary, the Mother of the Redeemer, but at the same time she also represents the whole Church, the People of God of all times, the Church which in all ages, with great suffering, brings forth Christ ever anew" [General Audience, Aug. 23, 2006].[84]

A senior apologist at "Catholic Answers" offers, "As Pope Benedict shows us, we don't have to make a forced choice between the possible meanings of what the Woman represents. In keeping with the richness of the way Revelation uses symbolism, to use Pope Benedict's phrases, she can be Mary and 'all Israel' and 'the whole Church' in different ways."[85]

My response: A queen, in a sense, "shares" the king's throne. Though Mary was a remarkable and godly individual, as I have already stated, she never has been and never will be the sole and unique

"Queen" of heaven this way. The innumerable throng who make up the bride of Christ (which includes Mary) corporately comprise the "Queen" of heaven, the bridal company who will share the authority of the King of kings for all eternity. In Revelation 3:21, Jesus promised:

> *"To him who overcomes I will grant to sit with Me on*
> *My throne, as I also overcame and sat down with*
> *My Father on His throne."*

Revelation 21:7 also foretells concerning all God's offspring: "He who overcomes shall inherit all things." If this throne-destiny belonged to Mary alone, these verses would be assigned only to her or primarily to her. Instead, they describe the destiny of all who overcome this fallen world by the grace of God.

This passage in Revelation seems to partially fit some aspects of who Mary was and is—especially how "she bore a male Child who was to rule all nations with a rod of iron"—and how the dragon sought to "devour her Child as soon as it was born" (Revelation 12:4-5, See Matthew 2:13-15). That's actually a pattern in Scripture; sometimes prophecies are layered, with more than one fulfillment. However, on the highest and most perfect level, I believe this passage primarily relates, not to the mother of Jesus, but to the bride of Christ, ("the Israel of God") which is made up of the redeemed of all ages. (Galatians 6:16)

4. What Jesus said to John at the cross:

One of the seven last statements of Jesus made from the cross was directed to John, the beloved disciple. It is found once in Scripture:

> *Now there stood by the cross of Jesus His mother, and*
> *His mother's sister, Mary the wife of*
> *Clopas, and Mary Magdalene.*
> *When Jesus therefore saw His mother, and the disciple*
> *whom He loved standing by, He said to His mother,*
> *"Woman, behold your son!"*
> *Then He said to the disciple, "Behold your mother!"*
> *And from that hour that disciple*
> *took her to his own home.*
> *(John 19:25-27)*

In explaining this passage, one Catholic author offers (in the Amazon description of his book, *Behold Your Mother*)— "From the cross Jesus gave us his mother to be our mother, too: a singularly holy model, consoler, and intercessor for our spiritual journey. Yet most Protestants, and too many Catholics don't understand the role that God wants her to play in our lives."[86]

My response: Pause and think deeply about this proposition for a moment. If Jesus had intended to communicate such a profound revelation, don't you think He would have plainly stated it, in words like the following:

> Behold your mother, John, and the mother of all who will ever believe in Me.

Rather than a cryptic concept inciting disagreement, it would then be heralded as an unquestionable and undeniable truth. No, Jesus was simply making sure His mother would be cared for after His departure. Period. That's all it meant. If not, the end of that passage in the Gospel of John would have also been more a far more clear, over-arching explanation. Instead of merely saying, "From that hour that disciple took her to his own home," it would have communicated:

> From that hour all the disciples realized that Mary would possess throughout the New Covenant era the role of being a "spiritual mother" for all believers.

However, not one of the Gospel writers or the Epistle writers ever implied such an unconventional idea. Not one.

The practice of petitioning Mary in prayer

The first prayer to Mary appeared around 250 A.D., so her role as an intercessor was not taught nor practiced in the original church. It is called the "Sub Tuum Praesidium" in Latin (*Beneath Thy Protection*). Translated from the Greek, it reads:

> *"Beneath your compassion, we take refuge, O Theotokos [God-bearer]: do not despise our petitions in time of trouble: but rescue us from dangers, only pure, only blessed one."*

The more commonly used and well-known prayer, associated with the rosary, is the "Hail Mary" (*Ave Maria*):

> *Hail Mary, full of grace, the Lord is with thee. Blessed art thou among women and blessed is the fruit of thy womb, Jesus. Holy Mary, mother of God, pray for us sinners now and at the hour of our death. Amen.*

Most Catholics are probably unaware of the history of the "Hail Mary" prayer, assuming it has been a part of church tradition and dogma from the very beginning. The Encyclopedia Britannica clearly explains its roots:

> "The first part, the words of the archangel Gabriel (Luke 1:28), appears in liturgies as early as the 6th century. The second part, the words of Elizabeth, the mother of St. John the Baptist (Luke 1:42), was added to the first part by about 1000 CE, the appositive Jesus being added some two centuries later, possibly by Pope Urban IV (reigned 1261–64). The closing petition came into general use during the 14th or 15th century and received its official formulation in the reformed breviary of Pope Pius V in 1568."[87]

So, the early church never promoted praying to Mary, even after her demise. In fact, this famous prayer, celebrated in song (*Ave Maria*) has only been around in its completeness for a little less than 500 years. Those who want an original and pure form of Christianity should surely consider these things. If it was not needed for over a millennium, it is not needed now.

Logical reasons why no one should ever pray to Mary

The same line of logic presented in Question #11 (concerning whether it is possible to petition the saints to pray in our behalf) applies to Mary as well. She is neither omniscient nor omnipresent—and both would be necessary for her to handle all the hundreds of millions of petitions that most likely ascend toward her from all over the globe in a single day. Only God Himself is capable of processing that much information—and much more indeed!

I would add this thought also. Can you imagine the billions who have religiously prayed the "Hail Mary" prayer, expecting her to intervene for them at "the hour of their death"? Now imagine how impossible it would be for her, even in a celestial state, to be personally aware of the time of each person's passing, and to be faithfully praying for him or her at that moment. Approximately 178,000 people die daily. If Catholics make up 17% of the world population, and if the statistics match perfectly, she would have to be personally involved in assisting 30,260 people every day as they pass from this world to the next (about twenty-one per minute). Do you really think that is possible?

Why would that even be necessary? Those who are truly saved, at death, pass "from death into life" (John 5:24). Though they are "absent from the body," they are "present with the Lord" (2 Corinthians 5:8). It is a seamless and immediate transition. No one in heaven needs to pray for true believers so that this change of location successfully takes place. It will happen flawlessly simply because it is a promise from the Almighty God Himself.

As I have commented before, repeating the "Hail Mary" over and over is bound to become mantra-like, monotone, mechanical, and sometimes, nearly mindless. We would never attempt conversation with another person by echoing the same statement, often while clutching beads to log a prescribed number of petitions. It would not only be an insult to the intelligence of the person; it would also be a futile way of trying to open a line of communication.

Real conversation is a flow of thought from one person to another that is very fluid, spontaneous, emotion-filled, and creative. It is not constructed with a series of predictable, memorized statements, droningly repeated tens of thousands of times during a lifetime, to somehow "earn" the person's attention and gain a response. As mentioned in the chapter on "Penance" and in Appendix #3, Jesus described this as a "forbidden" practice (and I quote again):

> *"And when you pray, do not use vain repetitions as the heathen do. For they think that they will be heard for their many words." (Matthew 6:7)*

Yes, I realize these are strong words—but the uttering of the "Hail Mary" prayer over and over, according to the Lord Jesus Christ's assessment, is nothing more than "vain repetitions," and the word "vain" means empty, useless, without effect, and to no purpose.

You may be thinking, *This author has already brought up this scripture and stated this argument. It is unnecessary for him to repeat it again.*

Exactly.

Repetition is unnecessary.

Final conclusions about Marian doctrines

Finally, it is clear most of the Marian doctrines of the Catholic Church (as explained in Questions #12-16) **cannot be labeled** "sound doctrine" (Titus 2:1)—and for the following three reasons:

1. They were not embraced by the early church.

2. They are often based on symbolic, metaphorical interpretations of scriptures that can be interpreted in more logical ways.

3. They are not plainly and clearly stated in the Bible, which is necessary for doctrines on this level of importance to be embraced and promoted as truth.

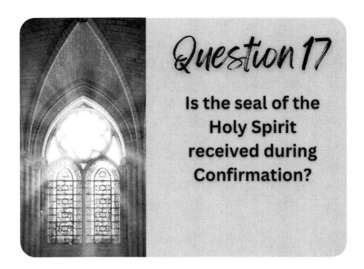

Question 17

Is the seal of the Holy Spirit received during Confirmation?

There are seven sacraments acknowledged and taught by the Catholic Church. *(For the full list, see Appendix #5.)* The three considered most important are Baptism, the Eucharist (Holy Communion), and Confirmation.

If you are unfamiliar with Catholicism, you may be wondering, *What is the purpose of Confirmation?* A Catholic website explains:

> "In short it is the full outpouring of the Holy Spirit as once granted to the apostles on the day of Pentecost. Confirmation brings Catholics a deepening of baptismal grace and unites us more firmly to Christ. It increases the gifts of the Holy Spirit and leaves an indelible mark on the soul just like baptism."[88]

Another writer, quoting the Catholic Catechism, shares:

> "The Holy Spirit dwells within us at baptism. Confirmation completes the grace we receive at baptism, since we receive a 'special strength of the Holy Spirit.'" (CCC 1285ff)[89]

A direct quote from the Catholic Catechism supplies the official doctrinal stance:

> "Like Baptism which it completes, Confirmation is given only once, for it too imprints on the soul an indelible spiritual mark, the 'character,' which is the sign that Jesus Christ has marked a Christian with the seal of his Spirit by clothing him with power from on high so that he may be his witness." (CCC 1304)[90]

Summarizing the primary points in these quotes, Catholics believe that five main things are imparted during Confirmation:

1. The full outpouring of the Holy Spirit as the apostles received,

2. A deepening of baptismal grace,

3. An awakening of the gifts of the Holy Spirit,

4. The seal of the Holy Spirit resulting in real Christian character,

5. Empowerment to be a more effective witness.

Is this true? Is there a spiritual outpouring, a supernatural reality, accompanying Confirmation that is historically-traceable, doctrinally-provable, and dramatically life-changing? Or is this sacrament just another religious ceremony that fails to deliver to adherents the reality of what is promised? Let's humbly and sincerely explore this important issue together.

The sacrament of Confirmation

The Confirmation ceremony is simple. Though some minor details may differ, normally, it is performed after a Mass by the bishop of a diocese, though he may appoint a priest to take his place. The bishop normally wears red liturgical garments to represent the fire of the Holy Spirit that came on Pentecost. A homily is presented, and various recitations and prayers are offered. (You can look up the details online.)

Each candidate is brought to the bishop individually by a sponsor, or the bishop may go to them. The candidate announces his or her confirmation name. The bishop makes the sign of the cross on a worshipper's forehead with special holy anointing oil, calls the candidate by his or her new name, and makes the proclamation, "Be sealed with the gift of the Holy Spirit" (a reference to Ephesians 1:13-14). The candidate says, "Amen." The bishop proclaims, "Peace be with you" and the confirmation candidate responds, "And with your spirit."

Back in the day when I was confirmed, the bishop would also give the candidate a soft slap on the cheek to represent a willingness to suffer for Christ. (I don't think this is usually done anymore.) Also, at times, it has been customary to kiss the bishop's ring as a sign of humility, submission, and respect toward the holy One he represents. This traditional anointing ceremony is presented as the means of the gifts of the Holy Spirit being awakened in a Catholic's life, and the impartation of greater strength to witness the faith.

When I was around eleven years old, I went through this ritual with all sincerity—at Blessed Sacrament Catholic Church in Norfolk, Virginia. However, for me, in all honesty, it was no more than that—a ritual. There was no supernatural reality, no encounter with the power of God, no transformation, no change of character, no awakening of the gifts of the Spirit, and no deepening of spirituality. In fact, nothing happened—nothing at all—except I received an additional middle name.

My encounter with the Holy Spirit

The wonderful things that were supposed to take place during the sacrament of Confirmation finally did occur—about nine years later under totally different circumstances. When I was twenty years old, about a year after being "born again," I was filled with the Baptism of the Holy Spirit in a very remarkable and unforgettable way. For about a year, I had fervently sought God for this Pentecostal/Charismatic in-filling and had not yet received it. Then, when I wasn't even expecting God to move for me, He did so—in a very powerful way.

It was an ordinary day. I had been working most of the day in a church office and was walking across the street to a Dairy Kreme restaurant to order a banana split. (That was before I got seriously health-minded concerning my diet.) I noticed a lady sitting at a concrete table outside the restaurant wearing a large back brace. I introduced myself as a minister, told her I believed in healing by laying on of hands, and asked if I could pray for her. She happily agreed, declaring that she, too, was a believer.

I laid my right hand on her forehead and lifted my left hand to heaven and began to intercede, declaring God's promises to heal and praising God for a miracle. Suddenly, and much to my surprise, the power of God—like spiritual fire—hit my left hand, moved down my arm, and exploded with intensity in my chest area. It was an indescribable heavenly ecstasy I had never experienced before (I understand why Peter called it "joy inexpressible" / 1 Peter 1:8.)

During that sacred moment, which was so much more intense than the traditional ceremony of my younger years, I began speaking in tongues. That phenomenon, also called glossolalia, is an inspired language of worship and was a common sign of the infilling of the Spirit in the early church. (See Acts 2:1-7; 10:44-48; 19:1-7, 1 Corinthians 14:2.)

Speaking in tongues is a gift of the Holy Spirit, referred to in Scripture as "diverse kinds of tongues" (1 Corinthians 12:10 KJV). This gift can manifest three ways:

1. Preaching in a known language of which the person speaking in tongues has no knowledge,

2. Giving a prophetic message that must be interpreted,

3. A heavenly language of worship that Paul implied can be "tongues of men and of angels" that is only understood only by God (1 Corinthians 13:1; 14:2).

Up until that moment, I had never experienced the power of God in such depth. But from that point forward, I have felt the reality of God's presence in a very tangible way, every day for over fifty years. It changed my walk with God radically. Other gifts of the Spirit were also stirred up in my life, which normally should happen. (See 1 Corinthians 12:1-11.)

Ordinarily, the baptism of the Holy Spirit is imparted with the laying on of hands by anointed leaders who have received the encounter themselves. (See Acts 19:1-7.) In my case, though, this empowerment came to me directly and personally from the Father above—and I am eternally grateful.[91] Since then, I have had the privilege of praying for thousands of people to receive the baptism with the Holy Spirit and have witnessed remarkable visitations of God's presence and power—

like the time, near Belpre, Ohio, when I spoke to about fifty young Catholic men studying for the priesthood. They were so hungry for God. They all expressed a desire to be born again, so they asked Jesus to come and dwell within their hearts. All of them prayed to be filled with the Holy Spirit as well and many received, with the evidence of speaking in tongues. I have often wondered what kind of fruit resulted from that glorious visitation of God in the years that followed.

The gifts of the Holy Spirit

When the baptism with the Holy Spirit is poured out on a sincere believer, God usually awakens other gifts. Catholicism teaches there are seven gifts of the Holy Spirit—wisdom, understanding, counsel, fortitude, knowledge, piety, and fear of the Lord.[92] Although these expressions of Christlikeness are valuable and to be desired, this is not the list nor the number of the primary gifts of the Spirit, as found in the Bible. According to Scripture there are nine primary gifts of the Holy Spirit:

There are diversities of gifts, but the same Spirit.
There are differences of ministries,
but the same Lord.
And there are diversities of activities,
but it is the same God who works all in all.
But the manifestation of the Spirit is given
to each one for the profit of all:
for to one is given the word of wisdom through the
Spirit, to another the word of knowledge
through the same Spirit,
to another faith by the same Spirit, to another
gifts of healings by the same Spirit,
to another the working of miracles, to another
prophecy, to another discerning of spirits, to another
different kinds of tongues, to another
the interpretation of tongues.
But one and the same Spirit works all these things,
distributing to each one individually as He wills.
(1 Corinthians 12:4-11)

These are supernatural gifts. For instance, the gift of the word of knowledge and the gift of the word of wisdom are not naturally acquired through study. Once received, the two gifts awaken within recipients a sensitivity to inspired revelations about situations in their own lives or the lives of others, or other important matters, like the correct interpretation of God's Word. Verses 28-31 of the same chapter (1 Corinthians 12) also mentions gifts of ministry positions (apostles, prophets, teachers) and administrative gifts. Even the gift of "helps" is referenced.

If "Jesus Christ is the same yesterday, today, and forever" as the Bible teaches, then the manifestations of the Holy Spirit should also be the same (Hebrews 13:8). The way the Holy Spirit moved in the early church is being replicated in our day among those who believe, both Catholics and non-Catholics. God does not change and there is no indication in His Word that His power stopped manifesting among believers after the original apostles died. Authentic New Testament Christianity should include the same supernatural reality that it did in the very beginning. Those who adhere to Cessationism dishonor God, by failing to promote His true work in the earth.

My Confirmation name (my patron saint)

There is another important aspect of Confirmation I have not yet fully examined. Participants in this sacrament always receive a new name—a Confirmation name—which the bishop or officiating priest affirms. It is the name of a patron saint with whom the confirmed person is supposed to have a special relationship the rest of his or her life. This new name is placed after the first and middle name and before the last name.

A person's patron saint is expected to be a source of faithful intercession and personal spiritual guidance. Usually, candidates for confirmation are encouraged to review the lives and characters of various saints to see which one they relate to the best. Each saint is described as having a unique area of expertise in which he or she is most effective. There is even a patron saint of television (St. Clare of Assisi / 1194-1253 A.D.) and a patron saint of the Internet (St. Isidore of Seville / died 636 A.D.) who both lived quite a long time before television and the Internet came into being. Isn't that paradoxical?

Even Catholics admit that choosing a Confirmation name is not biblical and does not come from the official Catholic liturgical book. Long lists are available of the primary fields, careers, or areas of influence assigned to specific saints. (You may peruse a lengthy list at this link.[93])

As I mentioned earlier in the book, I took the name Christopher as my Confirmation name. I was captivated by the intriguing story of this saint whose image on jewelry is very popular even among non-Catholics and non-religious people. As the legend goes, Christopher was a tall, muscular man (some accounts say over seven feet) who wanted to be dedicated to God. However, he did not feel he could consecrate his life in a priestly or monk-like fashion of fasting and praying. Instead, he devoted himself to the unselfish task of carrying travelers across a dangerous river on his shoulders, especially the weak, the young, or the physically challenged. As the story unfolds, one day, as he was carrying a child, mysteriously, the weight of his little passenger kept getting heavier, to the point where he barely made it to the other side and feared they both would drown.

Once on the other side, the Child revealed Himself as Jesus, then explained that the increase in weight Christopher experienced was the heavy burden of a fallen and lost world that He, the Son of God, carried. After revealing the meaning behind the visitation, the Christ Child vanished. Though his name was originally Offerus, at some point, the name Christopher, which means "Christ-bearer," was conferred on this saint. It is believed that later in his life, Christopher was martyred for his faith.

That's the name I embraced, because in my pre-teen years, before I even knew the Lord, I had a deep desire to bear Jesus' name to the world and share the burden of lost humanity. I seriously considered becoming a priest or a monk. I prayed to Christopher for several years, expecting his intervention and guidance, until I became more irreligious during my teens. Ironically, about the same time, the church released a statement that Christopher was, quite possibly, no more than a fictitious, legendary figure. What a shocking realization that was! At best, I felt my times of praying to him were probably a waste of my time and a fruitless attempt to communicate with a being in heaven (if he even existed). At worst, it was similar to the occult, New Age practice of contacting a "spirit-guide" to navigate life successfully. Participating in that kind of practice was prohibited in the Old Testament, so why would it be allowed during New Testament era? (See Deuteronomy 18:9-14.)

When King Saul tried to contact the prophet Samuel (who had passed on to the next world), he knew enough about the things of God not to attempt praying to that saintly representative of God himself. Instead, he attempted to penetrate the spirit world illegitimately, appealing to a witch (a spiritist, a woman with a familiar spirit) to contact Samuel. Ignoring God's rules this way did not benefit Saul at all. It may have even hastened his demise, for his life came to an end within a day's time. (See 1 Samuel 28:1-25.)

If people (Catholic or non-Catholic) think they are attempting to receive guidance from entities other than God Himself, most likely (as already stated under Question #11), they have opened themselves up to the influence of demonic beings called "familiar spirits." (See Leviticus 19:31; 20:6, 27.) These are evil spirits who are familiar with the individuals being addressed, and because of that, are able to impersonate them.

Remember, the devil and his evil underlings are masters of deception. "Satan disguises himself as an angel of light" (2 Corinthians 11:14 ESV). So, apparitions, voices, and spiritual sensations that seem legitimate can be completely false, if what happens is not according to the biblical standard. I know this may sound hard to receive, but I assure you, I am not being overly critical. Quite the contrary, I am deeply concerned for any person who trusts in this non-biblical practice. It is infinitely more important to seek the face of God and call on the name of Jesus. That is all you really need.

The real deal (the real seal)

The Bible does teach about the "seal of the Holy Spirit" being given to believers. However, it describes this grace being poured out at salvation, not with the baptism of the Holy Spirit. Read the following passage carefully:

> *In Him you also trusted, after you heard the word*
> *of truth, the gospel of your salvation; in whom also,*

> *having believed, you were sealed with*
> *the Holy Spirit of promise,*
> *who is the guarantee of our inheritance until the*
> *redemption of the purchased possession,*
> *to the praise of His glory.*
> *(Ephesians 1:13-14)*

This passage indicates that when we hear the Gospel, positively respond to it, and are genuinely saved, at that moment, God seals us with the Holy Spirit.

A seal is given as a sign of authenticity and authorization. For instance, a document is verified as being "authentic" when it bears the seal of a notary public, and often, that same document "authorizes" the person possessing it to do a certain thing, claim a certain benefit, or function on certain level. A seal transfers an image that is unique to, and identified with, the owner of the seal. The transferred image is an exact replication of the original image when the seal is pressed into foil, paper, wax, or some other malleable substance that is soft enough to receive an impression. All those details are highly symbolic.

Jesus revealed that He had been "sealed" by God, the Father (John 6:27). That means the image of the Father's character was fully expressed in the Son—so much so that He proclaimed:

> *"He who has seen Me has seen the Father." (John 14:9)*

Jesus was and ever will be "the image of the invisible God" (Colossians 1:15). So, a "seal," in one sense, is an image transfer, as well as an authorization or proof of authenticity.

In like manner, when repentant and believing people surrender to Jesus, inviting Him to be Lord of their lives and to live in their hearts, at that moment, the image of the character of Jesus is, in a sense, "pressed" into their regenerated spirits—so that these newly saved individuals experience a character change and begin to love what God loves and shun what He would shun. No wonder the Scripture declares:

> *Therefore, if anyone is in Christ, he is a new*
> *creation; old things have passed away;*
> *behold, all things have become new.*
> *(2 Corinthians 5:17)*

God's preservation plan

A seal can also be a means of protection from outside influence. Because the world continues to pull at those who convert to true Christianity, God seals those individuals with the character of Jesus. That way, hopefully, the divine nature in their hearts will be stronger than the lower nature in their flesh and the lure of a lust-driven world.

For the "sealed" believer, the love of God on the inside is stronger than the hate, anger, and prejudice on the outside. The peace of God on the inside is stronger than the stress, anxiety, and tension on the outside. The joy of God on the inside is stronger than the depression, shame, and discouragement on the outside. The holiness on the inside is stronger than the wickedness, immorality, and perversion on the outside. The divine wisdom on the inside is stronger than the foolishness, twisted logic, and deceptive beliefs on the outside—the light of God on the inside is brighter than all the dark things that pervade the entire human race.

This is God's preservation plan. Those He saves, He seals, because those He rescues from sin, He intends to keep for time and eternity. For this, those who are born again should be eternally thankful. (See Psalms 121, 2 Corinthians 1:22, Ephesians 4:30, Revelation 7:3.)

Question 18

Statues, icons, and devotional scapulars: Is their use acceptable in the sight of God?

God declared His Ten Commandments from Sinai, a mountain consumed with holy, heaven-sent fire. On that pivotal day in the history of God's dealings with mankind, His voice must have rolled like thunder across the desert dunes and plains, penetrating the hearts and minds of the Israelite people. What an intense scene—a sacred event that changed this world forever!

Those divinely authored mandates are listed in two main Bible passages: Exodus 20:2-17 and Deuteronomy 5:6-21. In both lists, there is an unmistakable ban on making images of things in heaven or on earth with the intent of bowing before them in worship. Here is the exact wording of that portion of God's holy mandate:

"I am the LORD your God, who brought you out of the
land of Egypt, out of the house of bondage.
You shall have no other gods before Me.
You shall not make for yourself a carved image—any
likeness of anything that is in heaven above,
or that is in the earth beneath, or that
is in the water under the earth;
you shall not bow down to them nor serve them.
For I, the LORD your God, am a jealous God, visiting
the iniquity of the fathers upon the children to the third
and fourth generations of those who hate Me,

> *but showing mercy to thousands, to those who love Me*
> *and keep My commandments." (Exodus 20:2-6)*

What a strong and stern divine utterance! Without question, God prohibited the worship of idols: manmade images—lifeless stone, wood, or metal "deities" that cannot see, hear, talk, move, or respond to worshipers in any way.

Now, here is the problematic issue—Have Catholics transgressed this commandment by the statuary they erect in their cathedrals? Or is God referencing the pagan practice of assigning identity, power and virtue to idolatrous images that have no true identity, power or virtue in and of themselves? I can answer with absolute assurance, Catholics do not do that (though some Protestants talk as if they do). So, is the use of statues, images, icons, as found in the Catholic tradition, right or wrong? That question cannot be answered with a simple "yes" or "no." In constructing a suitable response, let me start by asking another question that responds to a commonly voiced claim.

Were the Ten Commandments altered by the Catholic Church?

Protestants quite often accuse the Catholic Church of intentionally altering the Ten Commandments to omit this admonition against the making of images. Is such an allegation accurate or unfair? Let's compare the short form of the Decalogue as presented in both Protestant and Catholic literature, as well as the original passage in the Protestant and Catholic versions of the Bible. Here is the abbreviated version of the Ten Commandments, representative of the kind of wording found in most Protestant sources:

1. You shall have no other gods before Me.
2. You shall make no idols.
3. You shall not take the name of the Lord your God in vain.
4. Keep the Sabbath day holy.
5. Honor your father and your mother.
6. You shall not murder.
7. You shall not commit adultery.
8. You shall not steal.
9. You shall not bear false witness against your neighbor.
10. You shall not covet.[94]

Here are the Ten Commandments as presented in Catholic sources:

1. I am the LORD your God: you shall not have strange Gods before Me.
2. You shall not take the name of the LORD your God in vain.
3. Remember to keep holy the LORD'S Day.
4. Honor your father and your mother.
5. You shall not kill.
6. You shall not commit adultery.
7. You shall not steal.
8. You shall not bear false witness against your neighbor.
9. You shall not covet your neighbor's wife.
10. You shall not covet your neighbor's goods.[95]

Both these lists are humanly edited simplifications of what God originally spoke—for the sake of easier comprehension, retention, and memorization. If you read them carefully, you will notice, the second commandment in the Protestant version, banning the making of idols, is omitted in the Catholic version, and the tenth commandment in the Protestant version, about coveting, is expanded into two commandments in the Catholic version. However, (and this is important) the source passages (Exodus 20:2-17, Deuteronomy 5:6-21) in both the Protestant and Catholic versions of the Bible are essentially the same, and nothing is omitted.

The primary difference is definitely not the substance of what is written but how Catholics and Protestants divide up and number these Commandments. Unknown to many Bible readers is the fact that the original passage places all the Ten Commandments together without numbering them. Traditionally, Catholics label Deuteronomy 5:6-10 as the First Commandment, verse 11 as the Second Commandment, verses 12-15 as the Third Commandment and then a similar pattern ensues. Uniquely, Verse 21 is divided into the Ninth and Tenth Commandments, distinguishing the unlawful desire to commit adultery from the unlawful desire to dishonestly take goods that belong to another. In his writings on Exodus, the theologian Augustine suggested this particular division of the Commandments.

On the other hand, Protestants have traditionally assigned Deuteronomy 5:6-7 as the First Commandment, then verses 8-10 as the

Second Commandment, verse 11 as the Third Commandment and so on. Verse 21 is not divided, as in Catholicism, but joined together as the Tenth Commandment.

As already stated, in the Catholic version of the entire Bible, the Ten Commandments, as originally spoken by God, *does* include the admonition against the making and worshiping of idols. This curse-imparting divine directive has not been omitted. Since that is the case, is it even relevant to note the difference between the shorter renderings offered by both Catholics and Protestants? Yes it is, for one primary reason. Those Catholics who rarely read the Bible depend primarily on the Catechism or Catholic literature for their doctrinal views, so this omission may result in some being unaware of the admonition concerning images. That would make them less likely to question the legitimacy of statuary in their churches. However, it is just as true that Protestants who rarely read the Bible may be unaware of the two divisions of coveting that God warns against—a warning that becomes even more convicting when it is separated into both categories.

So, these two traditional presentations of Mount Sinai's mandates could both be slightly detrimental, but in different ways. My advice? Very simple—to both Catholics and Protestants alike. Read the Bible for yourself and discover the fullness of what God has spoken. Then you will be more certain of the details of God's communications to His own.

The motive behind the practice, explained by Catholics

Catholics insist that these statues, images, icons, and pieces of art are primarily a means of remembering certain events (like the Stations of the Cross) or revered personalities (saints and respected church leaders). "John Damascene's *Apologetic Sermons Against Those Who Reject Sacred Images* gives an authentic presentation of the Catholic attitude towards statues and pictures of Mary and the saints: 'If we were making images of men and thought them gods and adored them as gods, certainly we would be impious. But we do not do any of these things.'"[96] An explanation and defense, offered by Father Mitch Pacwa, quotes from the Baltimore catechism and the Council of Trent:

> "'We do not pray to the crucifix or to the images
> and relics of the saints, but to the persons they repre-

sent.' Catholic doctrine absolutely rejects the worship of anyone but God and rejects all worship of statues, whether of Christ or the saints. What the Church does allow is praying to the saints in order to ask for their intercession with the one true God. The Church also allows one to make statues to remind a person of Christ or the saint:

'Further, the images of Christ, of the Virgin Mother of God, and of the other saints are to be kept with honor in places of worship especially; and to them due honor and veneration is to be paid–not because it is believed that there is any divinity or power intrinsic to them for which they are reverenced, nor because it is from them that something is sought, nor that a blind trust is to be attached to images as it once was by the Gentiles who placed their hope in idols (Ps. 135:15ff); but because the honor which is shown to them is referred to the prototypes which they represent.

'Thus it follows that through these images, which we kiss and before which we kneel and uncover our heads, we are adoring Christ and venerating the saints whose likenesses these images bear' *(Council of Trent, Session XXV, Decree 2)*."[97]

I have also read two arguments from various Catholic sources like the following:

1. Religious images and icons are not considered to be objects of worship any more than the pictures of loved ones we carry around in our wallets.

2. In Washington D.C. there are statues of Abraham Lincoln and Thomas Jefferson in their memorial buildings, but we do not confuse the statuary with worship, so why would the statues of saints in Catholic churches be any different?

Responding from the perspective of a former Catholic

From my former-Catholic perspective, I believe there are major differences between the last two things mentioned. We do not bow before the pictures of our loved ones and we do not kiss the feet of Abraham Lincoln or Thomas Jefferson, neither do we present prayerful petitions before any of them.

Even though Catholics say they do not revere the statues themselves, they believe those images are a "point-of-contact" with individuals thought to reside in the spiritual world, with whom they believe they *can* engage prayerfully. So, the final purpose of the statues, images, and icons is what really matters, and that is the primary area of concern.

Protestants, who are usually quick to speak disparagingly of this practice, are often guilty of similar practices themselves. In many Protestant churches, there are pictures of Jesus and other famous Bible personalities, as well as doves and crosses (usually, without the image of Jesus crucified), adorning the walls of their buildings or in their stained-glass windows (if they have them).

Normally, however—except for the cross—no one bows before these forms or images. So, the two groups are not really approaching this practice with the same mindset. Far more sacredness and honor tends to be expressed by Catholics toward their images. But is it right or wrong to do so? Before fully answering that question, let's visit another related issue often offered as a defense by advocates of the Catholic point of view.

God commanded certain religious images to be made

Catholics often point out that there were two main times when God seemed to set aside His own rigid guidelines and commanded images to be made for specific religious purposes among the Israelites:

- The cherubim on the ark and on the curtains in the tabernacle of Moses,
- The brass serpent that Moses made for the healing of the snake bitten Israelites.

These two examples lead to a single conclusion. There have been times when certain manmade images were not only acceptable, but divinely inspired and divinely designed. So, why did God do that? Why did He seem to break His own rules?

The symbolism of the Ark of the Covenant

God instructed Moses to adorn the ark of the covenant with golden cherubim and to weave images of cherubim into the curtains and veils of the tabernacle. (See Exodus 25:18-19; 26:1, 31.)

The ark of the covenant was the earthly representation of a celestial reality. The mercy seat on the ark in the holy of holies represented a heavenly mercy seat, the very throne of the Almighty. In the tabernacle of Moses, the cherubim were pointed inward, toward each other, as if enraptured with the glory of God (something Jews call "the Shekinah") that rested on the lid of the ark between them.

So, the cherubim themselves were not to be the focus of attention, but representative of how the focus should always be on the glory of God. The cherubim on the curtains were not objects of worship or veneration, but a reminder to the priests that the sanctuary was a place where heaven and earth connected, and eternal things spilled over into the realm of time. Concerning the ark with its cherubim, Jeremiah prophesied that one day this sacred object would no longer be a focal point of religious devotion in Israel. Here is the prophetic passage:

> *"Then it shall come to pass, when you are*
> *multiplied and increased in the land in those days," says*
> *the LORD, "that they will say no more, 'The ark of the*
> *covenant of the LORD.' It shall not come to mind, nor*
> *shall they remember it, nor shall they visit it,*
> *nor shall it be made anymore.*
> *At that time Jerusalem shall be called The Throne of the*
> *LORD, and all the nations shall be gathered to it, to the*
> *name of the LORD, to Jerusalem. No more shall they*
> *follow the dictates of their evil hearts."*
> *(Jeremiah 3:16-17)*

This passage was a beautiful way of prophetically and symbolically describing the coming Messianic era when Jesus will reign from Jerusalem over a world that fully recognizes His Lordship and worships Him. When the throne of the King of kings is present in Jerusalem, the ark that symbolized that throne will no longer be relevant or important—for the fulfillment of the symbol is far greater than the symbol itself. Surely, it would benefit us if we moved closer to that mindset even now. Yes, the substance is always far more powerful and far more important than the shadow. So, did God break his own rule? Absolutely not! Because the prohibition against image-making always included image-worship. Aha! We are getting closer to truth.

The symbolism of the brass serpent

When the plague of serpents invaded the camp of Israel and many were bitten and dying from the venom, God commanded Moses to make a brass serpent and erect it on a pole. All the Israelites who set their gaze on the brazen serpent were healed of the otherwise fatal snakebites. (Read Numbers 21.)

Though no one knew it at the time, this was not only relevant for the crisis they were facing, but a symbol of a much greater deliverance yet to come. Jesus referred back to this event in describing how He would die and the role He would fill in healing people of the "venom" of sin, when He claimed:

"As Moses lifted up the serpent in the wilderness,
even so must the Son of Man be lifted up,
that whoever believes in Him should not
perish but have eternal life."
(John 3:14-15)

What a miracle that was originally! Tragically, though, many years after Moses made the brazen serpent, the Israelites began burning incense to it, as if it had some kind of innate, magical, supernatural power. Instead of simply honoring it as a historical artifact that was a point of contact for their faith in God during a crisis, they began treating it as an idol. Centuries later, when King Hezekiah was purging the land of idolatry, he realized this serpentine object had become a stumbling block to the people, so he told his soldiers to beat it into dust. As they were accomplishing that, he scornfully called it "Nehushtan" (meaning a piece of brass). (See 2 Kings 18:4.)

This righteous king was attempting to enlighten God's people that the object itself had no inherent divine power. God was their healer, not a brass serpent. So, something that was originally good shifted to something bad when it became idolatrous. At that point, it had to be removed, because it was given too much reverence.

In a similar, though certainly not as blatant way, I believe Catholics often express too much reverence for the statuary in their churches. This is especially true when the statues depict Mary or various saints and are used as a point of contact in the hope of presenting prayerful petitions to those revered individuals. That's when the images become a means of reinforcing false beliefs and erroneous practices that are not endorsed by the Word of God.

I know that is hard to receive, but I urge you to prayerfully consider the logic and the Bible-based revelation behind it. *(See Question #11 / "Can the saints in heaven be petitioned to pray in our behalf?")*

So, did God give rules to His people that He did not keep Himself? The answer is an emphatic "No!" In neither of these two examples was worship given to the object. The high priest did not pray to the cherubim or bow worshipfully before them in the holy of holies. Initially, the people did not worship the brazen serpent. They just gazed upon it. Their faith was inclined toward God. They were both symbols of higher spiritual truths and used to bring attention to the Most High God Himself. Read the original passage again:

> *"I am the LORD your God, who brought you out of the*
> *land of Egypt, out of the house of bondage.*
> *You shall have no other gods before Me.*
> *You shall not make for yourself a carved image—any*
> *likeness of anything that is in heaven above, or that is*
> *in the earth beneath, or that is in the*
> *water under the earth;*
> *you shall not bow down to them nor serve them.*
> *For I, the LORD your God, am a jealous God, visiting*
> *the iniquity of the fathers upon the children to the third*
> *and fourth generations of those who hate Me,*
> *but showing mercy to thousands, to those who*
> *love Me and keep My commandments."*
> *(Exodus 20:2-6)*

If you isolate just verse four (in bold print above), you could use that single sentence to outlaw all pictures made on cameras, all paintings, all sculptures, and even plastic kids' toys in the shape of animals or people. You could go far beyond God's original and intended meaning. It needs to be emphasized—for Catholics and Protestants alike—that the prohibition of images is inseparably tied to reverencing other gods beside the true God (verses three and four) and bowing down in worship to those images (verse five). Verse four does not stand on its own. There are plenty of teenagers who are overly obsessed with taking selfies on their smartphones—and that may be borderline idolatrous (I say that tongue in cheek)—but I do not believe that constitutes the breaking of this commandment.

Summing up the important points

On some of these issues, there are no rules set in stone (pun intended). It boils down to personal preferences. For the most part, I refrain from placing statues and images in our church. However, we do have a picture of Noah and the ark adorning one wall, a small ceramic eagle in the foyer, and pictures of worshipers with their hands lifted on the walls leading to the sanctuary—so where do you draw the line? Those are all "images." Then, I confess, there is the manger scene celebrating the birth of Jesus yearly. Of course, you will never see me bowing to the eagle, offering incense to Noah, or prostrate in prayer before the manger scene. That's the clincher. No attachment of worship or excessive veneration is offered.

I personally prefer not to display a cross with the form of the crucified Savior still on it. Why? Two reasons—because number one, no one knows what Jesus really looked like, and number two, I would rather emphasize that the Son of God has risen from the dead. He is no longer on the cross. But is it wrong for my Catholic friends to carry a crucifix in their pockets or wear one on a necklace, or have a picture of the crucified Christ in their homes? Though I would not do those things myself, I don't believe they are seriously wrong practices. If they love the One who died on the cross for us all, and if they use these things to remind them of His great love for us and the price He paid for our salvation—then "Hallelujah! We are gazing worshipfully the same direction!"

However, when it comes to images of Mary, or the saints, or in some cases, angels—in statue form, or icons, or even scapulars—that's another matter altogether and something I believe is definitely wrong in the sight of God, a practice that should be discarded. Speaking of scapulars, isn't it strange that in the Council of Laodicea (363-364 A.D.), the following mandate was given:

> "Neither the higher nor the lower clergy may be magicians, conjurors, mathematicians, or astrologers, nor shall they make so-called amulets, which are chains for their own souls. And those who wear these amulets shall be shut out from the Church." (Canon 36)[98]

An amulet is a protective charm worn to ward off evil, harm, trouble, illness, or even malevolent spirits. It is usually worn to bring good fortune or blessings. Yet, that sounds very similar to what certain devotional scapulars are supposed to accomplish (like the Brown Scapular of Our Lady of Mount Carmel that ensures its wearers escape from hell).

Was the governing body at the Council of Laodicea wrong? Or were they right? In this area of doctrine, they were right. We do not need physical objects to secure spiritual protection if we are in a covenant relationship with God. The promises of Psalm 121:5-8 are sufficient:

> *The LORD is your keeper; the LORD is your*
> *shade at your right hand.*
> *The sun shall not strike you by day,*
> *nor the moon by night.*
> *The LORD shall preserve you from all evil;*
> *He shall preserve your soul.*
> *The LORD shall preserve your going out and your*
> *coming in from this time forth, and even forevermore.*

If I have to choose between a small, rectangular piece of brown woolen cloth worn around my neck and the risen Savior living in my soul for protection, I definitely choose the latter—yes, I confess, "Give me Jesus!"

Question 19

Candles, incense, ashes, and holy water: Are these religious items authentic expressions of Christianity in its original form?

All the Catholic ceremonial items mentioned in this chapter are primarily an overflow from the Old Testament. Their use is not commanded, nor encouraged, nor even cited in the pages of the New Testament, except for the mention of ashes one time by Jesus—and even then, He was describing an Old Testament practice. That alone should be sufficient to cause sincere believers to at least question the value and legitimacy of these ceremonial practices. However, to be more fully convinced of what is true and right for the age in which we live, let's examine each one in detail.

The Old Testament lampstand

Though candles did not exist among the Israelite people in the wilderness journey, oil lamps as a source of light did. (The mention of "candlesticks" in some Bible versions is a mistake in translation.) Among many other responsibilities, the priests were commanded to keep the seven-stemmed, menorah lampstand in the tabernacle of Moses trimmed, lit, and shining its light constantly. It was never to go out. (See Exodus 27:20-21.) This unique lampstand, made of one piece of gold, was a symbol of the Word of God. This is verified by the often-quoted verse:

> *Your word is a lamp to my feet and a*
> *light to my path. (Psalms 119:105)*

So, the lampstand represented the light of truth shining among the children of Israel, guiding them during their wilderness journey. It also represented Israel's calling to shine the light of truth in world full of darkness, deception, paganism, and false religion.

The fire that was used to light the lampstand came from the altar, and the fire on the altar originally fell from heaven—so the light that lit up the holy place (a tent-like structure) had a supernatural origin. (See Leviticus 9:24.) No wonder the priests were commanded to always keep that lamp burning and its light shining. (See Exodus 27:20.) That was light sourced in heaven—irreplaceable.

The use of candles in churches

Like this ancient ritual, Catholics burn candles to represent their prayerful petitions being remembered in the presence of God or remembered by some saint who is being petitioned to pray in their behalf. A burning candle symbolizes an appeal that continually ascends before God, even when the one who lit that candle is going about his or her daily business.

Sometimes a candle is lit concerning a particular person, a particular circumstance, or a particular need being met that is an object of prayer. Votive candles can also represent vows memorialized before God, like the constantly glowing wick. Sometimes, "the faithful also light candles as a sign of gratitude to God for answered prayers."[99]

This religious practice may help believers visualize their prayerful petitions ascending before God perpetually, but it does not magically or supernaturally activate them, lengthen their duration, or insure a response from above. Why would burning candles cause a continued reminder in heaven of prayers uttered on earth when God is omniscient. Scripture declares, "His understanding is infinite" and "He knows all things" (Psalms 147:5, 1 John 3:20).

Burning candles do not enhance God's memory concerning petitions, capture His attention, impress Him, or motivate Him to move on the worshiper's behalf any more than the heartfelt uttering of the associated prayers. No such practice can be found in the pages of the Bible or in the history of the early church, as recorded in the book of Acts. So why should we implement it now?

Other religions use candles

Candle burning is a symbolic ritual found in many religions.

Zoroastrians "adore fire as the visible expression of Ahura Mazda, the eternal principle of light and righteousness."[100] "Prayer is emphasized at the individual level more than the communal level, with some Zoroastrians praying five times a day and reciting scriptures, always facing the sun wherever it is in the sky, or a candle or other light at night."[101]

One of the major calendar events in Hinduism is the annual "Feast of Lights" called Diwali—a festival that celebrates light overcoming darkness, good overcoming evil, and knowledge overcoming ignorance. Millions of candles and lamps are lit all around the world during this feast.

Buddhists encourage the use of candles in meditation because, "The candle flame symbolizes the inner light. It can serve as a continual reminder of our fundamental reality and the destiny of each and every one of us: Nirvana."[102]

Sacred candles are also very important and revered in darker, occult religious groups like Santeria (Cuba), Voodoo (Haiti), and Umbanda Spiritism (Brazil)—all three of which stem from a syncretistic mix of Catholicism and Yoruba African religion and honor numerous false deities. The burning of candles is utilized to invoke those imagined gods and to aid communication with beings in the spirit world.

Witches and Wiccans also use candles. As one professing witch commented, "Oh, candle magick. I love it so much. Most of my really intense spells incorporate candles because they're such an easy and powerful way of focusing energy, especially if you're using them over a period of time. If magick equals intention plus energy plus action, then candle magick is the action part of the equation. By working with candles, we have a visible way of seeing our magick at work."[103] Candles placed in the form of pentagrams are important in attracting and interacting with demon spirits. Here is a description from Wikipedia about the use of candles in Wicca:

> "In Wicca and related forms of Paganism, the candle is frequently used on the altar to represent the presence of the God and Goddess, and in the four corners

200 ~ The Beliefs of the Catholic Church

of a ritual circle to represent the presence of the four classical elements: Fire, Earth, Air, and Water. When used in this manner, lighting and extinguishing the candle marks the opening and closing of the ritual. The candle is also frequently used for magical meditative purposes."[104]

All of that is enlightening, isn't it (again, pun intended)? Zoro-astrians, Hindus, Buddhists, Voodoo priests, witches, Wiccans, and Pagans all use candles in their spiritual activities. I am certainly not implying that Catholicism is on the same level as any of those religions that do not celebrate what the Son of God did for us. Absolutely not! I am just showing the tendency in a wide variety of worldviews toward the use of candles because many adherents believe they are an enhancement, even an empowerment of the experience of prayer and meditation. However, those who truly know God and understand prayer don't need an aid like candle-burning.

Candlelight conclusions

So, is it right or is it wrong to burn candles in religious devotion? Let me respond to that single question with five answers:

1. If those burning candles believe spiritual power or effectiveness in prayer are augmented by the practice of lighting candles, then it is not right, nor is it acceptable in the sight of God. Candles have no power to accomplish anything.

2. If candles are placed before statues of Mary and various saints, as a memorial of a request for their help in intercession, it is an improper approach to prayer. Since Mary and the saints cannot respond to petitions, lighting candles before their statuary is a serious error—assigning spiritual power or abilities to depart-ed saints that they do not have. (See Question #12.)

3. If lighting candles is just an attempt at creating a more solemn, sacred atmosphere in a time of worshiping the true God, but no spiritual power is attributed to this action, then it is merely a matter of personal preference, but unnecessary.

4. If candles are lit as a memorial, a reminder of something God has done, it can be acceptable. For instance, Jewish worshipers burn candles during Hanukkah as a reminder of the miracle that happened when the Maccabees reclaimed and rededicated the second temple—and that is a joyous and blessed annual event (the Jewish Festival of Lights).

5. If candles are lit symbolically, like a unity candle during a marriage, it can be an artistic and even prayerful and beautiful way of depicting a man and woman becoming one before God. Of course, no actual power is attributed to the ceremony, so this is a pleasant emblem of a God-blessed union.

Having made these observations, both negative and positive, let it be summed up in a final statement. Those who have a relationship with the One who said, "Let there be light" in the beginning, and "I am the light of the world" when He walked the earth, do not need symbols such as "holy candles" to represent their spiritual connection with God (Genesis 1:3, John 9:5). Being "called out of darkness into His marvelous light" needs no representation in the form of candles (1 Peter 2:9). Walking "in the light" supernaturally is so much **greater** than representing it naturally; it requires only a born-again heart, on fire with devotion to God (1 John 1:7). However, if true worshipers choose to use candles in a merely symbolic way, doing so is appropriate and acceptable.

What about incense?

Once again, in the Old Testament, the use of incense was commanded during various rituals mandated by the Law. It had to be made in a specific way with specific ingredients for sacred use in the tabernacle of Moses and the temple of Solomon. Burning incense on the altar of incense in the holy place every morning and evening was an important part of the daily ritual in God's sanctuary. (See Exodus 30:1-38.)

Incense symbolizes prayer and intercession. It only emits its odor when it is set on fire, just as prayer must be set on fire with passion and praise toward God to be effective. Its smoke ascends upward, just as our prayers ascend upward toward heaven. So, the act of burning incense in the Old Testament era represented fervent petitions rising toward the throne of God from hearts set ablaze with devotion and holy desire. David used this metaphor when he cried:

> *Let my prayer be set forth before You as incense, the*
> *lifting up of my hands as the evening sacrifice.*
> *(Psalms 141:2)*

In the book of the Revelation, twenty-four elders in heaven are depicted offering "golden bowls full of incense, which are the prayers of the saints" (Revelation 5:8). Then three chapters later, ushering in the apocalyptic, final "seven trumpet" judgments, the symbol emerges again:

> *Then another angel, having a golden censer, came and*
> *stood at the altar. He was given much incense, that he*
> *should offer it with the prayers of all the saints upon the*
> *golden altar which was before the throne.*
> *And the smoke of the incense, with the prayers of the*
> *saints, ascended before God from the angel's hand.*
> *Then the angel took the censer, filled it with fire from*
> *the altar, and threw it to the earth. And there were*
> *noises, thunderings, lightnings, and an earthquake.*
> *(Revelation 8:3-5)*

So, incense is a dominant biblical symbol of sincerely seeking God, not only on earth, but also, in heaven. That is undeniable.

The history of the use of incense

As far as we know, incense was never used during worship gatherings in the early church. There is no record of this practice during the first four centuries. Apparently, it was shunned because of its connection to false religions, as honestly pointed out by one Catholic writer:

> "The offering of incense as viewed in the first few
> centuries of Church writings is usually negative. One
> of the most common ways to ask Christians to com-
> promise their faith was to force them to offer incense to

pagan gods. It is probable, therefore, that the practice of using incense in Christian worship was abandoned to avoid confusion among the faithful and to present a clear witness: incense offerings were associated with paganism and, therefore, abandoned by Christians. Incense in worship made a comeback in the fifth century once Christianity was firmly established."[105]

Pause for a moment and think deeply about that last sentence—was the use of incense in worship gatherings a sign that Christianity was more "firmly established" or was it a sign of "compromise" infiltrating the church at that point? Here's the back story revealing when its use in the liturgy was first recorded:

"The earliest documented history of using incense during a Catholic sacrificial liturgy comes from the Eastern branch of the Church. The rituals of the Divine Liturgies of Saint James and Saint Mark dating from the 5th century include the use of incense. In the Western Church, the 7th century Ordo Romanus VIII of Saint Amand mentions the use of incense during the procession of a bishop to the altar on Good Friday."[106]

So, it was not included in Christian worship services for nearly half a millennium and understandably so. Can you imagine the apostles and disciples in the upper room, saturating the atmosphere with incense smoke just prior to the rushing mighty wind of God's presence entering their midst and cloven tongues of fire appearing over them? (See Acts 2:1-7.) Nothing like that would have been necessary to attract the supernatural reality of such a powerful outpouring of the Holy Spirit. In the beginning years of the church, following that encounter with God, it would have been a major step backward to implement such a religious practice. God had lifted them dramatically out of the symbolic rituals of the Old Testament season into the spiritual realities of the New Testament era. Why return?

Countering that logic, a Catholic priest explains why incense has increasingly become a major part of the liturgy of the church:

"The usage of incense adds a sense of solemnity and mystery to the Mass. The visual imagery of the smoke and the smell remind us of the transcendence of the Mass which links heaven with earth, and allow us to enter into the presence of God. (Fr. Williams Saunders)"[107]

A Catholic writer, commenting on this quote, adds:

The Holy Sacrifice of the Mass transcends space and time, while the use of incense helps the worshiper to enter into this eternal reality through the use of the external senses. That is why incense—fragrant to the senses and visually compelling for the mind and heart—is such a powerful liturgical gift."[108]

So, the strong aroma and the swirling smoke are both assigned a certain power—the power of enhancing a worshiper's ability to have an encounter with the Almighty. If this is what the authors of the previous quotes intended, I disagree. The smell of incense and the sight of its smoke have absolutely no power to usher anyone into the presence of the heavenly Father, but the following things do:

Therefore, brethren, having boldness to enter
the Holiest by the blood of Jesus,
by a new and living way which He consecrated for us,
through the veil, that is, His flesh,
and having a High Priest over the house of God,
let us draw near with a true heart in full assurance of
faith, having our hearts sprinkled from an evil
conscience and our bodies washed with pure water.
(Hebrews 10:19-22)

So, we "draw near" to God by the "blood of Jesus" and by "the washing of water by the Word" (Ephesians 5:26). The "pure water" the writer of Hebrews referenced was surely a reference to God's Word. Compared to these two things, the smell of incense and the sight of its smoke are inconsequential. Yet those who promote the practice insist the following:

"Incense smoke symbolically purifies all that it touches. This is best illustrated by the richly symbolic practice in the Chaldean Rite of the Catholic Church. Those preparing to receive Holy Communion during the Holy Qurbono (Chaldean sacrificial liturgy) first purify their hands by holding them in smoke just above a bowl of burning incense. Similarly in the Maronite Rite of the Catholic Church, as they are being purified prior to liturgical use, the liturgical vessels — chalice, diskos (similar to the paten), and its asterisk (star) cover — are all inverted over the burning incense to catch the fragrant smoke."[109]

During the Mass, the ones holding a thurible (a censer suspended by chains) are often seen "incensing" people and objects in order to "sanctify" them during sacred ceremonies. Attributing this power to incense smoke is especially disturbing to me, because similar rituals are common and celebrated in many non-Christian religions.

Yoga, Meditation, and New Age Spirituality—When I was involved in yoga and far eastern meditation practices (in 1970, prior to my encounter with Jesus), we often burned incense in our gatherings. Also, several years ago, when I visited a large New Age and Yoga gathering to share Jesus with them, I saw a Tarot Card practitioner hold her cards over incense smoke to "cleanse" them before giving a reading to those seated around her. The reading of Tarot Cards is an occult divination practice which God would quickly label an "abomination," and is forbidden to believers (Deuteronomy 18:9-14).

What's the difference between "cleansing" Tarot cards and "cleansing" a chalice? Why would those professing faith in the Savior of all mankind use a methodology found in false, superstitious religions? Be assured, Tarot Card practitioners are not the only ones who implement the ceremonial use of incense. Examples abound. Some of the following descriptions may shock you:

Buddhism—"Buddhists regard incense as divine odor, and its smell is meant to evoke the presence of Buddhist divinities. Burning incense sticks works as a sensory way to sanctify the space and offering behaviors with mindfulness and awareness. During the ritual process, an individual waves three or more burned incense sticks overhead while bowing to the divine statues. The burning incense sticks are then vertically placed into a censer located in front of the statues. To date, incense burning has become an indispensable ritualistic practice for many people who believe in Buddhism."[110]

Hinduism—"The use of incense is a traditional and ubiquitous practice in almost all pujas, prayers, and other forms of worship. As part of the daily ritual worship within the Hindu tradition, incense is offered to God (usually by rotating the sticks thrice in a clockwise direction) in His deity forms, such as Krishna and Rama."[111]

Taoism and Shinto—"Incense holds an invaluable role in . . . Chinese Taoist and Japanese Shinto shrines for the deity Inari Okami, or the Seven Lucky Gods. It is reputed to be a method of purifying the surroundings, bringing forth an assembly of buddhas, bodhisattvas, gods, demons, and the like . . . In Chinese Taoist and Buddhist temples, the inner spaces are scented with thick coiled incense, which are either hung from the ceiling or on special stands. Worshipers at the temples light and burn sticks of incense in small or large bundles, which they wave or raise above the head while bowing to the statues or plaques of a deity or an ancestor. Individual sticks of incense are then vertically placed into individual censers located in front of the statues or plaques either singularly or in threes, depending on the status of the deity or the feelings of the individual."[112]

Islam—Incense is used in several ways in Islam, most notably the regular rite of purifying and cleansing the Ka'aba in Makkah. The purpose is to fill the air with a sweet aroma to inspire the souls of visiting pilgrims. According to a hadith of Muhammad, angels love fragrant scents and hate foul smells. [Note: The Ka'aba, a word meaning cube in Arabic, is the large square building draped in black silk, embroidered with gold, that is considered the holiest shrine in Islam located at the Great Mosque in Mecca. Muslims believe that Abraham originally built that famous mosque that contains "the black stone," purportedly given to Abraham by the angel Gabriel.]

Neopaganism—"Incense is also often used in Neopagan rituals to represent the element of air, although more modern approaches to incense magic demonstrate that incense actually represents all of the elements. This is attributed to the fact that incense smoke wafts through the air, is created through the use of fire, the incense materials are grown from the earth, and combustible incense is formed using water. It is also believed to release natural energy. Incenses of a wide range of fragrances are also used in spell and ritual for different purposes."[113]

Satanism—"Some forms of Satanism use incense to create an atmosphere that is capable of bringing 'demons' into the room, to perform such tasks as telling the future, healing the ritual practitioner or another person, and in some cases, Satanists believe they can 'curse' or 'hex' someone if the demons are willing to help. Although Satanism uses a variety of incense sticks, the one most commonly used is Patchouli (Graveyard Dust). Patchouli, when burnt in a small room or altar with several burning black candles, is said to bring forth those demons the practitioner wishes. Practitioners may bathe in water and then dress in black to perform these rituals, which may put the practitioner into a trance like state."[114]

Are you shocked by all these references? I am. But more than that, I am deeply troubled that fellow believers in the Lord Jesus Christ would embrace a practice so absent from the authentic New Testament church, so dominant in false religions, and so steeped in superstition. Surely, it is time to reevaluate this and other traditions that have often been unquestioned for centuries. Once again, I am not implying that Catholics, by adopting the use of incense in their liturgy, are on the same level as New Agers, Buddhists, Hindus, Taoists, Shintoists, Pagans, and Satanists. However, it should compel us to seriously question this practice. Realizing the prominence of the use of incense in these non-Christian religious ceremonies should make us even more reluctant to include it in anything associated with our blessed Savior.

Some final thoughts about the ceremonial use of incense

The only account in the New Testament of the priestly use of incense happened when the angel Gabriel appeared to Zacharias and prophesied to him concerning his wife, Elizabeth, her pregnancy, and the birth of the one later known as John the Baptist. Here's the account of that wonderful visitation:

So it was, that while he was serving as
priest before God in the order of his division,
according to the custom of the priesthood,
his lot fell to burn incense when he went into
the temple of the Lord.
And the whole multitude of the people was
praying outside at the hour of incense.
Then an angel of the Lord appeared to him,
standing on the right side of the altar of incense.
And when Zacharias saw him, he was
troubled, and fear fell upon him.
But the angel said to him, "Do not be afraid, Zacharias,
for your prayer is heard; and your wife Elizabeth will
bear you a son, and you shall call his name John."
(Luke 1:8-13)

That was the close of the Old Testament era and the beginning of a New Testament age in which things radically changed. After that holy visitation, and the miraculous birth that resulted, the offering of incense was never an important ritual again—never. In fact, a little over seventy years later, the temple was destroyed, and the altar of incense was lost to history. These once-important facets of Jewish religious ceremonies were left behind. God's New Covenant people were then moved up to a higher level of spirituality.

- **The temple**—The temple that once housed the ark of the covenant no longer exists, and instead, God's people are "the temple of the living God" (2 Corinthians 6:16).

- **The priesthood**—The priesthood is no longer exclusive and signified by certain clothing or an inherited position, for the entire body of Christ has the status of being a "holy priesthood," adorned with spiritual clothing (1 Peter 2:5).

- **The sacrifices**—Animal sacrifices are no longer required to atone for sin because the supreme sacrifice has taken place on Golgotha. Those who commit their lives to Him, and are crucified with Christ, become a "living sacrifice, holy, acceptable to God, which is our reasonable service" (Romans 12:1).

So, in this New Covenant era, God's people are now all three: we are the temple in which God dwells, we are the priests who minister to Him, and we are the sacrifices offered to Him. The other pieces of furniture in the temple are also spiritually fulfilled in us:

- **The menorah lampstand**—The body of Christ has now inherited the role (from the Messiah) of being "the light of the world"—shining our light openly and not behind a veil (Matthew 5:13).

- **The table of showbread**—Even as Jesus was "living bread," given to a human race starving for the truth, the body of Christ is now called to be "one bread," sacrificing their lives for the spiritual nourishment of others and to satisfy God's hunger for fellowship with the offspring of Adam (1 Corinthians 10:17).

- **The altar of incense**—Instead of literal incense being offered up daily, the body of Christ now sends up "spiritual sacrifices" to heaven, the sweet aroma of the "sacrifice of thanksgiving" and the "sacrifice of praise" (1 Peter 2:5, Psalms 116:17, Hebrews 13:15). We become "the aroma of life leading to life" (2 Corinthians 2:16).

Can you see how God has lifted these natural objects of worship upward to a far greater, far-more-important, supernatural level? We must keep this in mind if we are to properly interpret one of the last prophecies of the Old Testament foretelling the advance of the Gospel in all the world in this New Covenant era:

> *"For from the rising of the sun, even to its going down,*
> *My name shall be great among the Gentiles; in every*
> *place incense shall be offered to My name, and a pure*
> *offering; for My name shall be great among*
> *the nations," says the LORD of hosts.*
> *(Malachi 1:11)*

The "pure offering" is not a reference to animal sacrifices; it is symbolic first, of Jesus, and second, of those who also present themselves as "living sacrifices" to God. Likewise, the "incense" is not literal. It is fulfilled metaphorically as thanksgiving and praise ascend to God from every nation, race, culture, language, and people—all around the globe.

Ashes and holy water

Once again, the use of ashes and holy water also stems from an Old Testament ordinance, for the ashes were an essential ingredient in the "holy water" of that era. Consider the commandments given in Numbers 19 concerning the making and the use of something called "the water of purification" (Number 19:9). Basically, the priests were to find a "red heifer without blemish, in which there is no defect and on which a yoke" had never been placed (Numbers 19:2). It was to be taken outside the camp, sacrificed and burned totally, along with "cedar wood and hyssop and scarlet" (Numbers 19:6).

Then the ashes were mixed with running water and sprinkled with hyssop (a small plant) on those persons who needed to be cleansed from their uncleanness. Many different reasons were listed that rendered a person "unclean," including touching a dead person or being present when someone died. In fact, just about anything connected with death was considered unclean. (If you are interested in knowing the details, read all of Numbers 19.) The writer of Hebrews (probably Paul) commented on this practice and the superiority of the spiritual provision made for God's people in this era:

> *For if the blood of bulls and goats and the ashes of a*
> *heifer, sprinkling the unclean, sanctifies*
> *for the purifying of the flesh,*
> *how much more shall the blood of Christ, who through*
> *the eternal Spirit offered Himself without spot to God,*
> *cleanse your conscience from dead works*
> *to serve the living God?*
> *(Hebrews 9:13-14)*

The blood of Jesus, though invisible, is far superior to holy water that is visible. The holy water the priests of the Old Testament era used "sanctified" people and things to a very limited degree during that era (cleansing them from defilement and setting them apart as holy unto the Lord). However, the blood of the Lamb of God is infinitely more powerful in effecting this result. Unfortunately, though, people tend to trust in what they can see and feel naturally more than things that are spiritually discerned. Maybe that's why the world's first vending machine dispensed 'holy water.' It was just that important to people back then and still is now.[115] But the spiritual reality of being cleansed by the "washing of water by the Word" is so much greater, because that's how God is going to present to "Himself a glorious church, not having spot or wrinkle or any such thing, but that she should be holy and without blemish" (Ephesians 5:23).

Some biblical support for ashes

There is a big difference between cleansing *from God* (symbolized by holy water) and consecration *to God* (symbolized by ashes). In the Old Testament, there are several powerful scriptures that associate ashes with sincere and deep repentance. For instance, at the end of his season of crises, when Job experienced a visitation from God, he lamented:

> *"I have heard of You by the hearing of the ear,*
> *but now my eye sees You. Therefore I abhor myself,*
> *and repent in dust and ashes."*
> *(Job 42:5-6)*

It was a common practice, in ancient times especially, to accompany repentance with ashes as an admission that we physical human beings are but dust and ashes in the end, when mortality hits us with its final blow. So, the symbolic message is clear: to live for the things of this life, in the end, is vain and futile. The application of ashes is a reminder of that and represents a willingness to continue living on that level of awareness.

Another powerful example is the reaction of the King of Nineveh to Jonah's preaching when he walked through the city declaring "Thus says the Lord; in forty days Nineveh will be overthrown." The biblical account of that event is stunning:

> *Then word came to the king of Nineveh; and he arose*
> *from his throne and laid aside his robe, covered himself*
> *with sackcloth and sat in ashes.*
> *And he caused it to be proclaimed and published*
> *throughout Nineveh by the decree of the king and his*
> *nobles, saying, Let neither man nor beast,*
> *herd nor flock, taste anything; do not*

> *let them eat, or drink water.*
> *But let man and beast be covered with sackcloth,*
> *and cry mightily to God; yes, let every one turn from his*
> *evil way and from the violence that is in his hands.*
> *Who can tell if God will turn and relent, and turn away*
> *from His fierce anger, so that we may not perish?*
> *Then God saw their works, that they turned from their*
> *evil way; and God relented from the disaster that He*
> *had said He would bring upon them,*
> *and He did not do it.*
> *(Jonah 3:6-10)*

Jesus also seemed to indicate divine approval for the use of ashes when He gave a warning to two cities where He had preached and worked miracles, but they had not repented:

> *"Woe to you, Chorazin! Woe to you, Bethsaida! For*
> *if the mighty works which were done in you had been*
> *done in Tyre and Sidon, they would have repented long*
> *ago in sackcloth and ashes."*
> *(Matthew 11:21)*

So, of all the items covered in this chapter, ashes seem to be the one that is most acceptable in this present era.

Final conclusions about these four religious expressions

Well, we have arrived at the end of this unique chapter. Clearly, there are no directives concerning the use of candles, incense, or holy water—not at all. Other than ashes, I suggest these are all unnecessary ceremonial trappings. What we desperately need is another visitation of the power of God as they had in the upper room. We need to encounter God in a supernatural way—just like the Charismatic Movement of the 60s and 70s, as well as other great spiritual awakenings.

Visitations from above will change us dramatically, make us less dependent on religious externalism, and make us salt and light as Jesus commanded—true agents of change in this broken world.

Question 20

Relics: Are these ancient articles truly a source of God's power and blessing?

The word "relic" is derived from the Latin word *reliquiae,* meaning remains, and the verb *relinquere,* meaning to leave behind. In other words, they are the "remains" of holy and revered individuals that are "left behind."

True relics are thought to be a viable means of obtaining cures and miracles, not because of a power inherent in the relics themselves, but because of the holiness of the saintly individuals they represent. There are three main classes of relics, according to the usual Catholic standard:

- **First class**—physical objects associated with the Lord Jesus, or the physical remains of a saint (quite often, a martyr),

- **Second class**—objects that were owned or worn by various saints, or instruments of torture or execution that caused their deaths (their martyrdom),

- **Third class**—items in contact with things mentioned in either of the first two categories, even something contacting the grave of a saint.

Once obtained, relics must be properly stored and/or displayed. The sacred containers—often fashioned with superior craftmanship, ornately decorated, and expensively designed—are called reliquaries.

The history of the practice

The veneration of relics did not begin with Catholicism. It was practiced in ancient Greece, as part of their devotion to certain deities in their pantheon, upheld by various legends.[116] It has also been a respected tradition in Buddhism, a religion that started almost five centuries before Christianity. Buddhists have sacred temples called "stupas," which are said to house the remains of Buddha or other respected Buddhist teachers that emerged during the evolution of that worldview. After his death, the body of the Buddha was divided into eight parts to be enshrined in different locations as Buddhism spread. The claim is made that visiting those locations helps a person achieve enlightenment (nirvana) and escape the cycle of rebirths.

The Catholic Church, for hundreds of years, has practiced gathering and enshrining religious relics because of a belief that miraculous man-ifestations or spiritual benefits either have happened, or can happen, through being in their proximity, not by some magical influence, but by the power of God.

During the Middle Ages especially, if a city had a well-known church or cathedral whose leaders publicized the possession of fa-mous relics, the citizens felt they could expect special privileges, benefits, and protection through the intercession of those saints who were celebrated and enshrined. It often brought prestige to the local community and boosted its economy, because believers from far away would make pilgrimages to see the relics, in the hope of receiving su-pernatural intervention.

Since the onset of this custom in Catholicism, various traditions have evolved, like special feast days for certain saints when their relics are brought out and displayed before attending congregants, or special times when the reliquaries are carried in processions through a host city on the days when those saints are especially honored.

Though gathering and displaying relics has been a part of the Catholic Church protocol throughout most of its history, some have approached the practice with concern, like Jerome, a respected church theologian (347-520 A.D.), who cautioned, "We do not worship, we do not adore, for fear that we should bow down to the creature rather than to the Creator, but we venerate the relics of the martyrs in order the better to adore Him whose martyrs they are."[117] Apparently, this tradition became more popular and widespread after the Second Council of Nicaea in 787 A.D. when an official decree stated that "every altar should contain a relic."[118] The remainder of this chapter will hopefully help you decide if this is a legitimate Christian practice.

Biblical references used to justify the veneration of relics

The following biblical stories are often referenced by those who support the idea of the veneration of relics:

Elijah's mantle—What a remarkable story it is, how God carried Elijah up to heaven in a fiery chariot! Just as remarkable is the next phase of that story, how Elijah's mantle fell to the ground and his prophetic protégé, Elisha, picked it up and struck the waters of Jordan, saying, "Where is the Lord God of Elijah?" The river that had parted for Elijah parted once again for Elisha. So, in a certain sense, Elijah's mantle functioned as a relic, with its power passing immediately to the prophet's successor. (See 2 Kings 2:11-14.)

Elisha's bones—Elisha, the successor of Elijah, became one of the most gifted and influential prophets of God showcased in Scripture. He inherited a double portion of Elijah's anointing and was used of God to execute twice as many recorded miracles, including the multiplication of oil for the widow woman and the cleansing of Naaman, the leper. However, one of the greatest miracles God performed through Elisha did not take place during his lifetime. Here is the startling account:

> *Then Elisha died, and they buried him.*
> *And the raiding bands from Moab invaded the*
> *land in the spring of the year.*
> *So it was, as they were burying a man, that suddenly*
> *they spied a band of raiders; and they put the man in*
> *the tomb of Elisha; and when the man was let down*
> *and touched the bones of Elisha,*
> *he revived and stood on his feet.*
> *(2 Kings 13:20-21)*

If there was a video available showing the looks on the faces of the men when their friend's corpse came back to life, I would love to see it, wouldn't you? Maybe in heaven we will be able to relive these amazing moments when God powerfully intervened for His people.

Clothing from the apostle Paul—Miracles and supernatural intervention often happened in the early church, sometimes in random, unconventional ways. Consider the following:

> *Now God worked unusual miracles by the hands*
> *of Paul, so that even handkerchiefs or aprons were*
> *brought from his body to the sick, and the diseases left*
> *them and the evil spirits went out of them.*
> *(Acts 19:11-12)*

Those are the three main biblical stories that many Catholics offer as legitimizing "proof" of the practice of venerating relics. Two other stories are sometimes mentioned:

The woman with the issue of blood—This desperately sick woman was healed, not by Jesus intentionally touching her, but when she intentionally touched something that was touching Him (the hem of His garment). (See Matthew 9:20-22.)

Peter's shadow—People in Jerusalem put their sick on beds and couches on the side of the road, in the hope that Peter's shadow might pass over their loved ones, that they might be healed. Once again, they did not think this was going to happen because Peter touched them himself, but because something connected to Peter touched them (his shadow). It should be noted that no actual healings were ever recorded in the Bible resulting from this action, but if the people persisted in doing it, there must have been some manifestations of the miraculous that encouraged them to continue. (See Acts 5:15.)

So, that's about it, as far as biblical references are concerned. Do you think these examples are enough to justify the thousands of relics that have been preserved, protected, and promoted by the Catholic Church through the centuries? Quite often, respect for the concept of relics stems from the idea that something connected to a person who walks close to God can itself be a point of contact for the miraculous to happen. But why not just trust in the same God they trusted, and walk close to Him ourselves?

Relics of Jesus

There are only a small number of relics assigned to the Son of God. Four of the most well-known are as follows:

The veil of Veronica—This famous piece of cloth allegedly bears the facial image of Jesus, transferred when Veronica wiped the sweat off His face when He was carrying His cross on the Via Dolorosa (an event celebrated at the sixth station of the cross).[119] Is this true? Before answering you might consider that there are at least six conflicting claims concerning different veils purported to be the original. Who's to say which one is genuine, or if any of them are authentic? Many questions remain.

Pieces of the manger—In 2019, Pope Francis sent a thumb-sized piece of wood to Bethlehem to mark the beginning of the Christmas season. It was allegedly from the manger in which Jesus was born, with the larger piece remaining in Rome in a very elaborate and expensive gold and silver reliquary. However, some historians claim that the manger was most likely made of stone, not wood. Who's to say what the authentic manger looked like or if it even exists? The holy family had to flee into Egypt. I cannot imagine them hauling the original manger there and bringing it back to Nazareth (it didn't belong to them anyway). Moreover, after Joseph and Mary passed on to heaven, who inherited this object, passed it on, protected it from generation to generation, and continued to confirm its authenticity? Many questions remain.

Pieces of the cross—In the year 324, Constantine sent his mother, Helena, to Jerusalem to find the cross on which Jesus was crucified. The traditional story goes like this: Helena was told that the cross was under the pagan temple of Venus, which she ordered to be destroyed. After digging extensively, they supposedly "uncovered three crosses, one thought to belong to Jesus Christ, and the others belonging to the two thieves that died alongside Him. To test and see which one of these crosses truly belonged to Jesus Christ, they searched for a leper at the outskirts of Jerusalem. Once one was found, they returned back to the site of Golgotha, the place of Jesus' crucifixion. The leper was instructed to touch each of the crosses, one by one. He touched the first one and nothing happened. He touched the second one and still nothing happened. Finally, when he touched the third and final cross, the leper was instantly healed. It was this cross that healed the leper, and for that reason it is known as 'The True Cross.'"[120] However, who's to say if this story is true, especially since it seems highly unlikely that the true cross of Jesus could be correctly identified or even exist after nearly three centuries had passed? Besides, crucifixion was a popular mode of execution in Rome for many years, and most likely, thousands of crosses were used. Many questions remain.

The foreskin of Jesus—One of the most famous and controversial "relics of Jesus" is a piece of flesh authorities claim was the foreskin cut from Him when He was circumcised as an eight-day-old, Jewish boy (also called "The Holy Prepuce"). The earliest mention of the foreskin is found in the "Syriac Infancy Gospel, also known as the Arabic Infancy Gospel . . . a New Testament apocryphal writing concerning the infancy of Jesus. It may have been compiled as early as the sixth century, and was partly based on the Infancy Gospel of Thomas, the Gospel of James and the Gospel of Pseudo-Matthew."[121]

In the second chapter of that book (the Syriac Infancy Gospel— evidently fictional—written long after the fact) the story is told that Jesus was circumcised in a cave and an elderly Hebrew woman put the foreskin in an alabaster box of precious spikenard ointment which Mary, the sinner, procured later and poured out on the head and feet of Jesus, wiping it with her hair. An elaborately designed story, wouldn't you agree?[122] This written source is a spurious work, not in the ap- proved Canon of Scripture. Why lend it any measure of credibility?

The next major development in the progression of this narrative is the gifting of "The Holy Prepuce" to a pope: "On December 25, 800, Charlemagne was purported to have given it to Pope Leo III in gratitude for crowning him Emperor. When asked where he got the holy foreskin, Charlemagne responded that it had been brought to him by an angel as he was praying at the Holy Sepulchre. Another report claims that it was given to him as a wedding present by Empress Irene. Pope Leo III then took the foreskin and placed it in Sancta Sanctorum and there it remained until Rome was sacked in 1527."[123]

But where was "the Holy Foreskin" prior to that? "According to St Birgitta's *De Praeputio Domini* ('The Lord's Foreskin'), the Virgin

Mary kept the Holy Foreskin in a leather pouch, before giving it to St John. For the next seven centuries, it remained in the pouch, before someone – possibly an angel – brought it to Charlemagne's court at Aix-la-Chappelle."[124]

Being a very coveted relic that brought a lot of attention from the multitudes, at one point (depending on the sources you examine), there were anywhere from eight to eighteen different "foreskins" in various European churches with the possessors all insisting they were the stewards the true foreskin of Jesus. That makes you question, even more, the legitimacy of such a claim, doesn't it?

After its disappearance in 1527, when Emperor Charles V attacked Rome, the coveted foreskin was allegedly found about thirty years later in Calcata, a city just north of Rome, "disproving a theory by 17th century theologian Leo Allatius that it ascended into heaven to become the rings of Saturn."[125] There it was enshrined in the Church of the Holy Name. Every January 1st (during the Feast of the Holy Circumcision) "the local priest would lead a procession around the village with the holy relic held high."[126]

Eventually, "under pressure to banish Catholic practices that could be seen as culturally backward, the Vatican issued a decree in 1900 threatening excommunication to anyone who wrote about the holy foreskin, but it allowed the village of Calcata to continue its yearly procession. In 1983, just a few weeks prior to the Jan. 1 Feast of the Holy Circumcision, the local priest went to check on the relic, but it was missing."[127] The mysterious theft has never been solved. Who would steal such a thing? Who would buy it?

And there are other items associated with Jesus that are celebrated as "true relics'" like the "holy lance" that pierced his side, the crown of thorns, a piece of bloody cloth supposedly used to wipe his brow, the "holy sponge" that was used to give Him vinegar on the cross, the column where He was whipped, and a seamless garment (the "holy coat") for which the soldiers cast lots.

Why weren't any of these mentioned in the book of Acts? Surely, if they were legitimate and powerful, they would have been valued, displayed, celebrated, and promoted in the early church. But not one—I repeat—not one of these articles was ever mentioned! That's a good indication that they were probably just fabrications developed many years later, proof that people claiming to be religious will often go to great extents to use dubious promotional tactics to attract the multitudes, often with monetary gain in mind. Many questions remain.

More examples: relics of various saints

Below are some of the more famous relics that can be viewed by devoted believers to this day:

Mary's breast milk—In the Chapel of the Milk Grotto of Our Lady in Bethlehem, Israel, a vessel is displayed that supposedly contains the breast milk of Mary, the same source that nourished the baby Jesus. I find it hard to believe that virtuous Mary, the mother of Jesus, would supply a sampling of her breast milk for such a purpose.

The finger of the apostle Thomas—This severed finger is displayed in the Basilica di Santa Croce in Gerusalemme, Rome, Italy. Why would it be important since we don't even know if that finger belonged to Thomas, and most likely, it was never placed within the hand-wounds of Jesus?

The tongue of Saint Anthony—"St. Anthony died from Edema in 1231, and when he was exhumed in 1263 he had totally decomposed, except for, curiously, his tongue. The tongue was reportedly just as wet and incorrupt as it had been in his life, when he was celebrated for his oratory skills. He spent most of his life roaming Italy and France, giving sermons that captivated all of his audiences with a gripping power. He was canonized not too long after his death, but it was 30 years later when he was dug up to be reburied in a new basilica that his miraculous tongue was discovered. Now the tongue, as well as his jaw bone, are both displayed in the Basilica of Saint Anthony of Padua in elaborate gold reliquaries. The rest of his remains are entombed in a separate chapel."[128] Isn't the Word of God that Anthony preached far more important?

The blood of Saint Januarius—In the Catholic Cathedral in Naples, Italy, is a container of dried blood that supposedly belonged to a saint named Januarius that liquifies twice a year. Isn't the invisible blood of Jesus that flows through our souls to cleanse us from sin far more important and far more worthy of our enraptured attention?

The skull (or skulls) of John the Baptist—There are four different locations that each boast having the "skull" of John the Baptist: The Church of San Silvestro in Capite in Rome, the Cathedral of Amiens, France (90 miles north or Paris), the Residenz Museum in Munich, Germany, and the Umayyad Mosque (Muslim).[129] Of these four skulls, which one is the true skull of this great Old Testament prophet who ushered in the ministry of the Lord Jesus Christ? Should a devoted believer visit all four locations, hoping that at least one is them is correct? Can anyone know for certain? Are any of them genuine?

The skull of John in Amiens was supposedly brought back from Constantinople by a Crusader in 1206. That's over a thousand years after his beheading![130] "Other locations claim to have other body parts belonging to John the Baptist, including his right arm and right hand (with which he baptized Jesus)."[131]

We are told in Scripture that his disciples entombed his corpse (Matthew 14:10-12, Mark 6:24-29), but there is no historical proof that his body parts were ever divided up for display. I have one major response to all this information. Wouldn't it be far more important for us to have the message of John the Baptist, preparing the way of the Lord, declaring to the world that Jesus is coming again?

The big business of relics

The fact that reverencing relics turned into big business was part of what fueled Martin Luther's ire, motivating him to write His 95 theses. Most informed Christians are aware that he nailed his 95-point proclamation to the door of Castle Church in Wittenberg on October 31st, but few are aware that "the next day—All Saints' Day, 1 November 1517—an immense collection of more than 17,000 relics was going to be put on display so that "the faithful" could venerate them and receive indulgences for doing so. These relics included the following:

• A thumb of St. Anne,

• Some straw from Jesus' manger,

• A twig from the burning bush,

• One piece of the bread of which Christ ate with his disciples during the Last Supper[132]

222 ~ The Beliefs of the Catholic Church

Other items purported to be in this collection included a chunk of gold given to the baby Jesus by one of the Three Wise Men, a strand of hair from Jesus' beard, a few strands from the swaddling clothes in which the baby Jesus was wrapped, a piece of the land that was bought for thirty pieces of silver, and three pieces of the whip with which Jesus was flogged.[133]

Viewing each of the 17,000 items provided a 100-day indulgence, so the amount of indulgences a person could rack up was incredible. (Do the math: 17,000 relics x 100 days indulgence = 1,700,000 days of indulgences.) Although the Catholic Church now officially interprets this to mean 1,700,000 days' worth of penance, the people of that day most likely interpreted it as 1,700,000 actual days removed from a time of banishment to Purgatory. Divide that by 365 days in a year = that equals 4,657 years' worth of penance in exchange for much less suffering in the afterlife. Worth the trip and the expense, wouldn't you think? (I speak, tongue in cheek, of course.)

Eventually, Frederick the Wise, elector for the region of the Holy Roman Empire that included Wittenberg, built his collection of relics in Castle Church to "over 19,000 holy bones and 5,000 other items," which bumped it up to a whopping 2,400,000 days of indulgences (approximately 6,575 years).[134] By viewing the relics and "making the stipulated contribution," believers could reduce their purgatorial incarceration significantly, "while providing much needed financial support for Castle Church and the University of Wittenberg."[135] Most intelligent people in the 21st century—Catholics and non-Catholics alike—would agree: that has all the characteristics of a royal scam.

My final thoughts on relics

Now we come to the end of this chapter and I'm pausing prayerfully. This subject is a serious matter, first, because it is such an in-grained belief in Catholicism, and second, because so much hinges on whether or not this practice is legitimate. If relics are truly gifts from God, how dare I reject them or prevent others from having faith in them! That would be a terrible sin against our heavenly Father. But if relics are false and vain attempts at obtaining supernatural help, how dare I endorse them or even hold my peace and fail to expose the fallacy of this practice! Without hesitation, I feel compelled to explain three fundamental reasons why I no longer reverence these "hallowed" objects:

1. The unreliability of relics:

Because of the profit motive, there was evidently a great deal of deception and corruption that accompanied the sale of relics. Even a Catholic website admits how unreliable the process of identifying true relics became—and here's the explanation:

> "During the Middle Ages, the 'translation of relics' grew, meaning the removal of relics from the tombs, their placement in reliquaries, and their dispersal. Sadly, abuses grew also. With various barbarian invasions, the conquests of the Crusades, the lack of means for verifying all relics, and less than reputable individuals who in their greed preyed on the ignorant and superstitious, abuses did occur. Even St. Augustine (d. 430) denounced impostors who dressed as monks selling spurious relics of saints. Pope St. Gregory (d. 604) forbade the selling of relics and the disruption of tombs in the catacombs. Unfortunately, the Popes or other religious authorities were powerless in trying to control the translation of relics or to prevent forgeries. Eventually, these abuses prompted the Protestant leaders to attack the idea of relics totally. (Unfortunately, the abuses and the negative reaction surrounding relics has led many people to this day to be skeptical about them.)"[136]

I must admit, I am one of those "skeptical" ones, extremely skeptical. However, I am not a disbeliever in the supernatural. I know without a doubt that God moves in miraculous ways, and sometimes, in very peculiar ways. But I have also witnessed dishonest individuals taking advantage of gullible people who sincerely love God for their own gain.

Relics through the centuries have provided a "golden opportunity" for deceivers to manipulate those who are easily persuaded because they so desperately want a connection with God. But the God of truth has given us the Word of truth and the Spirit of truth to lead us and guide us into all truth and to bring us to the One who said, "I am . . . the truth" (John 14:6). Why should we put our trust in anything else?

2. The questionable source of most relics:

The majority of relics are allegedly the remains of those who have been canonized as saints by the Catholic Church, most of whom were martyred for their faith as well. However, under Question #10, sufficient biblical evidence was provided to prove that all who are born again are saints in the sight of God. In the light of that insight, the importance of being near those supposed body parts and personal items is dramatically reduced.

Under Question #11, the assertion was also made that "departed saints" cannot respond to believers who appeal to them in prayer, and none of them have "specialized areas" in which they assist. If that be true (and I believe it is), the importance of supposed "relics" is reduced even more. (Who created those categorizations anyway, and where did they get their information from?)

3. The normal one-time-use:

God's pattern normally is to use natural objects only one time, or only for a short season, for supernatural purposes, lest they be overly reverenced by human beings. The main objects mentioned in this chapter that God used to manifest the miraculous were Elijah's mantle, Elisha's bones, and Paul's handkerchiefs and aprons. As far as we know, the first item was used only twice, and the second, only one time as a point of contact for God to move, and after that, they disappear from the biblical narrative. Concerning Paul's personal effects, we have no record of what happened to them. Once their time of use was over, apparently, these items did not receive an undue amount of attention.

There are other biblical objects that were used supernaturally that support this premise. In Old Testament times, you never hear of shrines being built for Samson's jawbone, Gideon's lamp, or David's sling and the five stones that were in his pouch. God even personally buried Moses, most likely, so the Israelites would not be able to locate his corpse to mummify it and place it inside some ornately designed mausoleum, to which they could make annual pilgrimages. The Israelites were quite familiar with this kind of excessive devotion to deceased leaders, having witnessed it in Egypt with the Pharaohs.

The only holy objects that were preserved and enshrined were the ark of the covenant and its contents (the tablets of stone with the Ten Commandments, Aaron's rod that budded, and the golden bowl full of manna). However, the people were never able to view or touch these items. When the ark was carried into battle, they expected supernatural power to come to their aid, but there was a time when that failed in a very shocking way (See 1 Samuel 4:1-11.) Most of the time, the ark and its contents were hidden behind a veil in the holy of holies.

Then the unthinkable happened. The seed of Abraham were carried away into Babylonian captivity and the ark was either hidden or stolen. No one knows for certain what happened to it or where it was placed—though many theories and claims exist.

Seventy years later, the Jewish people returned to Jerusalem and rebuilt the temple. How disturbing and disheartening it must have been for them to make all that effort when there was no ark! When that impressive edifice was finished, lo and behold, the holy of holies was utterly empty. The forty-foot-high, forty-foot-wide, four-inch-thick veil was hiding a chamber with nothing in it but air. So why even have a temple? One of the primary purposes for the temple was absent from the picture. Then, when the crucifixion took place, something very unusual happened. Here's the remarkable biblical record:

> *And Jesus cried out again with a loud voice, and*
> *yielded up His spirit. Then, behold, the veil of the*
> *temple was torn in two from top to bottom; and the*
> *earth quaked, and the rocks were split.*
> *(Matthew 27:50-51)*

Maybe, just maybe, God tore the veil in two for more than one reason. First, it could have been a sign that now all people can have access into God's presence, but second, it also could have communicated something completely different and very profound. Could it be that God was impressing the Jewish people that even though the temple had been restored to an even more spectacular appearance—

226 ~ The Beliefs of the Catholic Church

its primary purpose was missing. It was supposed to be a shrine for the ark of the covenant on which the glory of God rested, and the holy of holies was supposed to be the impressive showplace for the relics the ark contained. But instead, nothing was there. Absolutely nothing! Maybe it was important for them to be stunned into acknowledging that reality, so they could move away from an archaic religious system that was no longer being used by God in the same depth it had been in the past.

God desired to move His people forward into something far better. First, He had walked among them in the form of His Son (and many of them missed that). Then, the next stage in God's plan was to cleanse them from all sin supernaturally by the precious blood of Jesus and to dwell within their hearts.

What an amazing and wonderful shift! But many missed it, because they refused to let go of their religious traditions—even though they gazed wide-eyed on an empty holy of holies and a veil that was ripped from top to bottom by God Himself.

Yes, the revered chamber was empty—and yes, this revered concept of relics may be just as empty. Instead of being so focused on objects from those who died in the ancient past, wouldn't it be better to keep our eyes on the holy One who rose from the dead and is alive forevermore? Relics are questionable, but His love, His goodness, and His power are unquestionably what we need.

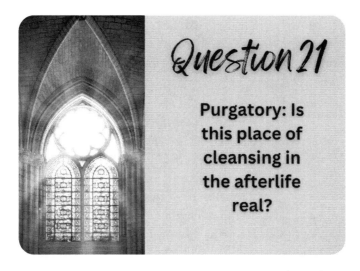

A ccording to the official catechism of the Catholic Church, Purgatory is for the "final purification of the elect" (CCC 1031). Here's an important and revealing quote:

> "All who die in God's grace and friendship, but still imperfectly purified, are indeed assured of their eternal salvation; but after death they undergo purification, so as to achieve the holiness necessary to enter the joy of heaven." (CCC 1030)[137]

The foundation of this Catholic belief is an acknowledgement that God is holy and to be in fellowship with Him, we, His people, must also be holy. Such a sincere desire to be pleasing to God is commendable. However, under the microscope of deeper examination, cracks and flaws in this theological concept quickly appear. Let's begin by inspecting the opening words of this catechism quote.

"All who die in God's grace"

Grace is unmerited love from God, something that cannot be earned by human effort or religious works. Grace comes into our lives in response to three complementary attitudes of heart: faith, humility, and sincere love for God. This threefold requirement is clearly revealed by the following scriptures:

Faith

*For by grace you have been saved through faith, and
that not of yourselves; it is the gift of God, not of works,
lest anyone should boast. (Ephesians 2:8-9)*

Humility

*God resists the proud, but gives grace to the humble.
(1 Peter 5:5)*

Sincere Love

*Grace be with all those who love our Lord Jesus Christ
in sincerity. Amen. (Ephesians 6:24)*

To "die in grace" is to die in a state of imparted righteousness, because Romans 5:21 promises that grace will "reign through righteousness unto eternal life by Jesus Christ our Lord." Such righteousness is not self-attained. On the contrary, it is "righteousness which is from God by faith" (Philippians 3:9). God made His Son "who knew no sin to be sin for us, that we might become the righteousness of God in Him" (2 Corinthians 5:21).

Did you get that? A true, born-again believer is granted the status of being just as righteous in the sight of the Father as Jesus, the firstborn Son—through identification. This divine righteousness comes as a gift along with the gift of grace as indicated by the following scripture:

> *For if by the one man's offense death reigned through
> the one [Adam], much more those who receive
> abundance of grace and of the gift of righteousness will
> reign in life through the One, Jesus Christ.
> (Romans 5:17)*

Seize this truth! Even as Adam passed a sinful status to his off-spring, Jesus passes a righteous status to His offspring. This is the highest expression of righteousness obtainable. No believer could ever become more righteous than "the righteousness of God," even after executing a thousand acts of extreme penance, or being subjected to ten billion years of suffering in Purgatory. Furthermore, by trusting in the true source of righteousness, all praise and all credit goes to "the God of all grace," not to any who aspire to please Him (1 Peter 5:10).

"All who die in God's . . . friendship"

My first reaction to this part of the Catechism quote is to say, "Real friends do not send their friends to a place of misery!" Quite the opposite, I can only imagine the Redeemer, with extreme pleasure, welcoming His "friends" into the splendor of heaven at the moment of their departure from this world.

Abraham was called "the friend of God" (James 2:23). I cannot imagine this Patriarch of the faith being banished to Purgatory at death, can you? Or what about Moses? Scripture affirms that the Lord spoke to this great prophet "face to face, as a man speaks to his friend" (Exodus 33:11). Surely, Moses was not subjected to further intense purification after his demise.

It is correct (according to Luke 16:19-31) that those who walked in a covenant relationship with God under the Old Testament, at death, temporarily went to "Abraham's bosom" in *Sheol* (the underworld location, also called *Hades* in the Greek). In that netherworld place (discussed under Question #11), there was an impassable gulf between the abode of the wicked and the abode of the righteous. Until Jesus paid the ultimate price of redemption on the cross, the redeemed of that era could not enter Paradise (the third heaven, the celestial abode of God). Nevertheless, Jesus described that temporary location (called "Abraham's bosom") as a place of "comfort," not a place of purgatorial purging. (Luke 16:25). That's an important point.

Continuing with the "friendship" idea, Jesus told His disciples:

> *"Greater love has no one than this, than to*
> *lay down one's life for his friends.*
> *You are My friends if you do*
> *whatever I command you.*
> *No longer do I call you servants, for a servant does not*
> *know what his master is doing; but I have called you*
> *friends, for all things that I heard from My Father*
> *I have made known to you."*
> *(John 15:13-15)*

Can you imagine Jesus continuing this passage by saying:

> By the way, I need to warn you, that even though
> I count you My friends, when you die, I will probably
> have to banish you to thousands of years of suffering
> in Purgatory until I see that you are perfect enough to
> enter heaven.

Quite the contrary, He awakened confidence in His followers by saying a little earlier in the same powerful discourse:

> *"Do not let your heart be troubled.*
> *Trust in God; trust also in Me.*
> *In My Father's house there are many dwelling places.*
> *If it were not so, would I have told you that I am*
> *going to prepare a place for you?*
> *If I go and prepare a place for you, I will come again*
> *and take you to Myself, so that*
> *where I am you may also be."*
> *(John 14:1-3 TLV)*

Surely, the early disciples who heard these exhortations died "in God's grace and friendship" (except for Judas), yet they were all still imperfect—just like the rest of us. However, when they transitioned from an earthly existence to the heavenly sphere, those imperfections were eliminated—instantaneously and supernaturally. It is unimaginable that those who were blessed to walk with the Son of God while He was on earth would not be allowed to walk with Him in heaven immediately after their demise.

To use an example already cited in the chapter on Absolution, Jesus promised the repentant thief who died next to him on Golgotha, "Assuredly, I say to you, today you will be with Me in Paradise" (Luke 23:43). Notice, Jesus used the word "today." He did not say, "After you have been purified in Purgatory for a lengthy season." All the repentant thief said was, "Lord, remember me, when You come into Your kingdom" (Luke 23:42). If someone being executed for a crime could go immediately to a joyous, celestial afterlife, simply because he expressed faith in the Messiah with one short request, the same kind of response would surely be extended to those who have devoted their hearts and lives to the Son of God for many years.

We should also consider—what about those believers who will be alive when Jesus returns? Surely some of them will still be imperfect. Will they be delayed in receiving their glorified bodies until they go through the purification of Purgatory? Or, as the Bible reveals, will that glorious transformation into immortality take place "in a moment, in the twinkling of an eye"? (1 Corinthians 15:52) I believe the latter, because my faith is not in my own goodness, but in "the Gospel of the grace of God" (Acts 20:24).

The source of our perfection

The Bible does not describe heaven as the dwelling place of those who have perfected themselves, but a place occupied by "the spirits of just men *made* perfect" (Hebrews 12:23, emphasis by author). It is God who grants us the status of being "perfect in Christ Jesus" (Colossians 1:28).

Admittedly, in our walk with God, we are commanded to reach for perfection in all that we say and do—even as our "Father in heaven is perfect" (Matthew 5:48). But all such efforts are expressions of worship, not attempts at earning a status of righteousness by religious self-effort. Ultimately, perfection comes as a gift from above. Jesus revealed this mystery when He interceded over all who would ever be part of the true church, declaring to the Father:

"I do not pray for these alone, but also for those who
will believe in Me through their word;
that they all may be one, as You, Father, are in Me, and
I in You; that they also may be one in Us, that the world
may believe that You sent Me.
And the glory which You gave Me I have given them,
that they may be one just as We are one:
I in them, and You in Me; that they may be made
perfect in one, *and that the world may know that You*
have sent Me, and have loved them
as You have loved Me."
(John 17:20-23)

Notice the Messiah never mentioned that His followers would be "made perfect" by going through many years of purgatorial suffering. He revealed this wondrous transformation would result from the privilege and power of their oneness with Him. If Jesus laid down his life "for His friends," the purchase price of His blood is sufficient to grant them access into Paradise at death, or His death was in vain. No wonder the Scripture boldly proclaims:

> *"Blessed are the dead who die in the Lord . . .*
> *that they may rest from their labors,*
> *and their works follow them."*
> *(Revelation 14:13)*

To be "blessed" means to be supremely happy, enriched with benefits, spiritually prosperous, and highly favored of God. To "die in the Lord" means to be under Jesus' headship and Lordship when we pass from this world. Do you think this verse describes people who are about to face the pain of Purgatory? No, not at all. If there was such a thing as Purgatory, this Bible promise would need to be rewritten to say something like the following:

> Blessed are the dead who die in the Lord (if they obtain a plenary indulgence for their sins prior to their demise and escape Purgatory, or—if they are only able to obtain partial indulgences before death—after they finish their designated time of purgatorial suffering), that they may rest from their labors and their works follow them.

Do you think this altered scripture sounds like a true assessment of what awaits a believer? Or have you arrived at the same Word-based conclusion being promoted in this chapter? I hope you have—but if you are not sure yet, there are still important, additional points that need to be made that are very convincing.

The surprising history of the doctrine of Purgatory

The concept of Purgatory cannot be found in the teachings of Jesus, the New Testament writers, or the early church leaders. Augustine of

Hippo (a theologian, respected by Catholics, who lived 354-430 A.D.) alluded to this concept, but even so, it did not become a popular belief until the end of the 12th century—over a thousand years after the birth of Christianity. During the fourteenth ecumenical council conducted in 1274 AD, this doctrine became one of the major stumbling blocks preventing a reunification of the Eastern Orthodox Church with the Catholic Church.

According to the Catholic Catechism, "The Church formulated her doctrine of faith on Purgatory especially at the Councils of Florence and Trent" (CCC 1031, Florence 1438-1439 A.D., Trent 1545-1563 A.D.). So historically, this concept is not only absent from the doctrinal foundation of the early church; it was never accepted by all those professing a biblical worldview in the centuries following.

Shadowy descriptions of a shadowy realm

What is Purgatory—really? How does it supposedly accomplish its intended purpose? Though described by many as a state of suffering, this afterlife location is usually not depicted in extreme terms, such as a scene of hellish torment. However, the Catholic Catechism does describe it as "a cleansing fire," whatever that means (CCC 1031). Contradictory speculations are common.

Purgatory is portrayed two primary ways: as a place of punishment and a place of purging for believers, to fulfill "the temporal punishment still due to the venial sins they committed while on earth."[138] Surprisingly and strangely, there is no authoritative stance that reveals the nature of exactly how this purging or purification takes place. It makes me wonder if those who believe in Purgatory, who unquestioningly accept the doctrinal stance of the church, have ever really subjected this belief to critical thinking and sincere biblical inquiry.

Usually, in this life, character development (or the "purification" of the heart) happens over a lengthy period by a process that is either negative or positive—or both. Let's examine these two processes.

Negative character development: through regret, repentance, recovery, and restoration—Unfortunately, human beings often yield to their lower nature, to lesser or greater degrees, and negative consequences almost always result. Painful outcomes cause the heart to be gripped with regret, and in the process, the value of making godly choices is learned. For true Christian believers, this process often involves grieving over failures, being convicted by God's Spirit, repenting before Him, praying for forgiveness, and submitting to God's will. In the process, Christlike character is awakened within. This is character development through regret, repentance, recovery, and restoration.

Positive character development through realization, resistance, and refusal—Those who are ethical, honest, and God-loving by nature usually desire righteousness for positive reasons, because of love for truth, the influence of the conscience, the conviction of the Holy Spirit, the reading of God's Word, the righteous example of others, or simply a desire to be pleasing to God and live a meaningful life. Thus, they make positive choices that result in overcoming the lower nature and in the development of Christlike traits without having to rebound from errors. When mistreated by others or damaged by the circumstances of life, they choose to forgive and they choose to trust, overcoming the temptation to be bitter or to doubt. This is all character development through realization, resistance, and refusal.

An important consideration

Dare to consider the following question—Would either of these processes even be possible in Purgatory? What is the condition of existence in that strange, netherworld location? I don't know of any Catholic author or expositor who has attempted to explain exactly how the purification of the soul is accomplished. Are mistakes allowed in Purgatory, so that repentance, recovery, and restoration can take place? Or does the reading of God's Word take place, so that realization and resistance against the lower nature can be awakened? Is there still a lower nature to overcome in that spiritual state? Is there a way of refusing the contamination of sin?

Do participants in the purgatorial process learn through the trial and error of human choices or the tension of challenging human relationships? Are the inhabitants of Purgatory subjected to temptations that must be resisted so the development of the divine nature can take place? Or is there just a constant, recurring reminder of the mistakes made during a previous earthly sojourn? Do the inhabitants of Purgatory just float around in a soulish state, suffering the torment of painful memories until they burn out? Think about it! There are no authoritative answers to these extremely important questions.

The "purification process" has never been explained in precise terms. It is a very vague and weak belief that crumbles when honestly inspected. Most of those who accept the idea of the existence of Purgatory just believe this purification will take place, but the means and the methods are never clarified, being just a matter of blind faith.

Recent popes, John Paul II and Benedict XVI, proposed that the term "Purgatory" does not indicate a place, but a condition of existence—which is even more vague and indefinable. In his 2007 encyclical *Spe salvi*, Pope Benedict XVI, referred to the words of Paul the Apostle in 1 Corinthians 3:12–15 about a fire that both burns and saves. He shared the opinion that "the fire which both burns and saves is Christ himself, the Judge and Saviour."[139] So Purgatory is "Christ Himself"? I'm shaking my head right now as I write these words, saying out loud, "There's absolutely no way that can be true!"

Of course, true believers are baptized with "the Holy Spirit and fire," and the Scripture declares "our God is a consuming fire" (Matthew 3:11, Hebrews 12:29). Though the fire of God is a dreadful thing to those who rebel against Him, it is a wonderful thing for those who love Him. It is the fire of love, the fire of transformation. (Read the Song of Solomon 8:6-7, Daniel 7:9-10, and Ezekiel 8:1-2.)

When Jesus returns, this fire will be witnessed in a spectacular way. The King of kings will be "revealed from heaven with His mighty angels, in flaming fire taking vengeance on those who do not know God, and on those who do not obey the gospel of our Lord Jesus Christ" (2 Thessalonians 1:7-8). But simultaneously, He will be manifested as a "refiner's fire" that will instantly purge His devoted people of the dross of the lower nature and transform them into eternal priests and glorified saints who bear His glorious image forever (Malachi 3:2). Once again, I did say "instantly." Here is one of my favorite verses about that glorious moment:

> *Beloved, now we are children of God; and it has not yet*
> *been revealed what we shall be, but we know that when*
> *He is revealed, we shall be like Him,*
> *for we shall see Him as He is.*

> *And everyone who has this hope in Him purifies*
> *himself, just as He is pure. (1 John 3:2-3)*

We will be dramatically changed, glorified, and made immortal (body, soul, and spirit), not after thousands of years of torturous treatment in some underworld location, but the very moment we rise from the graves to behold Jesus' beautiful face. Read verse three again, slowly and prayerfully:

> *Everyone who has this hope in Him*
> *purifies himself, just as He is pure.*

Lay hold to that. Seize it by faith. If you have the hope of the resurrection burning in your bosom, that is enough to "purify" you to the exceptional level of the Savior's own purity, and grant you entrance into Paradise. No other fire is needed, if you are truly devoted.

Did Jesus teach this concept?

It is important to reemphasize that Purgatory is often conceptualized, not just as a place of purging, but as a place of punishment, because sin during the earthly sojourn of believers can lengthen their time of "confinement."

The idea of Purgatory is based on the logic that some people who die are not so evil that they are deserving of hell, but they also have not committed themselves to God sufficiently to be worthy of heaven and the "beatific vision."[140] So, a transitional place of refining after death is deemed necessary.

The concept of an intermediate sphere of existence cannot be found anywhere in the Bible. Only two ultimate destinations in the afterlife are described: paradise or the lake of fire. Besides, the infinite bliss of heaven is not something we could ever earn by righteous works, religious devotion, or purgatorial suffering. Jesus made it very simple. He pledged:

> *"Most assuredly, I say to you, he who believes*
> *in Me has everlasting life."*
> *(John 6:47)*

If Jesus had believed and promoted the idea of purgatory, I imagine He would have worded that statement much differently—possibly, similar to the following statement:

> Most assuredly, I say to you, he who believes in Me has everlasting life, but usually, it will require a time of serious suffering and purging, possibly for thousands of years, in the pain of an intermediate state in the underworld. But it will be worth it in the end.

Thank God! That is not how the Savior described the next stage of our spiritual journey!

Validating Purgatory through the Book of Maccabees

Sometimes Catholics try to validate the doctrine of Purgatory by referencing 2 Maccabees 12:39-46. That passage describes Judas Maccabeus and his associates praying forgiveness for certain Jewish soldiers who had been killed in battle because it was discovered those men were wearing amulets associated with a false deity. He also took up a collection and sent it to Jerusalem as an atonement for their souls.

That book (which is not included in the Protestant Canon of Scripture) does not endorse what Judas Maccabeus did as a legitimate way of atoning for idolatrous sins. It just describes it as historical information. That may have been a custom among some Jews at the time. However, it is not commanded or approved anywhere in the other books of the Old Testament.

It is true when Moses took a census of Israelite men, each one was to give a half a shekel for the atonement of his soul, but that was a different situation and requirement altogether. (See Exodus 30:11-16.) So, using this reference in Maccabees as a supportive argument is not substantive at all.

Exegesis or eisegesis?

Exegesis is a theological term referring to the process of drawing out of a passage of Scripture its correct meaning and interpretation through a proper and thorough interpretive process. Eisegesis means imposing on Scripture the interpreter's own ideas or biases, rather than the true meaning of the text.

The strongest Catholic argument intended to uphold the idea of this "intermediate state" is based on 1 Corinthians 3:11-15. This has even been called "a go-to passage for many Catholics in support of Purgatory."[141] However, instead of being true to the text (exegesis), a pro-Catholic explanation has to be imposed on this text (eisegesis). Read it very carefully, prayerfully, and humbly, and see if you agree:

> *For no other foundation can anyone lay than that*
> *which is laid, which is Jesus Christ.*
> *Now if anyone builds on this foundation with gold,*
> *silver, precious stones, wood, hay, straw,*
> *each one's work will become clear; for the Day will*
> *declare it, because it will be revealed by fire; and the fire*
> *will test each one's work, of what sort it is.*
> *If anyone's work which he has built on it*
> *endures, he will receive a reward.*
> *If anyone's work is burned, he will suffer loss; but he*
> *himself will be saved, yet so as through fire.*
> *(1 Corinthians 3:11-15)*

Notice that this fiery determination of worthiness happens on a specific "Day." So, what day is being referenced as "the Day" when "the fire will test each one's work" before God? The answer is "the Day of the Lord"—the day when Jesus descends to reclaim this planet and resurrect His people. The fire of God will be so brilliantly expressed during this Second Coming of the Messiah that Isaiah claimed:

> *The light of the moon will be as the light of the sun, and*
> *the light of the sun will be sevenfold, as the light of*
> *seven days, **in the day** that the LORD binds up the*
> *bruise of His people and heals the stroke of their wound.*
> *(Isaiah 30:26)*

During that grand event, there will be an instantaneous determination made by the Creator concerning all the deeds of our lives. As I quoted earlier, "in a moment, in the twinkling of an eye" God will manifest Himself, assess our status, and if we have served Him, change and reward those He deems worthy—by the transformational power of God—into resurrected, glorified saints of the Almighty God (1 Corinthians 15:52). In that very day, we will "shine forth as the sun" in the eternal kingdom of our Father (Matthew 13:43),

These passages and promises do not imply a fiery confinement and refinement accomplished over hundreds or even thousands of years, but an instantaneous disclosure of the purity of works done in the name of Jesus Christ and in the name of Christianity. Only those religious works done sincerely, according to God's will, and in alignment with God's Word, will receive an eternal reward. All other religious works will be empty of eternal value and "burned up."

Most importantly, this passage could not be referring to the total world population; it only applies to those who have laid Jesus as the "foundation" of their lives. That would exclude people outside of the Christian faith, as well as those who are merely churchgoers (Christians in name only), who have not sincerely based their lives on a biblical belief system.

Ironically, some of the "wood, hay and straw" that will be burned up will most likely include many of the rituals, ceremonies, and traditions that have been developed in Christendom through the centuries that are not biblical but are the product of "the commandments of men" (Matthew 15:9). The "loss" that will be suffered is primarily the loss of those portions of people's lives devoted to erroneous biblical doctrines, concepts, and practices that did not promote the kingdom of God as He intended when He introduced the New Covenant.

Many cathedrals have been built and great religious institutions raised up that profess to be "Christian," yet do not promote true biblical salvation and the true revelation of God's Word. Much of that religious activity, though often performed worshipfully and sincerely, will be "burned up" at the coming of the Lord.

The believers themselves *may* be saved (if they have been born again and are genuinely devoted), but some of what they did in the name of Christianity, in the end, will be revealed as fruitless, non-biblical, uninspired, and not worthy of any eternal reward.

People in Purgatory Praying for Us? Seriously?!?

According to official Catholic teaching, not only are believers encouraged to pray for those suffering in Purgatory (a concept we will explore more fully in the next chapter on "Indulgences"); those who are confined to Purgatory supposedly are able to pray for people in this world. What? How could that be? Yet, the Catechism, in a section titled "Communion with the Dead," clearly states:

> "Our prayer for them [souls in Purgatory] is capable not only of helping them, but also of making their intercession for us effective." (CCC 958)

Are you shaking your head in unbelief right now? I am. We are called to pray for suffering souls who are not pure enough to enter heaven, so that their prayers for us may be more effective??? That doesn't make any sense at all. Prayer can only be "effective" if righteousness is the foundation of a believer's life. As the Scripture declares:

> *The effective, fervent prayer of a*
> *righteous man avails much.*
> *(James 5:16)*

If someone in Purgatory can pray an "effective prayer" (one that touches God's heart and brings forth the desired answer), then that righteous person definitely does not belong in Purgatory. Don't you agree?

In other religions, but not true Christianity!

In closing, it may surprise you that a belief in temporary, purgatorial, or "hellish" states (sometimes existing on many levels), is not confined to Catholicism. It is a dominant belief in Buddhism, Hinduism, Jainism, and other religions that teach a self-achieved "salvation" through the process of reincarnation. The law of karma demands that those who indulge in evil deeds must suffer, either in this life or in the afterlife, to cancel the spiritual debt incurred and to evolve spiritually before rebirth in this world can take place.

Of course, those false belief systems do not celebrate a crucified and resurrected Savior offering forgiveness as the centerpiece of their faith—so it is very understandable that they would base their hopes for the future on self-achieved character development and self-achieved salvation. However, that is not the good news of the Gospel.

The angel Gabriel told Joseph that Mary was with child by the Holy Spirit and that he was to call His name Jesus, "for He shall save His people from their sins" (Matthew 1:21). The angel did not say this Savior would punish His people for their sins in an afterlife location. If you are truly one of "His people," you can face death unafraid. Jude declared the amazing prophecy about Jesus' Second Coming:

> *Now unto him that is able to keep you from falling, and*
> *to present you faultless before the presence*
> *of his glory with exceeding joy,*
> *To the only wise God our Saviour, be glory and majesty,*
> *dominion and power, both now and ever. Amen.*
> *(Jude 1:24-25 KJV)*

Peter, the apostle, declared that on that wonderful day:

> *You will receive a glorious welcome into the eternal*
> *kingdom of our Lord and Savior Jesus Christ.*
> *(2 Peter 1:11 NCB)*

Quit being driven by fear. Start believing that the price Jesus paid on the cross is sufficient. Start confessing that "goodness and mercy" will follow you all the days of your life, that immediately after you pass through "the valley of the shadow of death," God will "prepare a feast" for you and you will "dwell in the house of the Lord forever" (promises from Psalm 23).

My concluding thoughts

As I finish this chapter, it is as if I hear, ringing in the cathedral of my own soul, the popular Gospel song, "On Christ the Solid Rock I Stand"—especially the following four lines:

> *My hope is built on nothing less*
> *Than Jesus' blood and righteousness.*
> *I dare not trust the sweetest frame,*
> *But wholly lean on Jesus' name.*

We who cling to the cross should abhor and reject any doctrine that steals from the power and the praise of what Jesus accomplished on that lonely hill of extreme suffering. Before He died, He cried with passion, "It is finished!" (John 19:30). He did not say, "It is somewhat finished—but not completely—because My followers will still have to suffer in the afterlife."

What He accomplished that day in our behalf was enough to take us from unrighteousness to righteousness, from earth to heaven, and from time to eternity. In response, we should lift our voices and worshipfully echo those three wonderful words again and again with absolute faith.

"It is finished"—the power of sin is conquered.

"It is finished"—nothing can be added.

"It is finished!"—our debt has been canceled.

"It is finished!"—we are forgiven for time and eternity.

"It is finished!"—the accuser has been cast down.

"It is finished!"—our salvation is secure.

Question 22

Indulgences: Can these reduce a person's time in Purgatory?

Catholics often go to great lengths to obtain merits, called "indulgences," so that they or their loved ones can exit Purgatory at an earlier time than what would otherwise be necessary. (Hopefully, you have read the last chapter before venturing into this one, since it lays the foundation for this entire concept.)

The word "indulgence" comes from the Latin word *indulgentia* which means leniency or kindness. So, indulgences are considered gifts from God, expressions of His leniency, patience, kindness, forgiveness, mercy, and love. The official Catechism explains:

> "An indulgence is a remission before God of the temporal punishment due to sins whose guilt has already been forgiven, which the faithful Christian who is duly disposed gains under certain prescribed conditions through the action of the Church which, as the minister of redemption, dispenses and applies with authority the treasury of the satisfactions of Christ and the saints. An indulgence is partial or plenary according as it removes either part or all of the temporal punishment due to sin. The faithful can gain indulgences for themselves or apply them to the dead."[142]

Let me break down that lengthy definition into five shorter points that hopefully make it easier to understand:

1. An indulgence removes the temporal punishment due to sin that has already been forgiven through Confession and Penance.

2. Indulgences are only granted when a Catholic fulfills certain actions or activities that the church authorizes for that purpose.

3. The church claims the ability to do this because of the infinitely inexhaustible treasury of good works and prayers from the life of the Lord Jesus and those who are perfectly united with Him in heaven: Mary and all the saints.

4. Indulgences are either partial (removing part of the punishment) or plenary (removing all the punishment) due to sin.

5. Catholics are taught that they can secure indulgences for themselves or for the dead—but not for other living Catholics.

Here's a more thorough explanation of the concept of "temporal punishment":

> "Temporal punishment for sin stands in contrast to eternal punishment for sin. Eternal punishment for sin is that punishment which is everlasting. Without end. Thus, eternal. That is the punishment due to mortal sin. Temporal punishment for sin is a punishment which will have a definite end, when the soul is purified and is permitted into heaven. Thus temporary. Temporal punishment for sin is that which is experienced in Purgatory."[143]

Of course, believers must be Catholic to earn indulgences and they must be in a state of grace. The Catholic Catechism explains:

> "An indulgence is obtained through the Church who, by virtue of the power of binding and loosing granted her by Christ Jesus, intervenes in favor of individual Christians and opens for them the treasury of the merits of Christ and the saints to obtain from the Father of mercies the remission of the temporal punishments due for their sins. Thus the Church does not want simply to come to the aid of these Christians, but

also to spur them to works of devotion, penance, and charity." (CCC 1478)

Although the doctrine and practice of obtaining indulgences is not found in the Bible, the claim is made that it has "a solid foundation in divine revelation which comes from the Apostles and develops in the Church with the help of the Holy Spirit."[144]

In other words, though not biblical in origin, it is still considered divinely inspired. However, regardless of denomination, the test of any doctrine is whether it can be found clearly stated in the written Word of God. The Bible is the "Rock" on which we must all build our lives. If "revelation" is not a part of this doctrinal, rock-solid foundation, it is most likely a mutation of the truth, or a deviation from the truth altogether.

The difference between a "plenary" and a "partial indulgence":

"A plenary indulgence means that by the merits of Jesus Christ, the Blessed Virgin Mary and all the saints, the full remission of the temporal punishment due to sacramentally forgiven sins is obtained. The person becomes as if just baptized and would fly immediately to heaven if he died in that instant. A partial indulgence means that a portion of the temporal punishment due to forgiven sin is remitted. Partial indulgences are received either by doing some act to which a partial indulgence is attached (e.g. praying a partially indulgenced prayer), or by the incomplete fulfillment of the conditions attached to a plenary indulgence."[145]

Only one plenary indulgence can be earned in a single day, but numerous partial indulgences can be earned. There are many sources (Catholic books, websites, articles, etc.) that supply lists of religious actions, authorized by the church, that allegedly result in the securing of indulgences.

The following examples and quotes, unless otherwise noted, are taken from the English version of the *Manual of Indulgences: NORMS AND GRANTS,* an authoritative resource put out by the "United

States Conference of Catholic Bishops" in collaboration with the Holy See (a term meaning the hierarchy of the church in the Vatican and its sphere of authority worldwide). This manual provides a very lengthy, detailed, and complicated overview of this religious belief and practice. I will only share a few of the options listed.

Plenary indulgences

There are "four prerequisites" for plenary indulgences to be activated. Those seeking such divine intervention must:

1. Have the interior disposition of complete detachment from sin, even venial sin,

2. Participate in Confession,

3. Receive Communion,

4. Pray for the intention of the Holy Father (the Pope).

These four prerequisites must be performed within days of each other, if not at the same time.[146] If these actions are taken, plenary indulgences are granted to the faithful who fulfill any of the following:

- "Who read the Sacred Scriptures as spiritual reading, from a text approved by competent authority and with the reverence due to the divine word, for at least a half an hour; if the time is less, the indulgence will be partial"

- "Who devoutly recite the Marian rosary in a church or oratory, or in a family, a religious community, or an association of the faithful"

- "Who visit [a sacred place] and there devoutly recite an Our Father and the Creed"

- "Who visit the Blessed Sacrament to adore the same for at least half an hour"[147]

- Who "attend a ceremony in honor of a new saint during the first year after canonization (available once)"[148]

- "Who make a three day retreat"[149]

Partial indulgences

Partial indulgences are granted to the Christian faithful who fulfill any of the following:

- "Who, led by the spirit of faith, give compassionately of themselves or of their goods to serve their brothers in need"

- "Who, at the celebration of the Easter vigil or on the anniversary of their own Baptism, renew their baptismal vows in any legitimately approved formula"

- "Who devoutly sign themselves with the sign of the cross, using the customary words: In the name of the Father and of the Son and of the Holy Spirit. Amen."

- "Who devoutly recite either the Apostles' Creed or the Niceno-Constantinopolitan Creed"

- "Who, in the particular circumstances of daily life, voluntarily give explicit witness to their faith before others"

- "Who, in a spirit of penance, voluntarily abstain from something that is licit for and pleasing to them"

- "Who invoke St. Joseph, spouse of the Blessed Virgin Mary, with a duly approved prayer"

- "Who devoutly visit one of the ancient Christian cemeteries or catacombs"

A plenary indulence, applicable only to the souls in Purgatory, is granted to the faithful:

- "Who on any and each day from November 1 to 8, devoutly visit a cemetery and pray, if only mentally, for the departed" (Any other time of year, doing this obtains only a partial indulgence for souls in Purgatory.)

- Who "on All Souls' Day . . . devoutly visit a church or an oratory and recite an Our Father and the Creed"

These quotes are just a small sampling of the many options provided to Catholics to obtain either plenary or partial indulgences.
Because all human beings falter, to smaller or greater degrees, those
who believe in this doctrine must constantly be monitoring their
acquisition of indulgences to escape the punishment of Purgatory
that will inevitably result from any sins or errors. Watching the clock
carefully is very important, too. Because if you accidentally read the
Bible for only twenty-nine minutes, you only get a partial indulgence,
but if you keep reading just another sixty seconds, a plenary indulgence
kicks in. Just sixty seconds of reading God's Word could determine
your destiny at death, if you happen to pass away shortly afterward.
Does that not strike you as a preposterous claim?

Of course, none of these instructions can be found in the Gospels
(the record of Jesus' teaching), nor the book of Acts (the record of how
the early church functioned), nor the epistles (that provides many rules
and for New Covenant believers). So, the whole laborious process is
totally absent from the original expression of authentic Christianity,
as recorded in the Bible. Then why do people believe in it?

Two questions that need to be answered

As I ponder the complicated details of this process of dealing
with personal sins, obtaining indulgences, and diminishing time in
Purgatory, two primary questions immediately come to mind:

**Question #1—How can spiritual cleansing and Christlike char-
acter be purchased through religious rituals?**

If Purgatory is for the purpose of cleansing, and cleansing should
result in the development of Christlike character ("the holiness necessary to enter the joy of heaven"), how can someone purchase that by
obtaining indulgences through various religious activities?[150]

No one can acquire Christlike character by simply repeating a
prayer or visiting an ancient cemetery; so how can anyone purchase
cleansing or Christlike character for themselves or for others who
have already passed on? Christian virtues are not commodities that

can be bought and sold; they result from personal commitment to a God-pleasing lifestyle over a lengthy period and from God's grace.

Question #2—How can intercessors who try to obtain indulgences for the dead know when the process is finished?

If Catholics attempt to earn indulgences for their loved ones, how can they tell when those persons are finally released to go to heaven and no longer require intercession? Of course, there would be no way of knowing if only partial indulgences are secured. If it was a legitimate process, there is a strong possibility that a Catholic could intercede for a loved one, obtaining indulgences for them, many decades after the process had already been completed.

The reason "temporal punishment" is supposedly required

The phrase, "temporal punishment" means something lasting only temporarily. So, here is the logic behind this concept in Catholicism. When a person repents, God removes the sense of guilt and the eternal punishment. However, even though guilt is wiped away, and the eternal punishment is canceled, temporal penalties may remain.

A passage of scripture that illustrates this is 2 Samuel 12. When Nathan the prophet confronted David over his adulterous affair with Bathsheba, David, in sorrow and brokenness admitted, "I have sinned against the Lord." Then Nathan responded, "The LORD also has put away your sin; you shall not die. However, because by this deed you have given great occasion to the enemies of the LORD to blaspheme, the child also who is born to you shall surely die." (2 Samuel 12:13-14). A Catholic commentator explains, "God forgave David, but David still had to suffer the loss of his son as well as other temporal punishments (2 Sam. 12:7-12)."[151]

This is also true with respect to penalties exacted for unlawful behavior in the legal systems of this world. Even if God forgives a truly repentant criminal, he or she may still need to serve time in prison to pay for crimes committed. So, yes, there really are consequences for sin or evil behavior, at times, that are not removed by God's forgiveness. That is unquestionable. But those consequences are in this life, not the next, if we are claiming salvation through Jesus. However, as pointed out by a Catholic writer seeking to validate this belief:

"When we first come to God we are forgiven, and when we sin later we are able to be forgiven, yet that does not free us from the penalty of physical death. Even the forgiven die; a penalty remains after our sins are forgiven. This is a temporal penalty since physical death is temporary and we will be resurrected" (Daniel 12:2).[152]

So far, I agree with this line of logic. However, just because there are consequences of sin that we encounter in this world, that does not prove that those who are forgiven of their sins in this life will yet face a time of suffering in Purgatory. How could that be true? Moreover, how could the securing of an indulgence on the part of a person living in this world hasten the purification of someone in the netherworld—when, as I have already pointed out, no one can buy character. It must be developed. If we cannot buy it for ourselves, we certainly cannot buy it for others.

Does this scripture support a belief in Purgatory?

This process of securing indulgences for the dead is neither logical, nor biblical. However, some Catholic theologians interpret 2 Timothy 1:16–18 to be supportive of the practice of praying for the dead. Paul seemed to make a prayerful plea in his letter to Timothy:

> *The Lord grant mercy to the house of Onesiphorus; for*
> *he often refreshed me, and was not*
> *ashamed of my chain;*
> *but when he arrived in Rome, he sought me*
> *out very zealously, and found me.*
> *The Lord grant to him that he may find mercy from the*
> *Lord in that Day—and you know very well how many*
> *ways he ministered to me at Ephesus.*

It seems that Onesiphorus had passed, and that Paul was expressing hope that the kindness Onesiphorus had shown to him would result in added mercy being granted to him in the Day of the Lord's return, when works are tried by fire.

This does not demonstrate the need of interceding for the dead; it just reveals a prayerful desire Paul harbored in his heart—that what

Onesiphorus had sown, he would also reap in the form of an eternal reward (just as the Bible promises—See 2 Corinthians 9:6, Galatians 6:7-8).

It would be like someone praying, "Oh God, return to my mother eternally a blessing for all the ways she sacrificed for me in her life." It is not actually necessary to pray that prayer for it to happen; it simply expresses a sincere desire based on gratitude.

Changing the "Good News" into the "Not-So-Good-News"

The Gospel is supposed to be "Good News" (in fact, that's what the word means). But the introduction of the idea of Purgatory changes it to the "Not-So-Good News." Read the following Scripture promise carefully to rediscover and reclaim the "Good News" (a passage already highlighted under Question #8):

> *My little children, these things I write to you, so that*
> *you may not sin. And if anyone sins, we have an*
> *Advocate with the Father, Jesus Christ the righteous.*
> *And He Himself is the propitiation for our sins, and not*
> *for ours only but also for the whole world.*
> *(1 John 2:1-2)*

The word "propitiation" means satisfaction for the demands of justice. Either Jesus' death and resurrection were sufficient to satisfy the demands of justice, or they were not. Hebrews 10:10 asserts that we have been "sanctified" (cleansed from the defilement of sin) "through the offering of the body of Jesus Christ once for all."

May I repeat those last three words again—"once for all." That was a price paid once for all those who trust in that price and nothing else needs to be added.

Important conclusions about indulgences

Indulgences are in direct conflict with the Gospel. We could never buy our way into a state of righteousness with money, even if we donated millions of dollars to the church for candles and special Masses. We could never earn eternal life, even if we racked up ten thousand hours of memorized prayers. The existence of such a doctrine indicates a serious failure to see the efficacy and sufficiency of what Jesus did on the cross as our means of justification. Of course, for me to make such a claim is a serious matter. During the Council of Trent (that convened from 1545 A.D. to 1563 A.D.), a curse (*anathema*) was pronounced over anyone professing the point of view I have expressed in this chapter. The following quote references that pivotal meeting:

> "Indulgences are part of the Church's infallible teach-
> ing. This means that no Catholic is at liberty to disbelieve
> in them. The Council of Trent stated that it 'condemns
> with anathema those who say that indulgences are use-
> less or that the Church does not have the power to grant
> them' (Trent, session 25, Decree on Indulgences)."[153]

The selling of indulgences is a practice that was started during the Crusades. It helped to raise money for the church at a time when expenses were escalating because of war, and it was used to encourage believers to enlist in this conflict. In fact, "the first known use of plenary indulgences was in 1095 when Pope Urban II remitted all penance of persons who participated in the Crusades and who confessed their sins. Later, the indulgences were also offered to those who couldn't go on the Crusades but offered cash contributions to the effort instead."[154] It was also a method utilized to raise funds to build St. Peter's Basilica in Rome. Such non-biblical practices were never implemented by the early church leaders.

One of the more famous back stories from the history of this doctrine involves a Dominican monk named Johann Tetzel (1465—1519) who would ride into a German town, set up a stage, and begin to appeal to the people to buy indulgences that would set their loved ones free from Purgatory.

An often-quoted statement attributed to him is, "As soon as the coin in the coffer rings, the soul from Purgatory springs." This blatant hawking of purchasable deliverance from the underworld was the offense that motivated an already zealous and sincere monk named Martin Luther to nail his Ninety-Five Theses to the door of Castle Church in Wittenberg, Germany.

That one act was one of the primary things that helped to ignite the fire of Reformation burning across Europe. Remember, the Reformation came through a Catholic, not a non-Catholic—a Catholic who was threatened with excommunication and execution—yet he boldly declared at the Diet of Worms (a gathering of church leaders in 1521):

> "Unless I am convinced by Scripture and plain reason - I do not accept the authority of the popes and councils, for they have contradicted each other - my conscience is captive to the Word of God. I cannot and I will not recant anything for to go against conscience is neither right nor safe."[155]

I agree with Martin Luther's assessment in this matter (though I certainly do not agree with everything he taught or did). If mere offerings could catapult a soul out of Purgatory sooner than what was deemed necessary, Jesus went to the cross in vain. We could all just buy our own soul's salvation if we had enough money to do so. If a portion of our salvation is purchasable—with money or religious practices—then all of it is purchasable.

Entertaining the idea that the glorious gift of eternal life could somehow be earned by human effort is a grievous insult to the suffering Savior who paid such an agonizing price to provide that gift freely. (See Romans 6:23.) Some leaders in the Catholic Church expressed partial agreement with this assessment in the Catholic Counter-Reformation and veered away from the original practice. Here's a good example:

> "In 1567, following the Council of Trent, Pope Pius V issued a decree declaring that it is forbiden to attach the receipt of an indulgence to any financial act, including the giving of alms."[156]

However, I am still concerned. What's the difference between buying indulgences with money and buying indulgences with some action, like quoting a prayer or reading the Bible, except for the church not benefiting monetarily?

The latter may not look as reprehensible to non-Catholics, but it is still the same basic principle.

(For a lengthier explanation of the words "Anathema Maranatha," the curses of the Council of Trent, and the new mindset among Catholics concerning these things, see Appendix #6.)

My encouragement to you

I encourage those who have trusted in these related concepts of Purgatory and indulgences to reconsider what is truly biblical. Hopefully, you will reach the conclusion that many Catholic and non-Catholic believers have reached, summed up by the Latin word *sola* which means alone. The *five solas* are the five things that alone are sufficient to bring salvation and eternal life—and each one stands *alone* in its unique area of dependency:

The Five Solas
Sola Scriptura (only Scripture)
Sola Fide (only faith)
Sola Gracia (only grace)
Solus Christus (only Christ)
Soli Deo Gloria (only for the glory of God)

To better understand these statements, let's add to each one of these powerful declarations the explanation of the opposite, false religious dependency it cancels:

Sola Scriptura (only Scripture) — not a catechism that
often teaches unbiblical doctrines
Sola Fide (only faith) — not a required membership
in any church organization
Sola Gracia (only grace) — not religious works like
penance and indulgences
Solus Christus (only Christ) — not a mediatorial
priesthood
Soli Deo Gloria (only for the glory of God) — not the
glory of any religious authority or institution

Yes, allow me to sum it up this chapter with passion by worshipfully shouting—"*The Bible alone, faith alone, grace alone, and Christ alone, for the glory of God alone.*"

I pray that this truth penetrates your heart in a powerful way and sets you free. May the love of God expressed through the crucifixion and resurrection of Jesus, and the truth of His Word, impact your heart and life in an unprecedented way—so that you may declare, along with millions of other Jesus-loving people, I am "free indeed!" (John 8:36)

(To bring a proper balance to the understanding of these final "Sola" declarations, read Appendix #8, "The Three Legs of Catholicism.")

Question 23

Is the concept of Limbo in Limbo itself?

There are two unique beliefs in Catholicism concerning the afterlife. The one we just considered is Purgatory, but there is another location in the spiritual realm referred to as "Limbo." The word "Limbo" is from the Latin word *limbus* which means edge or border and refers to a mysterious realm at the border of hell.

Limbo, as a theological concept, probably originated in Europe during the Middle Ages. However, it was "never defined as a church dogma, and reference to it was omitted from the official catechism of the church that was issued in 1992."[157] This unique doctrine was apparently developed to explain the fate of unbaptized infants. It was reasoned that because they had not yet reached the age of reason and accountability, and "had not committed sin," they were not worthy of hell. However, because original sin had not been removed, they would be deprived "of the 'beatific vision' (being face to face with God)."[158]

So there needed to be some "intermediate" spiritual location in the afterlife to accommodate them. (Catholic doctrine states that at an official baptism, "original sin" is removed, the indwelling of the Holy Spirit takes place, and the baptized infant is born again, receiving the gift of eternal life.)

Even though Limbo has never officially been a part of the doctrinal base of Catholicism, it is a traditional belief which many Catholics embrace, though details are sketchy and indefinable. There are no detailed descriptions of the conditions of existence in Limbo available in Catholic literature. This concept is not accepted among Protestants.

The "Limbo of the patriarchs"

There is also a Catholic concept theologically called "the Limbo of the patriarchs" or "the Limbo of the fathers." That was the chamber in the lower parts of the earth that Jesus descended to after His crucifixion where the patriarchs and the righteous from the Old Covenant era were dwelling.

According to Jesus' parable of "The Rich Man and Lazarus" (already discussed under Question #11), during that Old Testament era, there were two areas in the underworld separated by a "great chasm": the realm of the wicked who were subjected to fiery torment and the realm of the righteous in a peaceful region called "Abraham's bosom." Of course, I imagine this temporary abode of the righteous could not compare with the spectacular beauty, joy, and presence of God found in the third heaven. (See Luke 16:19-31.)

After Jesus died, he went and "preached the Gospel to the dead" in the "lower parts of the earth" (1 Peter 3:18-22; 4:6, Ephesians 4:9). Though we are not told fully what transpired, apparently, those in the underworld were given an opportunity to receive Jesus as their Lord and Savior and obtain salvation according to the New Covenant standard. Although Protestants would not call this temporary abode of the righteous the "Limbo of the patriarchs," most agree that this liberation from the underworld took place, based on the scriptures mentioned above. So, the first "Limbo" I mentioned has no scriptural proof, while the second "Limbo" is mentioned in the Bible, though not identified by that term—and quite possibly, it may not exist anymore, because of what Jesus accomplished.

Is there any hope for those who have not heard the Gospel? The primary passage that shines light on this shadowy area of biblical theology is Romans 2:14-16:

> *For when Gentiles, who do not have the law, by nature*
> *do the things in the law, these, although not*
> *having the law, are a law to themselves,*
> *who show the work of the law written in their hearts,*

their conscience also bearing witness, and between
themselves their thoughts
accusing or else excusing them
in the day when God will judge the secrets of men by
Jesus Christ, according to my gospel.

When this epistle to the Romans was written, the compilation of the New Testament had not yet taken place. If it had, surely Paul would have included the Gospels in this statement as well. One thing for sure: there are millions of people who have never been exposed to "the Law" (the first five books of the Bible) or "the Gospels" (Matthew, Mark, Luke, and John). They have never had the opportunity to accept or reject the truth on that level. So God, being a just God, will only judge them on the amount of light they have received: the "illumination" of the conscience. Their response to the conscience will either "accuse" them or "excuse" them on the Day when God will preside in judgment over all who have ever lived.

I personally believe that even then, if they have yielded to the influence of their conscience during their earthly sojourn, it will still be necessary for them to receive Jesus as Lord and be born again in order to enter Paradise. Of course, much of this is assumption and speculation. We don't know for certain—but we do know, without a doubt, that if someone receives the Gospel, and invites Jesus to be Lord of his or her life, the gift of everlasting life is immediately granted.

So, what is the conclusion of the matter? This is an area where we have little information. We do not know exactly how God will deal with those who die without ever hearing the Gospel. Neither do we know exactly how God will deal with infants and children who die before maturing enough to understand the concepts of sin, and separation from God, and how Jesus can be their Savior. But we do know that God is just, fair, loving, merciful, compassionate, and good, so we can trust that He has all these things under control, and He will certainly be compassionate concerning the future destiny of the most vulnerable and spiritually deprived among us.

First Communion was a very important,
sacred, and memorable day for me
(second boy from the right).

Question 24

What is the true symbolism and power of Holy Communion?

At the Last Supper, Jesus gave specific directions concerning the memorial His followers should conduct after His death and resurrection. Catholics call it the Eucharist (from the Greek *eucharistia* meaning thanksgiving). It is also reverently referred to as Holy Communion and is one of the seven sacraments.

There are four biblical locations where instructions concerning this wonderful, God-inspired, and God-blessed celebration of salvation can be found: Matthew 26:26-28, Mark 14:22-25, Luke 22:14-20, and 1 Corinthians 11:23-30. A few subtle, yet important differences exist in these accounts, so all four should be reviewed.

Let's read them together—carefully, thankfully, prayerfully, and worshipfully—regardless of how we interpret them.

Matthew's account:

> *And as they were eating, Jesus took bread, blessed and broke it, and gave it to the disciples and said, "Take, eat; this is My body."*
> *Then He took the cup, and gave thanks, and gave it to them, saying, "Drink from it, all of you.*
> *For this is My blood of the new covenant, which is shed for many for the remission of sins."*
> *(Matthew 26:26-28)*

Mark's account:

> *And as they were eating, Jesus took bread, blessed and*
> *broke it, and gave it to them and said,*
> *"Take, eat; this is My body."*
> *Then He took the cup, and when He had given thanks*
> *He gave it to them, and they all drank from it.*
> *And He said to them, "This is My blood of the new*
> *covenant, which is shed for many.*
> *Assuredly, I say to you, I will no longer drink of the*
> *fruit of the vine until that day when*
> *I drink it new in the kingdom of God."*
> *(Mark 14:22-25)*

Luke's account:

> *When the hour had come, He sat down,*
> *and the twelve apostles with Him.*
> *Then He said to them, "With fervent desire I have*
> *desired to eat this Passover with you before I suffer;*
> *for I say to you, I will no longer eat of it until it is*
> *fulfilled in the kingdom of God."*
> *Then He took the cup, and gave thanks, and said,*
> *"Take this and divide it among yourselves;*
> *for I say to you, I will not drink of the fruit of the vine*
> *until the kingdom of God comes." And He took bread,*
> *gave thanks and broke it, and gave it to them, saying,*
> *"This is My body which is given for you;*
> *do this in remembrance of Me."*
> *Likewise He also took the cup after supper, saying,*
> *"This cup is the new covenant*
> *in My blood, which is shed for you."*
> *(Luke 22:14-20)*

Paul's account:

> *For I received from the Lord that which I also delivered*
> *to you: that the Lord Jesus on the same night*
> *in which He was betrayed took bread;*

and when He had given thanks, He broke it and said,
"Take, eat; this is My body which is broken for you; do
this in remembrance of Me."
In the same manner He also took the cup after supper,
saying, "This cup is the new covenant in My blood. This
do, as often as you drink it,
in remembrance of Me."
For as often as you eat this bread and drink this cup,
you proclaim the Lord's death till He comes.
Therefore whoever eats this bread or drinks this cup of
the Lord in an unworthy manner will be guilty
of the body and blood of the Lord.
But let a man examine himself, and so let him eat of the
bread and drink of the cup.
For he who eats and drinks in an unworthy manner
eats and drinks judgment to himself, not
discerning the Lord's body.
For this reason many are weak and sick
among you, and many sleep.
(1 Corinthians 11:23-30)

Now, let's shine the spotlight of truth on these four accounts of a very profound, pivotal and prophetic climax in the life and ministry of the Son of God. First—the most controversial issue:

Which is the right: transubstantiation, consubstantiation, or sacred representation?

The teaching of the Catholic Church is that the bread and wine literally become the body and blood of the Lord Jesus (a doctrine called "transubstantiation," meaning a change in substance). Though the appearance and attributes of the elements remain the same, the underlying reality is changed.

For that reason, after a Catholic Communion service, any re-maining hosts (circular, flat, unleavened pieces of wheat bread) are treated with the utmost reverence and care, because it is believed that they have been irreversibly, supernaturally altered. It is interesting, however, that a recent poll by Pew Research found "just one-third of

U.S. Catholics (31%) say they believe that 'during Catholic Mass, the bread and wine actually become the body and blood of Jesus.'"[159] I recognize that assessment may or may not be completely accurate, but it is worthy of consideration.

A doctrinal modification held by some non-Catholic, Christian denominations is consubstantiation. That is the idea that the body and blood of Jesus are physically present with the elements. The elements themselves do not change, and the body and blood of Jesus cannot be recognized by appearance or taste, however, in some real and tangible way, they are present.

Do either of these two views convey what these important passages of Scripture mean, or instead, could the Communion elements simply be a tangible and physical representation of an intangible, spiritual mystery? Could Holy Communion simply be a divinely-authored allegory that reveals a much higher spiritual purpose in God's people?

A major key to understanding the symbolism

Before passing it to His disciples, Jesus said, "This cup is the New Covenant in my blood." The original cup, often referred to as a chalice, was most likely a metallic or stone vessel, created to be filled with a drinkable liquid. That cup itself was not literally the New Covenant, even though Jesus insisted, "This cup *is* the New Covenant." Neither was the New Covenant invisibly present within that cup. Could it have been just a natural object used to illustrate a supernatural truth? Was it merely a physical symbol of a spiritual reality?

Paul called the cup used in the Communion ritual the "cup of blessing," first, because that was the traditional name given to the third cup of wine drunk by Jews during the Passover meal, and second, because believers drink in the blessings, benefits, and promises of the New Covenant only because of the blood that Jesus shed (1 Corinthians 10:16). We receive God's blessings, then we become a blessing to others, and we bless God with our praise—so, it truly is a "cup of blessing."

If the cup does not *literally* become the New Covenant, isn't it logical to assume that the wine does not *literally* become the blood of Jesus, and therefore, neither transubstantiation nor consubstantiation are correct interpretations?

The metaphorical way Jesus taught

Jesus often described Himself with metaphors, symbols, and parables. For instance, He made statements like "I am the light of the world," "I am the door," "I am the vine," "I am the root," and "I am the bright and morning star" (John 8:12; 10:9; 15:5, Revelation 22:16). He never intended for His followers to interpret those statements literally. In like manner, when He made these statements concerning the bread and the wine, is it possible that He did not intend them to be interpreted literally either?

A special "Presence"

Many Christians believe sincerely that even though the Communion elements do not literally change into the body and blood of Jesus and are primarily symbolic, there is evidently a special Divine Presence attached to the offering of the bread and the wine confirming to the hearts of worshipers the reality of what the elements represent. This holy Presence—this expression of grace—edifies participants spiritually and often imparts special blessings to them during the Communion ceremony, even healing and deliverance, but no altering of the physical properties of the bread and wine take place.

The tense of Jesus' statements is so revealing

The tense of Jesus' statements at the Last Supper is very revealing. As He broke the bread, He used the present tense in declaring, "This *is* My body which *is* broken for you" and then, when He passed the cup, He claimed, "This *is* the New Covenant in My blood." That wording only makes sense if the communion ceremony was intended to be symbolic, for Jesus had not yet been crucified.

What if transubstantiation is the correct view? If it is, when the disciples partook of the bread and the wine, they were partaking of crucified flesh that had not yet been crucified. They were drinking blood that had not yet been shed. How could these things be? How could Jesus offer them His literal flesh to eat and His literal blood to drink when He was seated right in front of them—very much alive? If Jesus had been training His disciples in the doctrine of transubstantiation, He would have been very careful to put His words in the future tense. As He broke the bread, He would have foretold, "After I am resurrected, this *will literally become* My body which is going to be broken for you, and this *will literally become* My blood which is going to be shed for you." Only then would it have made sense for His disciples to interpret the meaning of the ritual that way.[160]

Communion can be celebrated at any time

When Paul shared the tradition of Communion with the Corinthian church, he quoted Jesus saying, "'This cup is the new covenant in My blood. This do, as often as you drink it, in remembrance of Me.' For as often as you eat this bread and drink this cup, you proclaim the Lord's death till He comes." The phrase "as often" implies the idea that believers can celebrate Communion anytime, anywhere, by themselves, or in group gatherings like home prayer meetings. It does not require that a Mass be conducted, or that a priest officiate the ceremony.

Official Catholic doctrine states that "this sacrament no one can effect except the priest who has been duly ordained in accordance with the keys of the Church, which Jesus Christ Himself gave to the Apostles and their successors."[161] Quite the contrary, an officiating priest is not a requirement; all truly devoted believers can even incorporate Communion into their own personal devotions. Such an idea may sound sacrilegious to some and novel to others. However, this is not merely a revolutionary concept; it is truly revelational, and wonderfully liberating.

What Jesus did *not* say

What Jesus said at the Last Supper concerning Communion is very important, yet what He did *not* say is just as significant. Even though this ritual was introduced to just the twelve apostles, the Savior never said that only they or a future mediatorial priesthood could administer the Communion ritual.

It was not until the First Council of Nicaea, beginning 325 A.D., that the rule was established (in Canon 18) that only bishops and presbyters (the priestly clergy) could conduct this ceremony.

Jesus also did not indicate that Communion would normally be celebrated in congregational gatherings held in cathedrals or churches.

Those things are humanly-authored, religious traditions superimposed on Jesus' original instructions.

Finally, Jesus did *not* say, "Do this to reproduce my death." He said, "Do this in remembrance of Me" (Luke 22:19). There is a huge difference between reproducing His death and memorializing His death. Paul did not say, "You reproduce the Lord's death," he said, "You proclaim the Lord's death till He comes" (1 Corinthians 11:26). The communion ritual was never intended to be a continuation of the crucifixion of the Messiah, but a marvelous and praise-filled celebration of the final price He paid to set us free.

In Catholicism, Communion is usually conducted at a gathering Catholics attend called "Mass." One explanation of that term, written by a Catholic, is as follows:

> "The English word 'Mass' comes from the Latin word *missa*, which means to be 'sent.' This Latin word has been used since the 6th or 7th century to describe the Catholic celebration of the Eucharist, our main liturgical service. The word is used during the conclusion of the celebration, when the priest or deacon says in Latin, *Ite, missa est*. The literal translation of that phrase is, 'Go, it has been sent.' Saint Thomas Aquinas wrote a commentary on these words and explained in his Summa Theologiae, 'And from this the Mass derives its name ... the deacon on festival days "dismisses" the people at the end of the Mass, by saying: "*Ite, missa est*," that is, the victim [Jesus] has been sent to God through the angel, so that it may be accepted by God.'"[162]

The "victim [Jesus] has been sent to God"? Could that possibly be true? Is there a continuation over and over, every time a Mass is celebrated, of the crucifixion and death of the Son of God? Why would that even be necessary since the "Spirit of holiness" resurrected Jesus from the grave to a renewed status of righteousness? (Romans 1:4) After that victory, why would an ongoing sacrifice be needed? Or was redemption accomplished "once for all"? The wording of the following passage (already quoted in Question #22) declares the latter to be the case:

For such a High Priest was fitting for us, who is holy,
harmless, undefiled, separate from sinners,
and has become higher than the heavens;
who does not need daily, as those high priests, to offer
up sacrifices, first for His own sins and then for the
*people's, for this He did **once for all***
when He offered up Himself.
(Hebrews 7:26-27)

The message after multiplication

There are other important and related passages that bring a more complete understanding of this hallowed concept of Communion, such as the teaching Jesus gave after He multiplied five loaves and two fishes to feed a large multitude that followed Him into a wilderness area.

Can you imagine what an incredibly powerful experience that was, to actually witness the bread and fish multiplying as the food was distributed? The Bible states there "were about five thousand men, besides women and children" (Matthew 14:21). So, the total number could have been 20,000 or more. Amazing! After miraculously supplying their meal, Jesus shared a profound message that prophetically foreshadowed the Communion ritual and its spiritual application in the New Covenant era to come. The insights He offered were so deep that "from that time many of His disciples went back and walked with Him no more" (John 6:66).

Many of those who heard these words were completely baffled. Therefore, it is not unthinkable that we still need the help of the Holy Spirit to draw out the revelation Jesus intended. Thankfully, John recorded the deep statements He used to unveil this divine mystery:

"I am the bread of life.
Your fathers ate the manna in the
wilderness, and are dead.
This is the bread which comes down from heaven,
that one may eat of it and not die.
I am the living bread which came down from heaven.
If anyone eats of this bread, he will live forever; and the

> *bread that I shall give is My flesh, which I*
> *shall give for the life of the world."*
> *The Jews therefore quarreled among themselves, saying,*
> *"How can this Man give us His flesh to eat?"*
> *Then Jesus said to them, "Most assuredly, I say to you,*
> *unless you eat the flesh of the Son of Man*
> *and drink His blood, you have no life in you.*
> *Whoever eats My flesh and drinks My blood has eternal*
> *life, and I will raise him up at the last day.*
> *For My flesh is food indeed, and*
> *My blood is drink indeed.*
> *He who eats My flesh and drinks My blood*
> *abides in Me, and I in him.*
> *As the living Father sent Me, and I live because of the*
> *Father, so he who feeds on Me will live because of Me.*
> *This is the bread which came down from heaven—not*
> *as your fathers ate the manna, and are dead.*
> *He who eats this bread will live forever."*
> *(John 6:48-58)*

Indisputably, in this passage Jesus used highly symbolic language. So, what did He really mean on the deepest level of revelation?

Jesus' flesh was the Word of God manifested

Jeremiah, the prophet, spoke of eating the Word of God when he worshipfully declared to the God of Israel:

> *"Your words were found, and I ate them, and Your*
> *word was to me the joy and rejoicing of my heart; for I*
> *am called by Your name, O LORD God of hosts."*
> *(Jeremiah 15:16)*

Various scriptures describe the Word of God as edible meal items like milk, honey, bread, and solid food (1 Peter 2:2, Psalms 119:103, Deuteronomy 8:3, Hebrews 5:12-14). Of course, none of these references are to be taken literally. Once again, they are poetical and metaphorical comparisons. They communicate in symbolic terms the encouragement that we should consume God's Word, digesting it into our inner being until it spiritually becomes a part of us.

Could it be that the idea of "eating Jesus' flesh" is also symbolic of the same thing? A logical sequence of thoughts leads to that conclusion. The first verse of the first chapter of the Gospel of John describes Jesus' original state, prior to the incarnation, in the following way:

In the beginning was the Word, and the Word
was with God, and the Word was God.
(John 1:1)

Then, verse fourteen of the same chapter describes an astounding and mysterious metamorphosis:

And the Word became flesh and dwelt among us, and
we beheld His glory, the glory as of the only begotten of
the Father, full of grace and truth.
(John 1:14)

So, Jesus was the Word made flesh. He was the entirety of the Word of God, from Genesis to Revelation, manifested in a human body. He was the total of all the written words of God ever recorded, as well as the total of all the living words of God that ever have been or ever will be spoken.

In figurative language, therefore, "eating His flesh" means eating the Word of God and digesting it spiritually into our inner being until we become utterly one with the Word. When we do, its stories, teachings, commandments, promises, and prophecies shape our character, determine our behavior, and guide our destiny. Remember the old saying, "You are what you eat." That's true both physically and spiritually.

If we "eat" the Word of God, we become expressions of the Word of God in this world, living examples of a Word-infused life. We each become "an epistle of Christ" (a love letter from God to those we contact) (See 2 Corinthians 3:1-3.) No wonder Jesus said, "Man shall not live by bread alone, but by every word that proceeds out of the mouth of God" (Matthew 4:4 MKJV).

Jesus' blood is infused with the Holy Spirit

Jesus gave the invitation, "If anyone thirsts, let him come to Me and drink" (John 7:37). What a blessed opportunity! The Messiah also claimed, "My blood is drink indeed!" (John 6:55) When these lofty, mystical statements are blended, understanding comes. To grasp this concept, however, we must first visit an Old Testament passage describing the blood of sacrificial animals offered during that era:

> *For the life of the flesh is in the blood, and I have given*
> *it to you upon the altar to make atonement for your*
> *souls; for it is the blood that makes*
> *atonement for the soul.*
> *(Leviticus 17:11)*

Pay attention to the beginning phrase, "the life of the flesh is in the blood." If the life of an animal is in the blood of an animal, then the life of a human being is in the blood of a human being. It logically follows that the life of God is also in the blood of God, and if God ever had blood, He had it in the veins of His only begotten Son.

This is verified by a declaration Paul made to the elders of the Ephesian church, revealing that true believers are "the church of *God* which *He* purchased with *His own blood*" (Acts 20:28, emphasis by author). Jesus' blood was not ordinary human blood; it was holy, untainted with sin, and full of divine life. The Holy Spirit is called "the Spirit of life" (Romans 8:2). If the "life is in the blood," then drinking Jesus' blood is symbolic of imbibing the life-giving Spirit of God.

Symbolically, we eat His flesh and drink His blood in the Communion ritual and that is a very holy privilege. However, it represents a much higher and much holier reality—the greater privilege of eating God's Word and drinking in God's Spirit, and by these, becoming one with the Everlasting Father.

Changed into the divine image

By these two things—the Word of God and the Spirit of God—we are daily being transformed as we partake of the divine nature. The Word of God reveals the personality of God. The Spirit of God expresses the personality of God. So, eating His Word and drinking in His Spirit result in absorbing God's personality, ingesting His character, and being changed into His image.

For instance, the Word of God reveals that His character overflows with love, joy, peace and righteousness. When we sincerely accept Him into our hearts and lives (just like we digest the bread and wine in our stomachs), we begin a process of becoming like Him: loving, joyful, peaceful, and righteous sons and daughters of God. The following two verses of Scripture powerfully illustrate this awe-inspiring truth in a wonderful blend:

We are transformed by the Word of God:

> By which have been given to us exceedingly great
> and precious promises, that through these you may
> be partakers of the divine nature, having escaped the
> corruption that is in the world through lust.
> (2 Peter 1:4)

We are transformed by the Spirit of God:

> But we all, with unveiled face, beholding as in a mirror
> the glory of the Lord, are being transformed
> into the same image from glory to glory,
> just as by the Spirit of the Lord.
> (2 Corinthians 3:18)

By the promises of God's Word, we partake of God's nature. As we gaze into the mirror of His Word, we see a reflection of the glorious Lord Himself and are changed into the same image by God's Spirit. (See James 1:23-25.) So, by the Word of life and by the Spirit of life, we become one with the Lord of life.

This is true communion on the highest level, portrayed by the sacredness of the Communion ritual. However, the thing symbolized is always more important and more profound than the symbol itself. The substance is always far more important than the shadow.

In the Old Testament, circumcision was important, but what it represented (having a circumcised heart, the cutting away of the lower nature) was far more important and essential. In the New Testament, water baptism is important, but what it represents (being immersed in death to self so that Jesus might live in and through us) is far more important and essential.

In a parallel way, Holy Communion is very important and very sacred, but what it represents is far more important, far more sacred, and far more essential—living a Word-infused, Spirit-infused life that is in tune with the purposes of God. It is very beneficial to celebrate Holy Communion often; it is far more beneficial to experience what Communion symbolizes, every moment of every day.

The power and beauty of true communion

As I related in the Introduction, the turning point of my life was the day I was truly born again. That's when I entered a personal relationship with the Lord Jesus Christ. More scriptures pertaining to this vitally important experience, and a deeper explanation, are shared in the Addendum. Titus 3:5 also calls this transformational encounter "the washing of regeneration."

There are two primary aspects to this regenerative experience: being begotten of the Word and being born of the Spirit.

- **Begotten of the Word**—When we first come to faith in Jesus, we are "begotten . . . by the Word of truth." (James 1:18 DRA). The word of God like seed is planted in our hearts and begets faith in us to receive the God of truth into our lives.

- **Born of the Spirit**—After we respond to the Word of God and repent, we can then invite God to come and dwell within our hearts and lives; if done sincerely, that is when we are "born of the Spirit" (John 3:5).

Through these two spiritual influences, we celebrate "Communion" daily on the highest level: communion with God and communion with fellow believers. The Greek word for communion is *koinonia*. The following scripture highlights this beloved, biblical term:

> *The cup of blessing which we bless, is it not the*
> *communion [Greek koinonia] of the blood of Christ?*
> *The bread which we break, is it not the communion*
> *[Greek koinonia] of the body of Christ?*
> *For we, though many, are one bread and one body;*
> *for we all partake of that one bread.*
> *(1 Corinthians 10:16-17)*

Oneness of heart: a New Covenant blessing

The word "communion" comes from the English word common. It means to share things in common, to be united in heart and mind. Communion is also related to the words commune, communication, and union.

In the Old Testament, God foretold the beauty of what we would experience in the New Covenant when He gave the following two promises:

> "*Then I will give them one heart* and one way, that
> they may fear Me forever, for the good of them and
> their children after them.
> And I will make an everlasting covenant with them,
> that I will not turn away from doing them good; but I
> will put My fear in their hearts so that
> they will not depart from Me."
> (Jeremiah 32:39-40)

> "*Then I will give them one heart,* and I will put a new
> spirit within them, and take the stony heart out of their
> flesh, and give them a heart of flesh,
> that they may walk in My statutes and keep
> My judgments and do them; and they shall be
> My people, and I will be their God."
> (Ezekiel 11:19-20)

This phrase "one heart" is only found three times in the entire Bible: the two prophecies just mentioned that were given by Jeremiah and Ezekiel, and the Scripture that indicates when these prophecies were fulfilled, in the grand spiritual awakening that followed the birth of the church in the book of Acts:

> Now the multitude of those who believed were of **one
> heart** and one soul; neither did anyone say that
> any of the things he possessed was his own,
> but they had all things in common.
> (Acts 4:32)

This oneness of heart can also be identified as "the communion of the saints": one of the most beautiful aspects of being in the body of Christ, something that is trans-denominational. As I shared under Question #1, the true body of Christ is not signified by an organization; it is a living organism. It is united, not by a church roll, but by a common experience of heart.

The mystery of *koinonia*

The Greek word *koinonia* is translated a number of ways, including the words communion and fellowship. Both these English words can mean: *to be joined together as one.* Consider the following examples:

> *That which was from the beginning, which we have*
> *heard, which we have seen with our eyes, which we*
> *have looked upon, and our hands have handled,*
> *concerning the Word of life—*
> *the life was manifested, and we have seen, and bear*
> *witness, and declare to you that eternal life which was*
> *with the Father and was manifested to us—*
> *That which we have seen and heard we declare to you,*
> *that you also may have* **fellowship** [Greek *koinonia*]
> *with us; and truly our* **fellowship** [Greek *koinonia*]
> *is with the Father and with His Son Jesus Christ.*
> *(1 John 1:1-3)*

> *But if we walk in the light as He is in the light, we have*
> **fellowship** [Greek *koinonia*] *with one another, and the*
> *blood of Jesus Christ His Son*
> *cleanses us from all sin.*
> *(1 John 1:7)*

> *God is faithful, by whom you were called into the*
> **fellowship** [Greek *koinonia*] *of His Son,*
> *Jesus Christ our Lord.*
> *(1 Corinthians 1:9)*

Finally, a prayer that I pray for all those who are seeking truth concerning all these important issues covered in this book:

The grace of the Lord Jesus Christ, and the love of
God, and the **communion** *[Greek koinonia] of the Holy*
Spirit be with you all. Amen.
(2 Corinthians 13:14)

So true spiritual "communion" [*koinonia*] is fellowship with the Father, the Son, the Holy Spirit, and with each other. It is both vertical and horizontal (which together forms a cross). This is the beauty of the New Covenant and the answer to Jesus' intercessory prayer that He prayed right before He was taken into custody and crucified:

"Father . . . I have manifested Your name to the men
whom You have given Me out of the world . . .
For I have given to them the words which You have
given Me; and they have received them, and have
known surely that I came forth from You; and they
have believed that You sent Me.
I pray for them. I do not pray for the world but for those
whom You have given Me, for they are Yours . . .
I do not pray for these alone, but also for those who will
believe in Me through their word;
that they all may be one, as You, Father, are in Me, and
I in You; that they also may be one in Us, that
the world may believe that You sent Me.
And the glory which You gave Me I have given them,
that they may be one just as We are one: I in them,
and You in Me; that they may be made perfect in one,
and that the world may know that You have sent Me,
and have loved them as You have loved Me."
(John 17:1-23 excerpts)

So again, this is the "unspeakable gift": oneness with the Father, with the Son, with the Holy Spirit, and with each other (2 Corinthians 9:15 KJV). Imparting this oneness to His people is the very reason Jesus went to the cross.

Experiencing this level of spirituality, this "Holy Communion," transcends denominationalism and many of our doctrinal differences. It far supersedes even the blessed ritual that mysteriously symbolizes how it is acquired. It is a rare treasure indeed to those who find it in this world. It truly is a taste of heaven on earth.

Finally, in closing, we should consider that it was no accident or chance happening that Jesus introduced the communion ritual during the Jewish celebration of Passover. There are many beautiful, symbolic connections between the two that you should explore. Just as Passover celebrated and memorialized the exodus of the Jewish people from bondage in Egypt on their journey to the Promised Land, this new "Passover Feast" has become a memorial of an even greater exodus out of the bondage of sin into the "Promised Land" of a life filled with God's blessing and God's purposes.

Catholicism teaches that the elements of Communion (the con-secrated bread and wine) actually contain the "soul and divinity" of the Lord Jesus Christ, that the bread is not dead flesh, and the wine is not spilled, lifeless blood (CCC 1374). However, I am convinced that it is actually God's people, the true Church, born-again believers—those who abide in true *koinonia* communion with the Lord—who contain the "soul and divinity" of Jesus—not in our mouths, or in our stomachs, but deep within our regenerated hearts.

Praise God for opening our eyes to these awe-inspiring truths!

Question 25

Does Extreme Unction truly prepare a person for eternity?

Extreme Unction is the fifth of seven sacraments. *(For the full list, see Appendix #5.)* Those two words mean "final anointing," so named because it is only administered to those persons who are seriously ill or close to death, usually from old age. It is also commonly referred to as "The Last Rites." It is only performed for those who are genuine in their desire for God; the Catechism declares that it should be withheld from those who persist obstinately in grave sin.

In the early 1970s, the name "Extreme Unction" was changed to "The Anointing of the Sick." According to the Catholic Catechism, "the special grace of the sacrament of the Anointing of the Sick has the following effects:

- The uniting of the sick person to the passion of Christ, for his own good and that of the whole Church,
- The strengthening, peace, and courage to endure in a Christian manner the sufferings of illness or old age,
- The forgiveness of sins, if the sick person was not able to obtain it through the sacrament of penance,
- The restoration of health, if it is conducive to the salvation of his soul,
- The preparation for passing over to eternal life." (CCC 1532)

The biblical words "unction" and "anointing" are synonymous. In older translations of the New Testament (like the KJV and DRA), the

280 ~ The Beliefs of the Catholic Church

same Greek word *chrisma* is translated both ways. (See 1 John 2:20, 27.) Both words also have a double-meaning:

1. **Natural and symbolic**—The word "anointing" or "unction" describes the application of oil, either by pouring or smearing, symbolizing a special prayerful act of consecration to God or the hope of receiving a special blessing from God.

2. **Supernatural and actual**—The word "anointing" or "unction" also describes the specific supernatural application of the power of the Holy Spirit to a person's life, a divine empowerment to accomplish a God-given purpose.

When a dedicated believer anoints a needy person with oil, it is a prayerful, symbolic act performed in the expectation that God will supernaturally respond and pour out the "oil" of the Holy Spirit to perform what is being requested. Interestingly, the Holy Spirit Himself is biblically referred to as the "oil of joy" and the "oil of gladness" (Isaiah 61:3, Psalms 45:7).

Anointing with oil does not cause this spiritual unction—this "oil of joy"—to be manifested; it is an expression of faith, a symbol of expectation that this grace *will be* manifested. It is a prophetic way of acting out a prayer. Here's a good example of that very thing from the epistle writer James:

> *Is anyone among you sick? Let him call for the elders*
> *of the church, and let them pray over him, anointing*
> *[Greek chrisma] him with oil in the name of the Lord.*
> *And the prayer of faith will save the sick,*
> *and the Lord will raise him up. And if he has*
> *committed sins, he will be forgiven.*
> *Confess your trespasses to one another, and pray for one*
> *another, that you may be healed. The effective, fervent*
> *prayer of a righteous man avails much.*
> *(James 5:14-16)*

As mentioned under Question #7, the word "elders" in this passage is translated from the Greek word *presbuteros*. For that reason, the New Catholic Bible uses the word "presbyters" for the word "elders," which, in Catholicism, is a status given only to recognized church authorities. The Catholic Catechism clearly states, "Only priests (bishops and presbyters) are ministers of the Anointing of the Sick" (CCC 1516).

"Elders" was probably a term referring to any recognized and respected ministerial leaders of the church in that day. However, laying on of hands is not confined to them in Scripture, for Jesus declared right before ascending to heaven, "These signs will follow those who believe . . . they will lay hands on the sick and they shall recover" (Mark 16:17-18). Therefore, genuine faith seems to be the main prerequisite.

Another passage used by Catholics to validate this practice of anointing the sick is found in the Gospel of Mark, chapter six. Jesus sent forth the twelve disciples to preach the kingdom of God and to go, two-by-two, to various cities in Israel:

> *So they went out and preached that*
> *people should repent.*
> *And they cast out many demons, and anointed with oil*
> *many who were sick, and healed them.*
> *(Mark 6:12-13)*

Of course, among the early disciples, the expectation when anointing with oil was for the anointing of the Holy Spirit to miraculously heal the sick. Although officiating priests pray for recovery of the health of the sick person if that would be conducive to his salvation, that is normally not the expectation at all.

The sacrament is only administered when death seems imminent. So, the primary reason for performing the sacrament is the hope that the person participating will be suitably prepared for a transition to the afterlife. According to the online Catholic Encyclopedia, the Council of Trent taught:

> "This sacred unction of the sick was instituted by Christ Our Lord as a sacrament of the New Testament . . . and the corresponding canon . . . anathematizes [pronounces a curse] on anyone who would say that extreme unction is not truly and properly a sacrament instituted by Christ Our Lord." (*See Appendix #6.*)[162]

However, Jesus never gave explicit instructions to His disciples to perform this ceremony on those who are dying.

What happens during the ceremony

The following is a basic description of what takes place during Extreme Unction according to directives given to the Western Church (Roman Catholicism):

> "The sacrament consists (apart from certain non-essential prayers) in the unction with oil, specially blessed by the bishop, of the organs of the five external senses (eyes, ears, nostrils, lips, hands), of the feet, and, for men (where the custom exists and the condition of the patient permits of his being moved), of the loins or reins; and in the following form repeated at each unction with mention of the corresponding sense or faculty: 'Through this holy unction and His own most tender mercy may the Lord pardon thee whatever sins or faults thou hast committed [*quidquid deliquisti*] by sight [by hearing, smell, taste, touch, walking, carnal delectation].'"[163]

There are some significant variations in different rites (or divisions) of the Catholic Church. For instance, in the ancient Aquileian Rite, twelve anointings were administered to those receiving the sacrament: the head, forehead, eyes, ears, nose, lips, throat, chest, heart, shoulders, hands, and feet. The Catechism also strongly recommends:

> "If circumstances suggest it, the celebration of the sacrament [Extreme Unction] can be preceded by the sacrament of Penance and followed by the sacrament of the Eucharist. As the sacrament of Christ's Passover the Eucharist should always be the last sacrament of the earthly journey, the 'viaticum' for 'passing over' to eternal life." (CCC 1517)

If those who receive this sacrament recover, they can receive it again later on, if that is deemed necessary.

Is Extreme Unction effective?

Protestant reformers rejected this sacrament for a variety of reasons. They insisted that even though it was loosely based on Scriptures, it was not truly instituted by Jesus, and the scriptures used for validation promise healing, not the sharing of physical sufferings with the crucified Savior. Also, because of abuses of the rite, in the twelfth and thirteenth centuries, it was a sacrament only accessible to the rich, which of course, is no longer the case.

But that was then, and this is now. In this twenty-first century, does Extreme Unction effectively prepare a dying person to transition from time to eternity? Only God knows a person's heart and the hearts of any attending priests. So blanket statements cannot be made. This sacramental ritual could cause a person's heart to be inclined upward toward heavenly things in the hope of claiming forgiveness and connecting with the Lord Jesus Christ. So, it could result in a genuine salvation encounter or a renewal of the same. However, some very important factors are omitted.

Catholicism teaches that Catholics are born again during baptism, which usually happens in their infancy. Under Question #3 and in the Addendum, I cover this fundamental issue at length. Unfortunately, many who have been raised Catholic were told they were spiritually regenerated when they were baptized, yet that is not the case. So quite often, they grow up to be unregenerated adults who have never experienced spiritual rebirth and a personal relationship with Jesus. Someone on the threshold of eternity, desperately needs to be led into this encounter by someone who has received it himself, for Jesus was emphatic in declaring:

> *"Most assuredly, I say to you, unless one is born of*
> *water and the Spirit, he cannot enter the*
> *kingdom of God."*
> *(John 3:5)*

He also revealed in no uncertain terms:

> *"This is eternal life, that they may know You, the only*
> *true God, and Jesus Christ whom You have sent."*
> *(John 17:3)*

So, the most vitally important questions that should be asked of a person on the verge of death are: "Do you know Jesus?" – "Have you received Him into your heart as your Lord and Savior?" – "Have you gone to God directly and repented before Him for all the sins you have committed in your life and received His forgiveness?" - "Have you been filled with the Holy Spirit?" – "Do you believe with all your heart in the power of Jesus' crucifixion and resurrection?" When it comes to those final few weeks, days, or hours in this world, real faith is the most important possession a person can have, because Jesus gave the easy-to-grasp promises:

"Most assuredly, I say to you, he who believes
in Me has everlasting life."
(John 6:47)

"I am the resurrection and the life. He who believes in
Me, though he may die, he shall live."
(John 11:25)

All the rituals and ceremonies that men have devised are completely inefficient when compared to the power of believing the Gospel (the good news of what Jesus promised to do in the lives of His followers). Certainly, the prayerful anointing of body parts has value, but it is not scripturally necessary. Also, a natural ritual cannot effect a spiritual reality, and the latter is far more important.

Deathbed confessions and deep repentance have great value. However, if the person goes directly to God Himself instead of entrusting the state of his or her soul to a priest, it would be far better. Also, uttering prayers to Mary or appealing to the saints at such a critical time is totally counterproductive and should definitely be omitted. Jesus needs to be the focus, not a recitation of the rosary. Just heartfelt prayers in line with the Word of God should be prayed.

Offering communion to a dying person is important, but truly partaking of what communion symbolizes is far more important: digesting God's Word and drinking in His Spirit into our inner being and being transformed internally. Believing that the wafer is actually the body of Christ would be an unhelpful misconception at a moment when extreme clarity is needed.

So, I am compelled to answer, "No, Extreme Unction is not the optimum way of assisting someone to navigate the transition from time to eternity, from this life to the afterlife. The room could be filled with religious deception, instead of the truth of God's Word—and if there is ever a time when people need an atmosphere of truth, it is the moment of their departure from this world."

Conclusion

What really matters

W ell, I have shared my heart with you on some very important biblical matters—not for the purpose of just asserting
my own belief system, but in the far greater hope that your
walk with God and your journey through life will be greatly blessed
as a result. If you are presently Catholic—especially if you are a priest,
monk, nun, or other church leader—and if you resonate with what
I have written (or at least, a portion of it), please let me know. Let's
communicate. Let's connect. Send me an email or a message on our
website: www.toCatholicswithlove.org.

Because I have departed from many of the Catholic beliefs I once
embraced, some may label me a "Protestant" now. However, I don't
really care for that title. It describes a person who primarily "protests"
religious beliefs and practices considered to be wrong. I would prefer
to be described as a "believer" and a "promoter"—one who "believes"
and "promotes" the truth of God's Word.

Since I encountered the Lord Jesus, I have never joined any denomination. When someone asks what church group I belong to, my
response is usually, "I prefer to simply call myself a follower of Jesus."
Really, that's the main thing we should all aspire to be—and what a
high calling it is!

Moreover, instead of the twenty-five major points emphasized
in this book being nailed to some church door, after the manner of

Martin Luther, I pray they will instead *become* a door—a gateway to spiritual growth and advancement through which many Catholics and non-Catholics will pass, to behold the glory of what the God of the Bible offers to all who sincerely seek Him.

Five things I really respect about Catholics is their desire:

1. To be pleasing to God,

2. To have religious structure in their lives,

3. To respect that which is holy,

4. To be holy,

5. And to believe God to move in supernatural ways.

While some Protestant denominations draw back from the supernatural, Catholics tend to rush forward with strong faith for the miraculous, for visitations from heaven, for manifestations of the Holy Spirit. That must be why there was such a surge of multiplied thousands of Catholics participating in the Charismatic Renewal that started in the latter 60s and continued through the 80s (I spoke in many Catholic Charismatic meetings back then). And it's still going on. That movement highlighted a renewed faith in the supernatural manifestations that were so prevalent in the early church (healing, miracles, prophecy, spiritual rebirth, the gifts of the Holy Spirit, spiritual dreams, and encounters with the Lord, like those chronicled in the book of Acts and 1 Corinthians 12:6-11).

I hope and pray that you are open-hearted in a similar way—ready to passionately pursue a deeper relationship with God. The upper room was the starting point for the church of the New Testament "Age of Grace," and it was immersed with the supernatural reality of the presence of God. God hasn't changed, so His people should still be having spiritual encounters of the heavenly kind.

In the next section, I'm going to share a few stories of some of my loved ones who were Catholic until my radical conversion experience. Then the Lord used me to reach out to them. Almost this entire book has been theology. Now, I intend to share real life stories—the supernatural reality of what God can do when people choose to sincerely believe the Word of God.

Epilogue

Real life stories

W hat a blessing it is to share in this epilogue amazing things God did in the very beginning of my walk with Him—for me personally and for my loved ones! These few accounts easily prove that Jesus Christ is "the same yesterday, today, and forever" (Hebrews 13:8). The miraculous way He moved in the early church is still being evidenced among His people now. During His earthly ministry, Jesus gave the wonderful promise:

> *"He who has My commandments and keeps them, it is*
> *he who loves Me. And he who loves Me will be loved by*
> *My Father, and I will love him and*
> *manifest Myself to him."*
> *(John 14:21)*

So, the Savior promises to reveal Himself to a special group of people—those who truly love Him. Relationship is primary. Membership in an organization is secondary and not even necessary. Sometimes He manifests Himself in natural ways; at other times, in supernatural ways. Sometimes what He does is simple and subtle; at other times, it is blatantly heaven-sent and powerful.

May these real-life stories build your faith to receive miraculous manifestations in your own life also, and the lives of those you love. God has promised to respond to those who seek His face.

Why I did not join the monastery

On the back cover of this book, I mention an important turning point in my spiritual journey. I was on my way to the monastery when "a miraculous, divine intervention." dramatically altered my spiritual path. You may be wondering what happened to deter me. Well, here's the back story.

About three months after I was born again, I was living in an inter-denominational Christian commune in Central Florida, working on a construction crew every day, then participating in Bible studies and prayer meetings every night, seven nights a week. Life was peaceful, purposeful, and predictable, but I had a longing to go deeper. My desire was to draw even closer to God, serving Him with every waking moment. Because of my upbringing as a Catholic, I assumed the best way to do that would be to live a cloistered life. So, I made plans to join the Monastery of the Holy Spirit in Conyers, Georgia. I had heard that the monks who resided there believed in the gifts and power of the Holy Spirit, so I thought it would be a good fit for me. At the time, I had very little understanding concerning the differences between Catholic doctrines and the pure biblical perspective, so I saw no conflict.

I quit my job. Then, since I would have no need of money or possessions at the monastery, I gave away everything I owned to the poor, and set out hitchhiking. Little did I know the danger that would soon be stalking me. About the third person who picked me up was a man who claimed to be a construction worker. He explained that he had to first pick up his check at the trailer on the construction site where he worked, then we would head out. With a believable grin, he assured me, "You won't have to catch another ride. I am going all the way to Atlanta anyway, so I will take you the rest of the way to Conyers." Unfortunately, it was all a ruse, a dangerous deception.

After spending about ten minutes in the company trailer, he came out and explained, "While they are processing my check, let me show you the area and describe what we will be building." It was quite a large construction site with big fields and wooded areas, so there was plenty of acreage to cover. As we were driving around, with no warning, suddenly this stranger took off across a big field much faster than he had been driving up to that point. I was getting very uneasy, very suspicious. Then, near a grove of trees, he slammed on the brakes and pulled out a large, long-bladed knife. As he laid it to my neck, he informed me in no uncertain terms of his intentions—robbing me, raping me, then killing me. Within a few tension-filled seconds, I quickly decided how to deal with the situation.

The first word to flash through my mind was, "Run!" But I immediately dismissed that idea, realizing he could easily run me down with his car. The next word that exploded in my spirit was "Preach!" I had never preached a sermon before, but I knew lots of basic information, so I went for it. I pointed my finger at the man's face, and with loudness and intensity, I declared statements like the following:

> "You need to get right with God! One day you're going to stand before God on the Day of Judgment and give an account for every deed done in your body. Apparently, you are going to be cut off from Him forever and condemned to hell, because you've chosen a life of evil and rebellion. You're possessed with evil spirits, but God can deliver you. You must repent of your sin and plead with Jesus to wash your heart clean in His blood and deliver you from your wicked life or you will perish forever."

Within just a few moments, the situation shifted drastically. Much to my surprise, this self-professed killer broke down sobbing and confessed, "You sound just like my momma!" Then the unthinkable happened. He handed me the knife, turned around, knelt down on the floorboard and begged me to pray for him. I was stunned. Rolling down the window, I threw the knife as far as I could, then I laid hands on the man's head, commanding the demons to come out of him. By the way, exorcism is something every consecrated believer should be ready to execute, when necessary, not just designated priests. It's the first sign mentioned in the commission Jesus gave to His followers. Right before ascending into heaven, the Messiah plainly stated:

> *"These signs will follow those who believe: in My name*
> *they will cast out demons . . ."*
> *(Mark 16:17)*

As the man on his knees groaned in repentance, I prayed that the blood of Jesus would wash him clean. We must have sought God at least fifteen or twenty minutes. Then he regained his composure, started up the car and drove out to the main street where he dropped me off. I have no idea what happened to him after that mind-boggling encounter. I never heard from him again. I hope he was truly converted and that his heart and life were dramatically changed. All I know for certain is how it affected me. I decided that life-threatening confrontation was a sign from above that I was not supposed to be a monk, so I returned to the commune, very thankful for God's amazing grace.

Not long afterward, I got involved studying the Gospels and the book of Acts, and I concluded Jesus did not intend for His disciples to live in the seclusion of a monastery or a convent, to spend the rest of their lives seeking Him. Quite the opposite, before He ascended back to heaven, He presented what has been termed, "The Great Commission," found in two of the Gospels:

> *And Jesus came and spoke to them, saying,*
> *"All authority has been given to Me*
> *in heaven and on earth.*
> *Go therefore and make disciples of all the nations,*
> *baptizing them in the name of the Father and of the*
> *Son and of the Holy Spirit,*
> *teaching them to observe all things that I have*
> *commanded you; and lo, I am with you always,*
> *even to the end of the age." Amen.*
> *(Matthew 28:18-20)*

> *And He said to them, "Go into all the world and preach*
> *the gospel to every creature."*
> *(Mark 16:15)*

These passages and others convinced me where my emphasis needed to be. I decided that true discipleship had to involve a passionate commitment to reach the people of this world with the true message of the Gospel, not to withdraw from them. That is what I have committed my life to accomplish for over fifty years. And now . . . the wonderful story of my parents' conversion.

My parents' response and their conversion

My father and mother, Andrew and Winnie Shreve (pictured above), lived about twenty miles away from the Christian commune where I lived, so I was able to visit with them often after I encountered the Lord. Thankfully, my mother became one of my first "converts," readily giving her heart to Jesus after I shared with her how to experience true salvation. My father, on the other hand, was very reluctant to discuss the Bible, especially my newfound insights.

Dad was a committed Catholic for about forty years. He enlisted in the Naval Air Force about the time World War II was ending. In the latter 40s, he flew planes in the famed "Hurricane Squadron." After that, he became an officer in the U.S. Navy, and commanded several destroyers in the Atlantic/Mediterranean fleet. He was well known for his strong commitment to Catholic, Christ-centered values. One time he even chose as a ship emblem the popular picture of Jesus standing behind a sailor at the helm of a ship ("Christ Our Pilot" by Warner Sallman). Unfortunately, though, something happened to discourage, weaken, or damage his faith.

Dad stopped attending Mass and seemed to internalize some kind of altered religious belief system. Whatever happened, he never divulged the details with any of us in the family. Evidently, he still had faith in God, but for some reason, church attendance went out the window. Even though he never backed away from his core values (like honesty, integrity, and morality), I was unsure whether he still embraced a Christian, biblical worldview. For twelve years, my mother and I just kept interceding for him. She even fasted forty days, seeking God in his behalf. Then it happened. God intervened—amazingly and powerfully.

The pivotal point arrived in the form of a painful problem. A vertebra slipped in Dad's neck and for seven days, his head was locked in a bowed position. After suffering for a week, he checked into the local hospital, hoping to get some relief. Little did he know, a profound miracle was about to take place.

Later that night he called and excitedly explained what had transpired, "Mike, I was laying there in the hospital bed with nothing to do. So, I thought to myself, 'My head's already in a bowed position; I might as well pray.'" (My first reaction was to laughingly offer, "Sounds like a subtle hint from heaven, Dad!") He continued his explanation, "I decided to go back to my earliest memories and thank God for every blessing, every beneficial thing, that had ever happened throughout my life. That took about two hours. Then I just decided to praise God just because He's God."

I blurted out, "Dad, that's a biblical concept. Psalm 100 tells believers to enter God's gates with thanksgiving and His courts with praise." He responded, "I don't know about that; all I know is what happened next." I was rapt with attention.

Dad recounted, "Suddenly, a golden cloud swept into the hospital room and the face of Jesus, beaten, bloody, and crowned with thorns, appeared in the cloud. Then the cloud shifted from a golden color to a crimson red and waves of that red light began pouring over me." He enthusiastically concluded, "I knew I was being bathed in the blood of Jesus and I knew I was being born again."

I was gripped with awe. My father wasn't even asking to be saved— he wasn't even asking to be born again—but when He approached God with a grateful heart, the windows of heaven opened. For about a month, every time he tried to relate what happened, or offer another detail, tears of gratitude would fill his eyes.

He was a changed man from that point forward. He eventually became an adult Sunday school teacher in an interdenominational country church in the little town of Canton, North Carolina, where he and my mother had built a retirement cabin. During his latter years, he spent a great deal of time joyously studying the Word of God.

More family salvation stories

After I encountered the Lord, I started confessing Acts 16:31 by faith. To the Philippian jailer, Paul had promised, "Believe on the Lord Jesus Christ, and you will be saved, you and your household." So, I started claiming all of them for the kingdom of God—my siblings, cousins, uncles and aunts—considering them all my extended "household," and sharing the Gospel with them any way that I could. Many of them gave their hearts to the Lord Jesus—including my grandmother— and had genuine spiritual encounters with Him. A few of them were blessed to receive remarkable, even miraculous visitations.

Sam's powerful deliverance and unique vision from God

One of my cousins was miraculously delivered of heroin addiction when I prayed with him to make Jesus Lord of his life. God orchestrated his salvation in a fascinating way. He was living a very dysfunctional life on the streets of Washington D.C. Though somewhat well-to-do prior to his drug problem, he had been reduced to just one possession: a dilapidated Volkswagen bug. His days were occupied doing anything it took to support his daily drug habit (about $200 to $300). Then God compassionately intervened.

One night after shooting up some heroin, he felt an overwhelming compulsion to go visit his "Uncle Andy" in Winter Park, Florida (my father). So, he took off driving, not even knowing for certain what address he was looking for. It is still a mystery to me how he actually found the house. He had no idea that I just "happened to be" staying with my parents that same weekend because of a speaking engagement in a nearby church (another example of "sacred synchronicity"—a God-incidence, not a coincidence). When I came home from the "Word and Worship Gathering" that night, Sam was sitting in the living room talking with my parents. I could tell he was high. After my folks went to bed, I got my Bible out and started sharing the Gospel.

In about an hour, Sam said, "I'm ready. Let's pray." We got down on our knees and began to seek God. After about ten minutes into our prayer session, Sam looked up at me with a surprised look on his face. He blurted out, "Something just happened to me. I'm not high anymore, and I feel the power of God's presence in the air all around me." I said, "Sam, that power feels even better when He comes on the inside." Excitedly, he said, "Let's keep praying."

After another ten minutes, something wonderfully unique happened. It was God speaking to Sam on his level. He opened his eyes and looked at me incredulously as he explained what he had just seen. Slightly stuttering with awe, he explained, "I think I just had a vision." Stunned, I responded, "Tell me about it."

He haltingly responded, "I saw me and the Lord in a wrestling ring. He had me in a half-nelson, a hold I couldn't break free from. My back was on the canvas and I was crying, "Uncle, uncle, uncle!" (which, of course, means, "I surrender!").

I knew what it meant. God was saying his days of rebellion against the commandments of the Lord were over. What a joyful moment! I informed Sam in the middle of my laughter, "Everyone else I know gets saved crying Jesus, but if you can't get delivered saying uncle, keep right on doing it.

It worked! Immediately, Sam was set completely free from heroin. Miraculously, he never went through cold turkey (the normal withdrawal symptoms). Sam traveled with me for a season, serving God with all his heart.

Chip and Kitty's dual miracle, physical and spiritual

Of all the family stories I could share, the following is one of the most profound. Another cousin, Chip Kleisath, was quite a skeptic when I first approached him with the Gospel of the kingdom. We were about the same age and both of us had been raised Catholic. Just like me, during his early teens, he had become somewhat irreligious. Another reason he quit church involved family conflict: his Jewish wife did not want their children raised Catholic. She was also heavily involved in various expressions of New Age spirituality, as well as the Jewish Kabbalah.

Chip worked for the post office, but just a few months prior, he had become disabled. One of his arms developed a strange condition causing it to lose its strength, wither and draw up to his side. Unable to do his job properly, he was subsequently laid off. The doctors were baffled. There was no explanation for his ailment. I was scheduled to preach in the Tampa, Florida, area where he and his family lived, so I called Chip to invite him to the services. I mentioned that we fully believe in miracles and pray for them to happen. During our phone conversation, he totally dismissed the idea of being healed by God's power, so I was quite surprised when he actually showed up at church that night, along with his Jewish wife who had never attended a Christian gathering before.

I preached a simple message on the kingdom of God and true salvation and gave an invitation. Chip rushed to the front, wide-eyed with expectation. Apparently, he was supernaturally drawn by the convicting power of God. When I laid hands on him, he fell out under the power of God and was immediately saved, filled with the Holy Spirit (speaking in tongues), and healed (his arm returned to normal). Even though I consider myself a person of faith, I was stunned at how quickly and thoroughly God moved.

Having never witnessed anything like that before, his Jewish wife, Kitty, was quite startled. She jumped up and was about to quickly exit the church, but God graciously intervened. She had been gazing at the cross on the back wall of the church, intrigued by that Christian symbol. Just as she rose from her seat, from the direction of the cross, she heard the audible voice of Jesus (Yeshua) saying, "I love you. I died for you. I am your Messiah." Instead of rushing out, she ran forward to the altar and was powerfully saved. Not long after that encounter with the God of Abraham, she enrolled in Christ for the Nations Institute in Dallas, Texas. Eventually, she became a teacher of "The Jewish Roots of the Church" at a large Charismatic church in Central Florida.

One night of divine intervention forever changed both of their lives, dramatically and wonderfully. Jesus first authored faith in their hearts, then He blessed them miraculously because of their faith, granting them entrance into His kingdom and an inheritance of its supernatural reality. As the Scripture attests, "The kingdom of God is not in word, but in power" (1 Corinthians 4:20).

Uncle Dick's amazing breakthrough

My father's kind-hearted, older brother, Dick, was Catholic and he lived in Baraboo, Wisconsin. The first few months after I became a Christian, I often prayed that God would send "just one born-again person" to witness to Uncle Dick (he had some serious challenges in his life that required God's help). Unfortunately, doubtful, negative, (untrue) thoughts kept whirling in my mind, like: *It's not going to happen. There aren't any born-again Christians in Baraboo.* After about a month of this internal struggle, whatever faith I had for divine intervention eroded away. So I decided to take matters into my own hands (when I should have prayed through and trusted God).

After repairing my vehicle and buying new tires, I drove all the way from Cleveland, Tennessee, to Baraboo (about 800 miles) not knowing that God had a grand surprise waiting on me. (I think He enjoyed the startled look on my face.) When I arrived, I discovered—not only had God answered my prayer, He fulfilled one of the most glorious passages in His Word—"Now to Him who is able to do exceedlingly abundantly above all that we ask or think, according to the power that works in us, to Him be glory in the church by Christ Jesus to all generations, forever and ever. Amen." (Ephesians 3:20-21)

About twenty-five Christians were on their way to the Wisconsin Dells for a retreat when their bus broke down in Baraboo, about two miles from my uncle's trailer. Uncle Dick's son-in-law, who just *happened* to be a bus mechanic, stopped to help them out. Unable to fix their vehicle, he towed it to his trailer to continue working on it. (He lived next door to Uncle Dick.) To the dismay of the church group, they found out it was going to take over a week to fix. Feeling sympathy for their dilemma, my uncle graciously invited them to stay in his trailer and conduct their meeting. So for the next seven days, they held three services a day: worshiping, singing, studying the Bible, and praying—and you guessed it, they prayed for Uncle Dick.

So, I learned a lesson about the power of the Almighty God. I asked Him to send only one person to witness for just one visit, and He sent twenty-five people for an entire week (wall-to-wall Christians). Now I know, no matter how great the obstacle, God is able to go far beyond my expectations. May God do the same for you as well.

Addendum

The wonder of being "born again"

Some of the Bible passages in this Addendum are the very ones that were shared with me on that pivotal day in the fall of 1970 when I found Jesus (or more correctly, when the Good Shepherd finally found me, one of His lost sheep). Now, it's my turn to joyously share these scriptures with you.

Even though I quoted from the following passage in the Introduction and under Question #3, let's review once again the story of Nicodemus who came to talk with Jesus about His identity as the Messiah, His teachings, and His miracles. Here is an excerpt from that important story in the Gospel of John:

> *There was a man of the Pharisees named*
> *Nicodemus, a ruler of the Jews.*
> *This man came to Jesus by night and said to Him,*
> *"Rabbi, we know that You are a teacher come from*
> *God; for no one can do these signs that*
> *You do unless God is with him."*
> *Jesus answered and said to him, "Most assuredly, I say*
> *to you, unless one is born again, he cannot*
> *see the kingdom of God."*
> *Nicodemus said to Him, "How can a man be born*
> *when he is old? Can he enter a second time into his*
> *mother's womb and be born?"*

Jesus answered, "Most assuredly, I say to you, unless
one is born of water and the Spirit, he cannot
enter the kingdom of God.
That which is born of the flesh is flesh,
and that which is born of the Spirit is spirit.
Do not marvel that I said to you, 'You
must be born again.'"
(John 3:1-7)

Notice, Jesus did not make this spiritual rebirth optional; He made it mandatory. As mentioned under Question #3, the official stance of the Catholic Church is that those baptized into the Catholic Church are "born of water and of the Spirit" during that sacramental ceremony. However, I can assure you that when I was sprinkled as a baby, I did not receive a spiritual rebirth. If that had truly happened, I believe I would have been a much better person growing up. This remarkable experience of regeneration did not occur until I consciously and sincerely received Jesus into my heart and asked Him to be my personal Lord and Savior at the age of nineteen.

The hidden meaning

Examining the original Greek of this key passage provides a wonderful insight. In the statement, "You must be born again," the word translated "again" is *anothen,* which literally means from above. It is even translated "from above" in other places in the New Testament. (See John 3:31; 19:11, James 1:17.) So, to be "born again" is to be "born from above." What does that mean?

Two prophetic passages about the New Covenant are especially powerful in unveiling this mystery: Jeremiah 31:31-34 and Ezekiel 36:26-27. Jeremiah's prophecy is wonderful in its imagery:

"Behold, the days are coming, says the LORD, when I
will make a new covenant with the house of Israel and
with the house of Judah
. . . I will put My law in their minds, and write it on
their hearts; and I will be their God,
and they shall be My people.
No more shall every man teach his neighbor, and every

man his brother, saying, 'Know the LORD,' for they all
shall know Me, from the least of them to the greatest of
them, says the LORD. For I will forgive their iniquity,
and their sin I will remember no more."
(Jeremiah 31:31, 33-34)

The same God who wrote the law in tablets of stone on Mount Sinai promises to write His law in the hearts of His people in this New Covenant era. That speaks of something external becoming something internal.

Instead of a character demand on the outside (religious rules and laws), God promises a character change on the inside (spiritual rebirth). The new nature that is imparted during this holy encounter awakens within newborn believers a genuine love for the things God loves. That is what it means to become a "new creation in Christ" (2 Corinthians 5:17).

God also pledged in Jeremiah's prophecy that His New Covenant people would know Him personally and that He would never remember their sins again. The blood of the Old Covenant animal sacrifices could never change the nature of the participants in those rituals or take away their sin. It only "atoned" for their sin (which means a temporary covering). However, the blood of Jesus removes sin entirely, forever.

The mystery deepens in its profoundness in Ezekiel's prophecy. God spoke through that Old Testament prophet concerning what He would do for His people in the coming New Covenant era, saying:

"I will give you a new heart and put a new spirit within
you; I will take the heart of stone out of your flesh
and give you a heart of flesh.
I will put My Spirit within you and cause you to walk
in My statutes, and you will
keep My judgments and do them."
(Ezekiel 36:26-27)

So, to be "born from above" is to receive the impartation of a "new spirit" and the infilling of God's Spirit. These two gifts are absolutely wonderful and they make us "complete in Him" (Colossians 2:10).

Eight complementary concepts

To tie this all together, let's go through eight necessary steps that lead a person to this life-changing spiritual rebirth that Jesus talked about and the prophets foretold:

1. Truly repent before God (express genuine sorrow for sin and an intention to depart from sin):

> *"Repent therefore and be converted, that your sins may*
> *be blotted out, so that times of refreshing may come*
> *from the presence of the Lord."*
> *(Acts 3:19)*

2. Confess your faith in Jesus' death and resurrection:

> *That if you confess with your mouth the Lord Jesus and*
> *believe in your heart that God has raised Him from the*
> *dead, you will be saved.*
> *For with the heart one believes unto righteousness, and*
> *with the mouth confession is made unto salvation.*
> *(Romans 10:9-10)*

3. Sincerely call on the name of Jesus:

> *For "whoever calls on the name of the Lord shall be*
> *saved." (Romans 10:13)*

4. Respond to Jesus' invitation to enter your heart and life:

> *"Behold, I stand at the door and knock. If anyone hears*
> *My voice and opens the door, I will come in to him and*
> *dine with him, and he with Me."*
> *(Revelation 3:20)*

5. Believe that the Savior now dwells within:

> *That Christ may dwell in your hearts through faith.*
> *(Ephesians 3:17)*

6. Believe that you become a part of the family of God:

> *But as many as received Him, to them He gave*
> *the right to become children of God, to*

those who believe in His name:
who were born, not of blood, nor of the will of the flesh,
nor of the will of man, but of God.
(John 1:12-13)

7. Declare you are now a child of God and God is your Father:

And because you are sons, God has sent forth
the Spirit of His Son into your hearts,
crying out, "Abba, Father!"
(Galatians 4:6)

8. Expect Jesus' intercessory prayer over the church of this New Covenant era to be answered in you individually:

"O righteous Father! The world has not known You, but
I have known You; and these have known that You sent
Me. And I have declared to them Your name, and will
declare it, that the love with which You loved Me
may be in them, and I in them."
(John 17:25-26)

These last two verses from John 17 are the climax of an amazing 26-verse intercessory prayer Jesus prayed toward the close of His time on earth. He petitioned the Father concerning the disciples who were with Him then, as well as all those who would yet follow Him in this Age of Grace.

You should read that prayer in its entirety. It includes so many wonderful promises and provisions. However, the closing line of the Messiah's petition reveals a primary key to true Christianity: being filled with God's love and experiencing the personal indwelling of His Son.

The prayer that connects

If this wonderful, spiritual impartation has never happened to you, or if you are unsure, you should pray and seek the face of God now. Remember, Jesus encouraged us all with the following words:

"Ask and it will be given to you; seek and you will find;
knock and it will be opened to you." (Matthew 7:7)

Here is a prayer you can pray, or at least, use as a general pattern of prayer. As you speak it from your heart, be creative! Use your own wording! Add phrases important to you! Be spontaneous! Be passionate and full of praise! Be full of faith and expectation!

> *"Lord Jesus, I surrender to You as Lord of my life. I believe You died on the cross for the sins of humanity and I believe three days later, You rose from the dead victoriously. I repent of my sins and ask You to come and dwell in my heart. I claim the promise that Your precious blood will wash away all my transgressions. By faith, I receive the gift of grace, the gift of salvation, and the gift of eternal life, and I humbly ask to be 'born again.' From this day forward, I intend to serve You with all my heart as a true disciple. And I believe when You return, I will rise to meet You, resurrected and glorified, to dwell with You forevermore. Amen."*

If you approach God with sincerity, He will respond to you. The promise Jesus gave nearly two thousand years ago is still valid today:

> *"He who comes to Me I will never cast out."* (John 6:37)

You may have a real supernatural encounter when you seek God using this approach (which is wonderful when it happens), then again, you may not *feel* anything. True salvation is not always accompanied by a spiritual sensation. However, it always results in changed hearts and changed lives, and it always happens because you believe:

> *For by grace you have been saved through faith, and*
> *that not of yourselves; it is the gift of God, not of works,*
> *lest anyone should boast.*
> *(Ephesians 2:8-9)*

Though you have been "dead in trespasses and sins," you will be made "alive together with Christ"—as you pray in faith (Ephesians 2:1, 5). It really is that simple. God wanted it simple. The Bible even describes this as "the simplicity that is in Christ" (2 Corinthians 11:3).

Appendixes 1-10

Appendix #1 / The Apostles' Creed

The following statement of faith is referred to as "The Apostles' Creed," not because the apostles authored it (though some Christians believe they did), but because it is supposedly a summary of what they taught. Though it initially surfaced midway through the second century, "the oldest form of the creed appeared in approximately AD 340. The fullest form of the creed came into being around 700 AD."[164] Several statements and/or their traditional interpretations are contested by Christians of various denominations and persuasions. Those questionable lines are indicated by bold italic print.

I believe in God, the Father almighty,
creator of heaven and earth.
I believe in Jesus Christ, his only Son, our Lord,
who was conceived by the Holy Spirit
and born of the virgin Mary.
He suffered under Pontius Pilate,
was crucified, died, and was buried;
he descended to hell.
The third day he rose again from the dead.
He ascended to heaven
and is seated at the right hand of God the
Father almighty.

*From there he will come to judge
the living and the dead.
I believe in the Holy Spirit,
the holy catholic church,
the communion of saints,
the forgiveness of sins,
the resurrection of the body,
and the life everlasting. Amen.*

The word "catholic" comes from the Greek adjective *katholikos* which means universal. Protestants who quote this creed, say it is a reference to the whole body of Christ throughout the world, while Catholics interpret it as a reference to the Catholic Church globally.

Appendix #2 / Traditional prayers

The following three prayers are prayed during the recitation of the rosary and are often assigned during Penance.

The "Our Father" prayer:

> *"Our Father in heaven, hallowed be Your name. Your kingdom come. Your will be done on earth as it is in heaven. Give us this day our daily bread. And forgive us our debts as we forgive our debtors. And do not lead us into temptation, but deliver us from the evil one."*
> *(Matthew 6:9-13 NCB)*

The King James Version also adds at the end of this prayer, "For Yours is the kingdom and the power and the glory forever. Amen."

The "Hail Mary" prayer:

> *"Hail Mary, full of grace, the Lord is with thee. Blessed art thou among women, and blessed is the fruit of thy womb, Jesus. Holy Mary, Mother of God, pray for us sinners now, and at the hour of our death. Amen."*

The "Glory Be" prayer:

> *"Glory be to the Father, and to the Son, and to the Holy Spirit. As it was in the beginning, is now, and ever shall be, world without end. Amen."*

Appendix #3 / More reflections on repetitious prayer

Some meaningful observations concerning the practice of repetitious prayers have already been shared under Questions #9, #12, and #16. In two of those chapters, the following statement Jesus made right before sharing "The Lord's Prayer" was emphasized:

> *"When you pray, do not use vain repetitions as the heathen do. For they think that they will be heard for their many words.*
> *Therefore do not be like them. For your Father knows the things you have need of before you ask Him."*
> *(Matthew 6:7-8)*

That one command should be sufficient in determining how we approach the concept of prayer. There is a great difference between religion and relationship. Religion thrives on repetitious rituals and memorized prayers. On the other hand, predictable patterns in liturgical worship can help to make participants more familiar with certain spiritual concepts, help to create an atmosphere of the sacred, and guide a congregation toward greater unity—so such practices are not always ill-advised. In one of my books titled, *65 Promises from God for Your Child,* I offer a suggested prayer of declaration at the end of each chapter, just as I did a few pages back in the Addendum. So, I am not completely disinclined toward this approach. However, I do not claim that quoting those prayers are necessary for the promise to come to pass, or that they must be spoken exactly as written.

To be considered is the fact that God authored the Aaronic prayer found in Numbers 6:24-27, a prayer-declaration often quoted by both Jews and Christians, so He is in favor of this method at times. However,

He never instructed His people to repeat this prayer numerous times in one setting. A real relationship with God usually results in worship that is more free-flowing, more individually inspired, more spontaneous, and thus, more authentic. Some prayers used in the Catholic liturgy have remained unchanged for centuries (as well as other Christian denominations). Can you imagine how God must feel, after hearing the echo of the same petitions, week after week, month after month, year after year, and decade after decade, generated from multitudes around the globe who approach His throne according to a prescribed pattern? How disingenuous that must seem to Him at times!

The potential ineffectiveness of such an approach is magnified even more when those prayers are read almost mindlessly from a bulletin or a prayer book. Often, the mind can be engaged without the heart. Again, think of it from God's perspective. Sometimes, the reading of prayers may be help a person to focus and "jumpstart" a time of seeking God—but how would you feel if someone could not talk to you without reading from an established script.

Of course, certain biblical worship words or phrases may be heard repeated often during a truly spiritual prayer session, like "Praise God," "Praise the Lord," "Hallelujah," "Hosanna in the highest," "I worship you, Lord," or "I love You, God"—but not in a rigid, ritualistic way. Just like a man and his wife might use certain phrases toward each other often to express their mutual affection—so it is for lovers of God. Though the words and phrases may be similar at times, the depth of feeling and genuineness behind those words is fresh every time.

The Bible admonishes us to "pray without ceasing," so there should always be an inclination of the heart upward 24/7 (1 Thessalonians 5:17). If we strive to accomplish such a goal, inevitably, repetition is going to take place even if it is not planned or prearranged. In this area of doctrine, therefore, in all honesty—it is very hard to draw a line between what is advisable and what is not.

Scriptures often used by Catholics to support this tradition

Several passages of Scripture are often used by Catholics to lend support to the practice of praying repetitious, ritualistic prayers. Let's visit each of these occurrences.

The Lord's Prayer

The primary example is, of course, "The Lord's Prayer" (partially addressed under Question #9). When Jesus instructed His disciples to "pray in this manner," we should consider the strong possibility that He did not mean, "Pray this prayer word-for-word, exactly as I have given it." Instead, do you think He could have been simply instructing us to use a similar structure or pattern in approaching the Father? *(To explore this possibility, read Appendix #4.)*

This divinely inspired prayer is truly a gift. Speaking it word-for-word, slowly, in a heartfelt way, once or twice during any given prayer session, is unquestionably an effective way of connecting with the Father. However, repeating it ritualistically, numerous times, in nearly a mantra-like fashion, is surely not what Jesus intended. Doing so reduces it to a mechanical formula ineffective in touching the heart of God.

Four more examples: the two blind men, the ten lepers, the widow woman, and the repetition of Psalm 136

Four more scriptural references are used at times in Catholic writings to support the practice of repetitious prayer: the story of the two blind men, the healing of the ten lepers, "The Parable of the Persistent Widow," and Psalm 136. I will comment on all of these. First, the account of the blind men:

> *When Jesus departed from there, two blind men*
> *followed Him, crying out and saying,*
> *"Son of David, have mercy on us!"*
> *And when He had come into the house, the blind men*
> *came to Him. And Jesus said to them,*
> *"Do you believe that I am able to do this?"*
> *They said to Him, "Yes, Lord."*
> *Then He touched their eyes, saying, "According to*
> *your faith let it be to you."*
> *(Matthew 9:27-29)*

Even though the blind men may have repeated this simple plea numerous times ("Son of David, have mercy on us"), it was not a

310 ~ The Beliefs of the Catholic Church

rigid religious ritual that they repeated for many years. Rather, it was a desperate cry for help at an opportune moment, and most likely, interspersed with other similar prayerful pleas that are not written in this account. Now, let's focus on the story of the ten lepers:

> Now it happened as He went to Jerusalem that He
> passed through the midst of Samaria and Galilee.
> Then as He entered a certain village, there met Him ten
> men who were lepers, who stood afar off.
> And they lifted up their voices and said,
> "Jesus, Master, have mercy on us!"
> So when He saw them, He said to them, "Go, show
> yourselves to the priests." And so it was that as they
> went, they were cleansed.
> And one of them, when he saw that he was healed,
> returned, and with a loud voice glorified God,
> and fell down on his face at His feet, giving Him thanks.
> And he was a Samaritan.

Once again, even though Luke recorded one cry ("Jesus, Master, have mercy on us!"), it does not mean that phrase was *all* they uttered in petitioning the Savior. When one returned to thank Jesus, falling at His feet and glorifying God, you can be sure, his praise was not according to a prearranged script. It was real. It was spontaneous, and it was passionate (and shouldn't that often be the case with all of us). Now, the parable of the widow woman:

> Then He [Jesus] spoke a parable to them, that men
> always ought to pray and not lose heart,
> saying: "There was in a certain city a judge who
> did not fear God nor regard man.
> Now there was a widow in that city; and she came to
> him, saying, 'Get justice for me from my adversary.'
> And he would not for a while; but afterward he said
> within himself, 'Though I do not fear God
> nor regard man, yet because this widow
> troubles me I will avenge her, lest by her
> continual coming she weary me.'"

Then the Lord said, "Hear what
the unjust judge said.
And shall God not avenge His own elect who cry out
day and night to Him, though He bears
long with them?"

Jesus never implied that the widow woman repeated her petition to the unjust judge with exactly the same words every time she came before him. There are numerous ways to express the request she made. So, once again, this story cannot be used as proof. Now, let's visit Psalm 136. Here are the first four verses of that 26-verse, Old Testament song:

Oh, give thanks to the LORD, for He is good!
For His mercy endures forever.
Oh, give thanks to the God of gods!
For His mercy endures forever.
Oh, give thanks to the Lord of lords! F
or His mercy endures forever:
To Him who alone does great wonders,
for His mercy endures forever.
(Psalms 136:1-4)

As you can see, each verse ends with the statement, "For His mercy endures forever." This pattern continues in each of the twenty-six verses of the psalm. Does that prove the acceptability of repetitious, ritualistic prayers? No, it does not—first, because a psalm is simply a biblically-based song, and quite often in song lyrics, certain phrases are repeated. That's normal. Second, it is a musical celebration of a certain theological truth, a joyous declaration of faith, not a prayerful petition expressed directly toward God. Now, Jesus in Gethsemane.

The Garden of Gethsemane

In various Catholic articles on this controversial subject, several times I have seen Jesus' prayer in the Garden of Gethsemane offered as proof that repetitious prayer is not only acceptable, but advisable. However, for reasons I will cite, I do not believe this is a proper application. Let's read the whole passage—the last line is most important to this discussion:

Then Jesus came with them to a place called
Gethsemane, and said to the disciples,
"Sit here while I go and pray over there."
And He took with Him Peter and the two sons of
Zebedee, and He began to be
sorrowful and deeply distressed.
Then He said to them, "My soul is exceedingly
sorrowful, even to death. Stay here and watch with Me."
He went a little farther and fell on His face, and prayed,
saying, "O My Father, if it is possible,
let this cup pass from Me; nevertheless,
not as I will, but as You will."
Then He came to the disciples and found them sleeping,
and said to Peter, "What! Could you not
watch with Me one hour?
Watch and pray, lest you enter into temptation. The
spirit indeed is willing, but the flesh is weak."
Again, a second time, He went away and prayed,
saying, "O My Father, if this cup cannot pass away
from Me unless I drink it, Your will be done."
And He came and found them asleep again,
for their eyes were heavy.
So He left them, went away again, and
prayed the third time, saying the same words.
(Matthew 26:36-44)

Several points need to be made concerning this lengthy passage. First, this was not a prayer Jesus memorized in advance and repeated ritualistically in order to properly secure a deliverance. It was a product of the passion of the moment. The cross was imminent, so avoiding it, if possible, dominated Jesus' conversation with the Father.

So it is possible that Jesus apparently did not prayerfully address other things. In a similar way, how many times I have nearly gotten in an accident on the highway and said something several times in the tension of the moment like, "Oh Jesus, help us! Oh Jesus, help us! Oh Jesus, help us!" If someone riding with me in the car heard me do that, I don't think they would jump to the conclusion that I normally practice repetitious, ritualistic prayer, memorized in advance.

Furthermore, just because we have this brief record of a portion of Jesus' impassioned plea, it does not prove that He only prayed these words while seeking the Father in Gethsemane. He may have cried out many ways that were not recorded. The disciples kept falling asleep, so they were most likely oblivious to the majority of what Jesus said and only remembered this part. Notice verses 39 and 42 (in bold letters) are slightly different and the latter is not just an echo of the former.

Finally, Jesus was heard repeating this prayer a mere three times— yes, let me say it again, a mere three times. That is certainly not sufficient evidence to justify repeating certain prescribed prayers tens of thousands of times ritualistically over a period of many years.

The worshiping cherubim

The strongest argument in favor of repetitious, ritualistic prayer can be found in John's account of the activities that take place in the heavenly throne room.

Let's read an excerpt from the book of the Revelation:

> *Before the throne there was a sea of glass, like crystal.*
> *And in the midst of the throne, and around the throne,*
> *were four living creatures full of*
> *eyes in front and in back.*
> *The first living creature was like a lion, the second living*
> *creature like a calf, the third living creature had a face*
> *like a man, and the fourth living*
> *creature was like a flying eagle.*
> *The four living creatures, each having six wings, were*
> *full of eyes around and within. And they do not rest day*
> *or night, saying: "Holy, holy, holy, Lord God Almighty,*
> *who was and is and is to come!"*
> *(Revelation 4:6-8)*

Because these descriptions are very similar to the heavenly beings Ezekiel identified as cherubim in the first and tenth chapters of his book, that is probably their true identity. Taken literally, it seems that for all eternity, these heavenly beings will repeat this same phrase over and over and over—with no other words ever being uttered by them and possibly, nothing else being done. However, this isolated passage is surely not telling the whole story. There are likely many other worship phrases that flow out of these cherubim besides this one recorded statement—phrases John did not record. Who can say for certain?

The main issue is not how often or how ritualistically they speak this worshipful utterance, but the fact that they never stop adoring the Almighty. The Bible tells sons and daughters of God to pray without ceasing while we are here in this world (which is very challenging to achieve), yet here in this celestial scene, we witness this constancy as a living reality. And won't that be what makes heaven heaven—an atmosphere of constant praise and undisturbed ecstasy in the presence of God, something far greater than anything we have ever experienced on earth? Surely that is the most important takeaway from this passage.

Salvation is not of works

Paul tells us that salvation is "not of works, lest anyone should boast" (Ephesians 2:9). Repetitious, ritualistic prayers in many situations could be placed in the category of "religious works" that do not save us. Often-repeated prayers become mindless and monotonous—both to God and to us. As a boy especially, I would rush through the prayers assigned to me as my penance after Confession, sometimes slurring the words, not hardly thinking of their true meaning. My main motive was to finish as quickly as possible and get away from the shame and embarrassment of having just "spilled the beans" to a priest in a confessional. (Now admit it—if you were raised Catholic, you probably did that, too.)

God is not impressed by our ability to rattle off memorized supplications. He is not coerced into measuring out His grace according to the number of times we say them. He wants His people to pray from the heart, in a genuine way, expressing their innermost feelings to Him in a flow of words that is sincere and conversational—as unpracticed and unpolished as the conversations we have with fellow human beings. Our heavenly Father is not an energy force, a machine, or a computer into which we insert the right formula for the desired outcome to take place. He is a person, and He desires a personal relationship with us. Heaven must rejoice over those who pray to the true God in the way that blesses Him the most!

Appendix #4 / Praying "The Lord's Prayer" creatively

In His often-quoted "Sermon on the Mount," Jesus gave the following prayer to the church to pray. Imagine the profoundness of such an impartation: God Himself—incarnate in this world—teaching His sons and daughters how to pray just so He can graciously and powerfully respond. That really is intense! If He told us what to pray, surely, He intends to answer when we pray that prayer. Here it is:

"Our Father, who is in Heaven, hallowed be Your
name. Your kingdom come; Your will be done, on earth
as it is in Heaven. Give us this day our daily bread. And
forgive us our debts as we also forgive our debtors. And
lead us not into temptation, but deliver us from the evil.
For Yours is the kingdom, and the power,
and the glory, forever. Amen."
(Matthew 6:9-13 MEV, See Luke 11:1-4)

"The Lord's Prayer" can be quoted word-for-word, sincerely from the heart, and be an effective way of communicating with God. However, as I mentioned in the previous Appendix article, it seems very unlikely that Jesus intended His followers to repeat it numerous times in one setting or always as it was originally spoken, without any variation. In corporate gatherings, yes, at times, that is necessary for everyone to pray in unison. But private times of prayer are a different matter. Remember, Jesus prefaced this beloved prayer with the directive, "In this manner, therefore, pray"—which could mean, "Use a similar approach." (Matthew 6:9).

Improvising with "The Lord's Prayer"

I encourage you to explore this unique approach: using "The Lord's Prayer" as a basic outline—a spiritual template—that highlights key concepts, line-by-line, that can be expanded during a time of seeking God's face. With each phrase, express fresh, creative, worshipful utterances, related in meaning to the original words. Also, instead of using the archaic English, you might try using more familiar modern-day words. Instead of saying, "Our Father which art in heaven, hallowed be Thy name," say something more normal to you like:

- **"Our Father in heaven, Your name is holy."**

Then—after making that statement—expand on its meaning by celebrating the Fatherhood of God, then by celebrating various names given to Him in Scripture, as in the following example:

> *"Oh God, You are my Everlasting Father. You are the Father of mercies and the God of all comfort. You are the Father of lights in whom is no shadow of turning. I believe You love me like a Father, provide for me like a Father, and protect me like a Father."*
>
> *"You are El Shaddai, the Almighty God. There is nothing too hard for You. You are Yahweh-Rapha, the Lord my healer. You are Yahweh-Tsidkenu, the Lord my righteousness. You are my Rock and my refuge; I hide myself in You. You are the Alpha and the Omega, the Author and Finisher of my faith. You are the Lord of hosts, the God of an army of angels, poised and ready for battle. You are the King of kings and Lord of lords, the Maker of heaven and earth. Oh holy is Your name!"*

By rehearsing the Fatherhood of God, you are immersing yourself in His love for you, and by rehearsing His beautiful names and titles, you are "hallowing" His name—reverently acknowledging the holiness of His name and praising various aspects of His name with your whole heart. The next phrase is both a prayer and a proclamation:

- **"Your kingdom come."**

After making this powerful request, you may want to prayerfully describe what God's kingdom is, and the ways it can manifest in your life. For instance, Romans 14:17 says that, "The kingdom of God . . . is righteousness, peace, and joy in the Holy Spirit." So after this line, it would be a logical time to pray, "Father, fill me with Your righteousness. Let me be strong in upholding Your righteous standards in this world. Then, let me be filled with Your joy and Your peace until these expressions of Your nature overflow to others." Next comes submission to the Father and to your own individual purpose:

- **"Your will be done on earth as it is in heaven."**

With this statement you can intercede for various nations, communities, and people to conform to God's will. You can also seek a personal revelation from God of His will for your life, or a more complete manifestation of what you already feel is His will. Next, the provision plea:

- **"Give us this day our daily bread."**

After praying that line, you could also pray about specific material needs you may have and the provisions God has promised His people in the Bible. Identify certain things you need in your life naturally and spiritually as well (like healing for your body which Jesus said is "the children's bread"—Matthew 15:26). Next, the big hurdle:

- **"And forgive us our debts as we forgive our debtors."**

At this juncture, you need to dig deep into the darker areas of your inner being. Find any roots of bitterness or unforgiveness and uproot them by releasing those who have harmed you from the "debt" they owe. Forgive them, not from the mind, but from the heart. (See Matthew 18:35.) That does not always mean a restoration of relationship (which is impossible in some cases), but it does mean letting go of the resentment, anger, and in some cases, even the desire for revenge. At times, this brings deep healing to the heart.

- **"And lead us not into temptation, but deliver us from the evil."**

Pray protection for yourself and for your family, deliverance from the evil that streams from your own lower nature, from the world that surrounds us, and from all demonic plots and plans. Pray for strength to resist and strength to endure and overcome. Lift up specific areas of personal concern.

- **"For Yours is the kingdom, and the power, and the glory, forever. Amen."**

Acknowledge that any good done in any of the areas you have mentioned are for the sake of the kingdom of God, by the power of God, and for the glory of God. Mention specific ways you want to help advance God's kingdom, by impacting certain people and influencing specific places with the Gospel. Assure God that any breakthroughs that happen or any answers that come will be for His glory alone—

then spend time praising and glorifying God, worshiping Him in advance, believing that what you have requested, you will receive.

Once you do this, you will realize all the more the power of being spontaneous and creative in the presence of God. But be careful—praying "The Lord's Prayer" in this non-ritualistic, non-repetitious way can itself become ritualistic and repetitious if you let it. So, purpose when you pray to be open to the inspiration of the moment—always in agreement with biblical revelation, but always sensitive to that inner creativity that comes as a gift from God and should flow back to Him in the form of adoring worship.

Appendix #5 / The Seven Sacraments

Below you will find the list of the seven sacraments as defined within Catholicism, and the chapters in which I examine each one:

1. Baptism—Question #3

2. Eucharist (Holy Communion)—Question #24

3. Confirmation—Question #17

4. Reconciliation—Questions #7-9

5. Extreme Unction (The Anointing of the Sick)—Question #25

6. Matrimony—Not addressed in this book

7. Holy Orders (Priesthood)—Questions #4-6

In the Catholic Encyclopedia, sacraments are described "outward signs of inward grace, instituted by Christ for our sanctification."[165] It is also believed that "in every sacrament three things are necessary: the outward sign; the inward grace; Divine institution."[166]

In other words, sacraments are external and visible symbols that represent something internal and invisible that God accomplishes through His grace. However, Catholics tend to believe that the sacraments are not just symbols of "grace" that come to a believer. Rather, they cause that grace to be manifested. Drawing from the Council of Trent, the Catechism states:

"The Church affirms that for believers the sacraments of the New Covenant are necessary for salvation." (CCC 1129)

Based on this statement, by the standards of Catholicism, to be saved, first, it is necessary to be Catholic, and second, it is necessary to be in good standing with the church by participating in the sacraments.

Appendix #6 / The Catholic Counter-Reformation, the Council of Trent, and the Anathema curses

"The Counter-Reformation, also called the Catholic Reformation or the Catholic Revival, was the period of Catholic resurgence that was initiated in response to the Protestant Reformation. It began with the Council of Trent and largely ended with the conclusion of the European wars of religion in 1648."[167]

The Council of Trent started on December 13, 1545, and ended on December 4, 1563, convened by Pope Paul III. It was held at a time when tensions were flaring higher than the flames enveloping thousands who were burned at the stake for their heartfelt religious beliefs. Capital punishment for heresy was commonplace. Both sides were guilty of atrocities worthy of condemnation in the sight of heaven. Catholic authorities threatened to execute Martin Luther, but according to historians, Martin Luther advocated a fierce response toward Anabaptists because of their rejection of infant baptism.

The vast majority (if not all) of those who presently claim to be Christians, both Catholics and non-Catholics, would agree that such atrocious behavior is totally unacceptable, reprehensible, ungodly, and a disturbing misrepresentation of the Gospel to a world that desperately needs a demonstration of the love of God, even between Christians who differ in their doctrine. During that era of escalating religious hostilities, John Knox, a leader of the Scottish Reformation, wisely pointed out:

*"You cannot antagonize and persuade
at the same time."*[168]

If the opposing sides had only been willing to meet at a theological table with humility, calmness, kindness, and mutual respect—and if all parties had sought truth above personal opinion, religious affiliation, or church tradition—things could have gone much differently.

Most people who are sincerely religious have the same longing: to truly be right with God and experience communion with Him— so we should identify with that same heart-cry even in those whose doctrines and practices differ from our own. We can disagree and still love one another and interact with civility and patience. Consider the following simple request, voiced to the children of Israel by the Creator Himself, during a time of apostasy:

> *"Come now, and let us reason together . . ."*
> *(Isaiah 1:18)*

Pause for a moment and consider how amazing it is that God would word His invitation this way. If the Almighty Himself was willing to condescend and "reason" with His people who were not in a good condition spiritually, how much more should we be willing to "reason" with each other, respecting one another as fellow human beings made in the likeness of God!

The water is no longer boiling

During the Council of Trent, over 100 "*Anathema*" curses were pronounced on those who dared to profess interpretations of biblical doctrine that contradicted the canonical beliefs upheld by the Catholic Church. This subject is usually a big issue for non-Catholic Christians who become aware of these curses and understandably so.

The language is very intense. However, it's been almost 500 years and the boiling religious tension that existed then between Catholics and Protestants has simmered down to a relatively cool state in comparison. Furthermore, the original intention—the interpretation of what those "curses" were supposed to mean—was probably much different among the Council of Trent participants who agreed to them than what most Catholics profess to believe now. Because of the historical value, and the existence of common misconceptions on both sides of the table, I feel we should at least visit this controversial topic.

Fifteen of the "Anathema curses" of the Council of Trent

Instead of listing all the "*Anathema* curses" of the Council of Trent, a sampling of fifteen should be sufficient to impart an understanding of the original wording and tone.

The Priesthood

"If any one saith, that there is not in the New Testament a visible and external priesthood; or that there is not any power of consecrating and offering the true body and blood of the Lord, and of forgiving and retaining sins; but only an office and bare ministry of preaching the Gospel, or, that those who do not preach are not priests at all; let him be anathema" (Session Twenty-three, Canon I).[169]

The Sacraments

"If any one saith, that the sacraments of the New Law were not all instituted by Jesus Christ, our Lord; or, that they are more, or less, than seven, to wit, Baptism, Confirmation, the Eucharist, Penance, Extreme Unction, Order, and Matrimony; or even that any one of these seven is not truly and properly a sacrament; let him be anathema" (Session Seven, Canon I, "On the Sacraments in General").[170]

"If any one saith, that the sacraments of the New Law are not necessary unto salvation, but superfluous; and that, without them, or without the desire thereof, men obtain of God, through faith alone, the grace of justification; though all (the sacraments) are not indeed necessary for every individual; let him be anathema" (Session Seven, Canon IV, "On the Sacraments in General").[171]

"If any one saith that the sacraments of the New Law do not contain the grace which they signify, or that they do not confer grace on those who place no obstacle to the same, let him be anathema" (Session Seven, Canon VI, "On the Sacraments in General").[172]

Infant Baptism

"If any one saith, that in the Roman church, which is the mother and mistress of all churches, there is not the true doctrine concerning the sacrament of baptism; let him be anathema" (Sessions Seven, Canon III).[173]

The Holy Eucharist (Holy Communion)

"If any one denieth, that, in the sacrament of the most holy Eucharist, are contained truly, really, and substantially, the body and blood together with the soul and divinity of our Lord Jesus Christ, and consequently the whole Christ; but saith that He is only therein as in a sign, or in figure, or virtue; let him be anathema" (Session Thirteen, Canon I, "On the Most Holy Sacrament of the Eucharist").[174]

Penance (Confession / Reconciliation)

"If any one saith, that in the Catholic Church Penance is not truly and properly a sacrament, instituted by Christ our Lord for reconciling the faithful unto God, as often as they fall into sin after baptism; let him be anathema" (Session Fourteen, Canon I, "On the Most Holy Sacrament of Penance").[175]

"If any one denieth, that, for the entire and perfect remission of sins, there are required three acts in the penitent, which are as it were the matter of the sacrament of Penance, to wit, contrition, confession, and satisfaction, which are called the three parts of penance; or saith that there are two parts only of penance, to wit, the terrors with which the conscience is smitten upon being convinced of sin, and the faith, generated (a) by the gospel, or by the absolution, whereby one believes that his sins are forgiven him through Christ; let him be anathema" (Session Fourteen, Canon IV, "On the Most Holy Sacrament of Penance").[176]

Confirmation

"If any one saith, that the confirmation of those who have been baptized is an idle ceremony, and not rather a true and proper sacrament; or that of old it was nothing more than a kind of catechism, whereby they who were near adolescence gave an account of their faith in the face of the Church; let him be anathema" (Session Twelve, Canon I, "On Confirmation").[177]

The sacrifice of the Mass

"If any one saith, that in the mass a true and proper sacrifice is not offered to God; or, that to be offered is nothing else but that Christ is given us to eat; let him be anathema." (Session Twenty-two, Canon I, "On the Sacrifice of the Mass").[178]

Praying to the Saints

"If any one saith, that it is an imposture to celebrate masses in honour of the saints, and for obtaining their intercession with God, as the Church intends; let him be anathema" (Session Twenty-two, Canon V, "On the Sacrifice of the Mass").[179]

Purgatory (Justification)

"If any one saith, that, after the grace of Justification has been received, to every penitent sinner the guilt is remitted, and the debt of eternal punishment is blotted out in such wise, that there remains not any debt of temporal punishment to be discharged either in this world, or in the next in Purgatory, before the entrance to the kingdom of heaven can be opened (to him); let him be anathema" (Session Six, Canon XXX, "On Justification").[180]

Indulgences (Satisfactions)

"If any man saith, that the satisfactions, by which penitents redeem their sins through Jesus Christ, are not a worship of God, but traditions of men, which obscure the doctrine of grace, and the true worship of God, and the benefit itself of the death of Christ: let him be anathema" (Session Fourteen, Canon XIV, "On the Most Holy Sacrifice of Penance").[181]

Extreme Unction (Final Anointing, The Anointing of the Sick)

"If any one saith, that Extreme Unction is not truly and properly a sacrament, instituted by Christ our Lord, and promulgated by the blessed apostle James; but is only a rite received from the Fathers, or a human figment; let him be anathema" (Session Fourteen, Canon I, "On the Sacrament of Extreme Unction").[182]

"If any one saith, that the sacred unction of the sick does not confer grace, nor remit sin, nor comfort the sick; but that it has already ceased, as though it were of old only the grace of working Cures; let him be anathema" (Session Fourteen, Canon II, "Extreme Unction").[183]

The biblical foundation of the concept

Evidently, in every one of these fifteen declarations, the word *anathema* is emphasized. But what does that term mean? This unique word (pronounced an-ath'-e-mah) is found in Paul's first epistle to the Corinthians:

> *If any man love not the Lord Jesus Christ,*
> *let him be Anathema Maranatha.*
> *(1 Corinthians 16:22 KJV)*

For some reason, the translators of both the King James Version and the Douay-Rheims (Catholic) Version of Scripture chose to retain the original Greek words *Anathema* and *Maranatha* in the English translations of this verse. *Anathema* means "cursed." *Maranatha* means, "Our Lord come!" So, uttering the phrase *Anathema Maranatha* is most likely a prophetic way of declaring a person "cursed" at the "coming of the Lord." Some translations, however, shift the meaning slightly by altering the punctuation. A good example is the Complete Jewish Bible which places a period after *Anathema*, dividing the statement into two separate thoughts:

> *If anyone does not love the Lord, a curse on him!*
> *Marana, ta! [Our Lord, come!]*

In the King James Version, *anathema* is actually translated into the English word "accursed" four other times in the New Testament: Romans 9:3, 1 Corinthians 12:3, and in the following two verses, Galatians 1:8-9:

> *But even if we, or an angel from heaven, preach any*
> *other gospel to you than what we have preached to you,*
> *let him be **accursed** [Greek anathema].*
> *As we have said before, so now I say again, if anyone*
> *preaches any other gospel to you than what you have*
> *received, let him be **accursed** [Greek anathema].*

This Greek word stems from the Hebrew word *kherem* meaning anything devoted or consecrated to God for destruction, something unredeemable. At times, it was used for various animal sacrifices, but it was also used in very serious ways, such as the prophetic declaration over the city of Jericho, described as "accursed" in the King James Version of the Bible and "doomed by the LORD to destruction" in the New King James Version (Joshua 6:17).

According to various modern Catholic teachers, the *Anathema* declarations of the Council of Trent were merely announcements of excommunication, not decrees of divine judgment causing crumbling chaos in the lives of the guilty (as some Protestants assume). It is also often proposed that these curses of excommunication were pronounced only over wayward Catholics, not non-Catholics. However, that seems unlikely, since Paul insisted even angels preaching a false gospel are to be anathematized—indicating something far more dreadful than excommunication from the church. It must have meant banishment from the very presence of God and the overwhelming negative consequences of spiritual darkness.

Catholics now insist the *Anathema* proclamations were for the purpose of inciting repentance and were not an assignment to ultimate destruction and damnation, because only God has the authority to make such a severe determination. That's true, that only God has such authority. However, by the Catholic standard, excommunication (separation from the church), unless rescinded, would ultimately result in eternal separation from God in the next. So, denying such a connection is simply linguistic juggling.

A lot has changed in the last five centuries. The following excerpt from an excellent Catholic article brings up some important points on this subject that should help to pour water on the fire. (Of course, the coals may still sizzle.) Concerning the one-hundred-plus *Anathema* proclamations of the Council of Trent, this writer offers:

> "Among ecumenical councils, this usage began with the first—I Nicea (A.D. 325)—which applied the formula to those denying the divinity of Christ. Since then the formula has been used by all ecumenical councils that have issued dogmatic canons . . . Over time, a distinction came to be made between excommunication and anathema. The precise nature of

the distinction varied but eventually became fixed. By the time of Gregory IX (1370–1378), the term *anathema* was used to describe a major excommunication that was performed with a solemn pontifical ceremony. This customarily involved the ringing of a bell, the closing of a book, and the snuffing out of candles, collectively signifying that the highest ecclesiastical court had spoken and would not reconsider the matter until the individual gave evidence of repentance.

Such solemnities have been rare in Church history. They remained on the books, however, as late as the 1917 *Code of Canon Law*, which provided that, "Excommunication . . . is called anathema especially when it is imposed with the solemnities that are described in the Roman Pontifical" (CIC [1917] 2257 §§ 1–2)

Yet the penalty was used so seldom that it was removed from the 1983 *Code of Canon Law*. This means that today the penalty of anathema does not exist in Church law. The new Code provided that, "When this Code goes into effect, the following are abrogated: 1° the *Code of Canon Law* promulgated in 1917 . . . 3° any universal or particular penal laws whatsoever issued by the Apostolic See, unless they are contained in this Code" (CIC [1983] 6 §1). **The penalty of anathema was not renewed in the new Code, and thus it was abrogated when the Code went into effect on January 1, 1983.**[184] (bold emphasis by the author of this book)

Alright, that's wonderful! Praise God! But wait just a moment! Even if *anathema* curses, at one point, had to be personally applied by a pope performing a special ceremony, that does not apply to what happened at the Council of Trent. Those curses normally started with the simple three-word phrase, "If any one," not an expanded wording, "If any one mentioned specifically by the pope during a proper excommunication ritual." Moreover, going back to the apostle Paul, the *anathema* declarations in his epistles did not have to be activated by any additional apostolic ritual or personalized to be potent. Nor were they uttered only concerning those who once embraced the faith. So those points unravel quickly. Acknowledging that the *anathema* penalties were abrogated in 1983 is a strong and helpful statement. That means, thankfully—if that is true and if it is a belief that is universally accepted throughout the Catholic Church—that they are no longer considered to be in effect. However, some Catholic authors speak of them as if they are still operational. So why should we even consider them now?

Four important reasons:

1. To show how unyielding and serious the official Catholic stance was in 1563 concerning the doctrines and practices associated with these curses,

2. To underscore the seriousness of offering a different opinion on any of these critically important matters,

3. To make it known that the modern Catholic view has apparently softened—that Protestants should not continue to make this issue a source of contention—and that the original anathema declarations are supposedly no longer the official Catholic standard,

4. To show the somber and serious resolve that must accompany a presentation such as this book that I have authored.

Most of the primary doctrinal positions offered in this book were addressed, to one degree or another, by the curses of the Council of Trent. So, even though they have apparently officially been abrogated, still, if there was any possibility these proclamations had some kind of residual, lingering effect—and if there were any possibility that I am wrong in anything I have written and the traditional Catholic positions are right, it should make me very reluctant to publish this manuscript.

If by some remote chance, the curses were still operational—and if they meant more than just excommunication—then if I am wrong, those curses would all converge on my life and engulf me, not only for time, but for eternity.

However, if I am right (and of course, I believe with all my heart that I am), any lingering five-century-old curses will fall powerlessly around me and the truths I have shared will be healing waters to thousands of precious Catholic people who are thirsty for authentic New Testament Christianity. This is my hope and my prayer.

My final response to the Council of Trent curses

So, what is my response to these curses proclaimed at the Council of Trent? Very simple. No concern at all. No sense of foreboding. No fear. No worry. No outrage. Just peace, and patience, and love.

Most modern Catholics would say the same thing—that they no longer embrace such a mindset or subscribe to the same kind of language (even though I have discovered in many Catholic sources deep appreciation and respect for the Council of Trent, its conclusions, and its accomplishments).

I look back and recoil in horror at the way many Protestants and Catholics treated each other during that time when the initial breach took place. Thank God, we have grown culturally, socially, and spiritually since that tumultuous era.

Prior to discovering the truths of God's Word for myself, I embraced many false religious beliefs, including non-Christian world-views. Yet God was very patient with me—and He led me step-by-step. So, it makes sense that I should be just as patient with others, doing my utmost to lead them to the truth with graciousness, even those who unfortunately "oppose themselves" by rejecting the true revelation of God's Word (2 Timothy 2:25). Hopefully, those who disagree with me will be equally patient with me and we will be able to calmly discuss these vitally important matters.

In His first recorded sermon, Jesus advised His followers to maintain an attitude that both Catholics and non-Catholics should enshrine in their worldview:

"Bless those who curse you!" (Matthew 5:44, Luke 6:28)

Whether we agree on doctrinal issues or not, if we show this kind of Christlike love to each other, the world will certainly be a much better place to live.

Appendix #7 / The Sabbath Controversy: Saturday, Sunday, or something different?

Since the beginning of the Church Age, controversy has swirled around the issue of the proper day of the week Christians should claim as their "Sabbath" (their day of rest and corporate worship toward God). Is Saturday or Sunday the correct choice for true New Covenant believers? Was this ancient tradition corrupted and even paganized at a certain point in church history, as some believers insist? Is it necessary to make a choice between these two options, or is there a third explanation that is profoundly deep and wonderfully uplifting? These questions need to be answered. However, I do not provide a full response in this book for two reasons:

1. Worshiping corporately on Sunday is not just a Catholic tradition; most Protestant churches also gather on the first day of the week. This book focuses more on issues that relate primarily only to Catholicism.

2. Fully examining all the facets of this subject requires a lengthier article than I have room for in this book. So a more thorough version has been posted on two of our main websites:

Under "Writings" on www.toCatholicswithlove.org

Under "Biblical Writings" on www.thetruelight.net

Here is a brief overview of the pertinent points:

When God spoke the Ten Commandments from Mount Sinai, the fourth commandment (the third for Catholics) was "Remember the Sabbath day, to keep it holy" (Exodus 20:8). Without question, that was a reference to Saturday: the seventh day of the week.

Some believers contend that Christians are still required to hallow Saturday as the Sabbath, just as God originally required, and gather to worship on that day. Why, when, and how did the shift to Sunday worship take place anyway?

In the early days of Christianity, believers gathered on the first day of the week (Sunday), probably because of the following reasons:

- First, because it was the day that Jesus rose from the dead and it was the day that the Holy Spirit fell in the upper room. Since that was the timing of the birth of the church and the beginning of the New Covenant era, it must have seemed fitting to early believers to meet weekly on that day (see Acts 20:7 and 1 Corinthians 16:2).

- Second, early believers probably intentionally gathered at a different time than when Jews met at the synagogue, so that Jews who were not yet converted could more easily attend and hear the Gospel.

- Third, there was increasing tension between the two belief systems, traditions, and modes of worship, with severe persecution rising against the church by traditional Jews. This forced a fissure between the two groups that grew over time.

Then, in 321 A.D., after supposedly experiencing a Christian conversion, the emperor Constantine passed a law requiring that Sunday be the day of rest each week throughout the Roman empire. Although Christianity was finally accepted and even celebrated, unfortunately, that law was also an official recognition of sun worship (Sun-day): a pagan practice. So, Christians and Pagans began hallowing the same day. This was only one facet of various ways paganism began infiltrating the church at that time.

About forty years later, during the Council of Laodicea held in 364 A.D., the following declaration was ratified by Catholic leaders, putting the nail in the coffin of a Saturday Sabbath for all who professed Christianity (Canon 29):

> "Christians shall not Judaize and be idle on Saturday, but shall work on that day; but the Lord's day they shall especially honour, and, as being Christians, shall if possible, do no work on that day. If, however, they are found Judaizing, they shall be shut out from Christ."[185] [The phrase "shut out" means anathematized, excommunicated.]

Those who made such a radical decision should have reread Paul's convincing exhortation to the Roman church:

> *Who are you to judge another's servant? To his own*
> *master he stands or falls. Indeed, he will be made to*
> *stand, for God is able to make him stand.*
> **One person esteems one day above another; another**
> **esteems every day alike.** *Let each be fully*
> *convinced in his own mind.*
> *He who observes the day, observes it to the Lord; and*
> *he who does not observe the day,*
> *to the Lord he does not observe it.*
> *(Romans 14:4-6)*

Another apostolic directive given to the Galatians by Paul is even more convicting and convincing:

> *You observe days and months and*
> *seasons and years.*
> *I am afraid for you, lest I have*
> *labored for you in vain.*
> *(Galatians 4:10-11)*

One of his most revealing insights was shared with the Colossian church:

> *So let no one judge you in food or in drink, or*
> *regarding a festival or a new moon or sabbaths, which*
> *are a shadow of things to come,*
> *but the substance is of Christ.*
> *(Colossians 2:16-17)*

Two things about this statement should draw our attention:

First, the word "sabbaths" is in the plural, so Paul was talking about more than just the seventh day of the week. It was also a reference to seven other "Sabbath" days during the year when Jews are to refrain from work (the first and last day of the Feast of Unleavened Bread, the Feast of Pentecost, the Feast of Trumpets, the Day of Atonement, and the first and last days of the Feast of Tabernacles). All of these feast days were both memorials of past events in Israel's history and prophetic foreshadowings of far greater things God was yet to do in the future. For instance, the Feast of Pentecost was a memorial of the visitation, fifty days out of Egypt, when God spoke the Ten Commandments from Mount Sinai, on fire with His presence, to the entire nation of Israel. However, the annual feast was also prophetic of a more glorious event yet to come.

Fifty days after Jesus' resurrection, during the Feast of Pentecost, that same holy fire consumed a group of believers in the upper room and the Spirit of God preached the Gospel out of them in tongues to Jews from many countries, launching the New Covenant era—a time when God promised to write His commandments, not in stone, but in the hearts of His people (see Acts 2:1-7, Jeremiah 31:31-34). What God did on that day for the disciples in the upper room was "the substance" (the far more important and profound end result); the Feast of Pentecost celebrated yearly by the Jews was "the shadow"—a symbolic way of forecasting something better that was yet to come.

Second, even as the seven sabbatical feast days were prophetic of greater, more important, more profound things in the future, so the Old Testament tradition of a weekly Sabbath was also "a shadow of good things to come" (Hebrews 10:1 KJV). The "shadow" was just a time of physical rest, once a week, that enabled Jews to focus on spiritual matters; the "substance" is the supreme privilege of entering the rest of God—every minute, of every hour, or every day. Jesus invited us to enter this supernatural rest in the following beloved passage:

> *"Come to Me, all you who labor and are heavy laden,*
> *and I will give you rest.*
> *Take My yoke upon you and learn from Me,*
> *for I am gentle and lowly in heart,*
> *and you will find rest for your souls.*
> *For My yoke is easy and My burden is light."*
> *(Matthew 11:28-30)*

Now we no longer are confined to one day a week. Jesus, our "Lord of the Sabbath," causes us to rest in God continually (Luke 6:5). It really is all about Jesus! No wonder Hebrews 4:9 promises, "There remains, therefore, a Sabbath rest for the people of God" (ISV). This is far more than a single weekly event; it is a constant experience of heart for those who truly know the Son of God as Lord of their lives—which is far more important and far more profound.

Meeting on a weekly basis

Does this mean we should refrain from meeting with others in the body of Christ weekly? Absolutely not! Because the Bible exhorts:

> *And let us consider one another in order to stir up love*
> *and good works, not forsaking the assembling of our-*
> *selves together, as is the manner of some, but exhorting*
> *one another, and so much the more as you see the Day*
> *approaching. (Hebrews 10:24-25)*

This is not something Christians are bound to legalistically, but something we should implement lovingly and worshipfully—not because we have to, but because we want to. It should be our joy to gather with fellow believers. Whether that happens on Saturday, or Sunday, or every day of the week is truly irrelevant.

What matters most is possessing what the Sabbath symbolizes: being at peace *with* God and receiving the peace *of* God that passes understanding, then abiding in that peace toward God and toward others every day of our lives. It means confidently trusting God to do a complete and eternal work in us—with no doubt, no fear, no worry, and no anxiety. "God rested on the seventh day from all His works" (those manifested and those yet to be) and "we who have believed do enter that rest" (Hebrew 4:3-4, see verses 1-11).

In Old Testament times, God's people went to the temple, to the priests, to offer a sacrifice, on special feast days. In the New Testament, we become the temple. We become the priests. We become the sacrifice, and our celebration is not on designated days; it is constant, and will continue for all time and eternity.

Important Bible passages for further study on this subject:
- Multiple Sabbath days (Exodus 31:12-13),
- Rewards of Sabbath-keeping under the Old Covenant (Isaiah 58:13-14),

- How Jesus magnified the law (Matthew 5:21-45, John 4:21-24),
- What Jesus said about the Sabbath (Mark 2:23-28, Luke 6:1-5).

Be sure to read the full article on one of our websites. It goes into much more detail about this controversial subject.

Appendix #8 / The Three Legs of Catholicism

The "three legs" of Catholicism (also called the three "pillars") are as follows: Sacred Scripture, Sacred Tradition, and the Magisterium. The authority of the Catholic Church rests on these three things.

Sacred Scriptures

The "Sacred Scriptures" for a Catholic includes seven books that are not in the Protestant Bible. There are seventy-three (73) total, as compared to sixty-six (66) in the approved Protestant Canon of Scripture. (The word "canon" means measuring line, stick, or rule.) In the Catholic Bible there are forty-six (46) books in the Old Testament instead of thirty-nine (39). Both Bible versions have the same twenty-seven (27) books in the New Testament.

The seven extra books in the Catholic Bible are called the Deuterocanonical books (meaning second canon). Protestants often refer to them as "the Apocrypha" (meaning hidden or secret). Those books are Tobit, Judith, Baruch, Sirach (also called Ecclesiasticus), 1 Maccabees, 2 Maccabees and Wisdom (also called Wisdom of Solomon), as well as additions to Esther, Daniel, and Baruch. These were included in the Septuagint, the Greek translation of the Old Testament from the Hebrew that was produced in the third century B.C. but were not in the original Hebrew Bible.

The Septuagint also resulted in the Psalms being in a different order in the Catholic Bible. Both Bibles contain a list of 150 psalms. However, the Protestant Bible, which was based on the original Hebrew, divides Psalm 9 into two psalms (Psalms 9 & 10). Then it combines Psalms 146 and 147 into one. As a result, the psalms in between are numbered differently.

Some Catholics claim that Martin Luther was under a curse because he transgressed the warning of Revelation 22:18-19 by removing these seven deuterocanonical books to form the Protestant Bible. However, that accusation is evidently wrong—because that passage in the book of the Revelation only refers to that particular book of the Bible. It reads as follows:

*For I testify to everyone who hears the words of the
prophecy of this book: If anyone adds to these things,
God will add to him the plagues that are
written in this book;
and if anyone takes away from the words of the book
of this prophecy, God shall take away his part from the
Book of Life, from the holy city, and from the things
which are written in this book.*

If that curse was a reference to the entire Bible, then it was a grave transgression to add the twenty-seven books of the New Testament to the Old Testament canon of Scripture. Because it is generally believed the book of the Revelation was written around 97 A.D., yet the first known list of the twenty-seven accepted and respected New Testament books came around 367 A.D. (The 39th Festal Letter of Athanasius)

This subject becomes very complicated very quickly, but it does not warrant the concerns that arise from it. Why? Because none of these differences between the two Bibles significantly affect the portions of the Word of God that are most important to us, the parts containing primary doctrines concerning our eternal salvation, being forgiven of sin, and entering and maintaining a relationship with the true God.

Though some Catholic-leaning students of the Bible claim that 2 Maccabees 12:39-46 validates the doctrine of Purgatory, and 2 Maccabees 15:14-17 upholds the idea of praying to the saints, these two claims are clearly refuted in Chapters 11 and 21 of this book. "Sacred Scripture," even the Catholic version with its seven extra books, ironically, can be used to disprove many primary Catholic doctrines. Therefore, claiming this as one of the three legs of Catholicism could very well prove ultimately counterproductive.

The true Word of God is "forever settled in heaven" (Psalms 119:89). Once discovered, it should also be "forever settled" in our hearts—above and beyond the traditions of men and the hierarchy, not only of Catholicism, but of any Protestant denomination. However, "Sacred Traditions" and "The Magisterium" are assigned an equal standing in the Catholic Church. Let's visit those two complementary legs now.

Sacred Traditions

Evidently, "Sacred Traditions" guided the early church long before the New Testament "Sacred Scriptures" were written and preserved for future generations. The early church did not have the twenty-seven books from Matthew to Revelation (though they may have had some of the single epistles and gospels). However, they did have traditions handed down by their respected leaders, the original disciples and apostles. Note these two communications from the apostle Paul:

> *Therefore, brethren, stand fast and hold the **traditions***
> *which you were taught, whether by word or our epistle.*
> *(2 Thessalonians 2:15)*

> *Imitate me, just as I also imitate Christ.*
> *Now I praise you, brethren, that you remember me*
> *in all things and keep the **traditions** just as*
> *I delivered them to you.*
> *(1 Corinthians 11:1-2)*

In the beginning, the only way Christians could "earnestly contend for the faith which was once delivered unto the saints" was by clinging to the oral traditions they received and passed on from trusted sources (Jude 1:3). These covered a whole array of Christian beliefs and practices. However, not all religious traditions are good, even if they stream from "trusted sources" (like the Sanhedrin Court in Jesus' day). Some may be extremely helpful, while others are extremely harmful. Carefully read the following accusation that the Jewish rulers hurled toward Jesus and the searing rebuke He flung back at them:

> *Then the scribes and Pharisees who were from*
> *Jerusalem came to Jesus, saying,*
> ***"Why do Your disciples transgress the tradition of the***

elders? For they do not wash their
hands when they eat bread."
*He answered and said to them, "**Why do you also***
transgress the commandment of God
because of your tradition?
For God commanded, saying, 'Honor your father and
your mother'; and, 'He who curses father or mother, let
him be put to death.'
But you say, 'Whoever says to his father or mother,
"Whatever profit you might have received
from me is a gift to God"—
then he need not honor his father or mother.'
Thus you have made the commandment of God
of no effect by your tradition.
Hypocrites! Well did Isaiah prophesy
about you, saying:
'These people draw near to Me with their mouth,
and honor Me with their lips, but their
heart is far from Me.
and in vain they worship Me, teaching as
doctrines the commandments of men.'"
(Matthew 15:1-9)

Just because something can be labeled "traditional" does not mean
it is good or bad. Peter even addressed some family traditions in a very
negative way (though many "family traditions" are positive and good):

Knowing that you were not redeemed with corruptible
things, like silver or gold, from your aimless conduct
*[your worthless way of life] **received by***
tradition from your fathers,
But with the precious blood of Christ, as of a lamb
without blemish and without spot.
(1 Peter 1:18-19 NKJV, CJB)

So we, as believers, must have discernment and we must be dis-
criminating. We must tenaciously cling to some traditions and hurl
other traditions as far away from us as possible. We need God's help

in knowing the difference. A Catholic ministry in Canada defends this second leg of Catholicism by asserting:

> "Sacred Tradition faithfully preserves and tran-
> mits the entirety of the Gospel or Deposit of Faith in
> a living way in the Church, through the Apostles and
> their successors (the Bishops), all accomplished in the
> Holy Spirit, and it is every bit as authoritative as Sacred
> Scripture (see CCC 76-78 and 81-82)."[186]

Repeat that last phrase slowly. You might even want to read it out loud, "Sacred tradition . . . is every bit as authoritative as Sacred Scripture." That's a bold statement—too bold for me. The same article goes on to say, "Unquestionably, the Church in the first 400 years of Christianity was very much a church of Oral (Sacred) Tradition." **But that was then, and this is now.**

Early Christians had to depend on oral sacred tradition, but now, we have the entire Word of God. The vast majority of the traditions that were initially handed down orally in the beginning of Christianity are now preserved in written form in the New Testament. In light of this, two important questions need to be asked:

1. If modern Catholic traditions cannot be found in the Word of God, should they still be embraced?

2. If modern Catholic traditions actually contradict the Word of God, should they be deemed acceptable, and the Word of God relegated to an inferior position?

The answer to both of these questions should be a loud, resounding "No!" At this juncture in the evolution of the church, if traditions are not in alignment with the Bible, they should be labeled spurious and manmade—worthy of being discarded. A very appropriate way to end this section is by quoting Colossians 2:8—which incidentally is part of the written Word of God:

> *Beware lest any man spoil you through philosophy and*
> *vain deceit, after **the tradition of men**, after the*
> *rudiments of the world, and not after Christ.*

Let that warning echo many times in our hearts"—Beware lest any man spoil you" (robbing you of your most precious possession: the glorious inheritance you have received from the King of glory).

The Magisterium

As shared under Question #2, the word "Magisterium" is from the Latin word *magister* meaning teaching. Within Catholicism, it means three primary, related things:

1. The authority to teach the doctrine of Christ,

2. The authorities in the Catholic Church who declare those doctrines (the pope—who is the Bishop of Rome—as well as all the other bishops in the church, united together),

3. The authorized teachings themselves.

The "Magisterium" is a reference only to those teachings of the church considered infallible. "Ordinary magisterium . . . refers to the ordinary teaching of the popes and bishops as they conduct their ministry. Sometimes, though, they teach in an especially solemn way that is referred to as an act of the extraordinary magisterium. In the case of popes, this term is reserved only for instances when a pope infallibly defines a truth" (when the pope speaks *ex cathedra*).[187] "All other instances of papal teaching are termed 'ordinary.'"[188]

Catholic teachings on faith and morals established by an ecumenical council are also considered "extraordinary Magisterium." Another related descriptive term is "universal Magisterium," a reference to authoritative teachings that are established throughout the entire church worldwide. "Loyal submission of the will and intellect" is expected of all Catholics to those doctrines established through the Magisterium.[189]

Once again, the question must be posed—What if teachings from the Magisterium go contrary to the Word of God? Do we dare propose that this third "leg" of Catholicism is of equal height with the Bible? Or can we be even more daring and admit that men are subject to error, so the Bible must be our supreme authority? The Magisterium from one era to the next has been known to contradict itself, such as the promotion of "the idea that the soul enters the body some time after conception vs. more recent magisterial teachings that say ensoulment happens at conception. Both things having been taught at the level of ordinary universal magisterium."[190] The proper definition of when that happens is a serious issue. The fact that the Magisterium in two eras can differ on such an important matter shows clearly that the officials and the doctrines of the Magisterium can be seriously flawed.

Remember, the Sanhedrin Court and the rabbinical authorities in Jesus' day were considered the "Magisterium" of that era—yet they missed it horribly, even to the point of crucifying the Son of God. Could history repeat itself? Of course, just as there were noble and sincere, God-loving Jewish authorities in high positions of authority in the Sanhedrin in Jesus' day (like Nicodemus and Joseph of Arimathea), so there are many noble and sincere, God-loving priests, nuns, monks, and bishops now. You may be one of them. I urge you to be courageous. Dare to embrace truth, no matter what the cost.

Appendix #9 / Get connected online

The Catholic Project / www.toCatholicswithlove.org

The address says it all. Our website has been created as a space for Catholics to explore concepts important to them, comparing the Catholic belief system to biblical Christianity, as well as connecting with other former Catholics who have experienced the joy of being born again and filled with the Spirit of God. We love you and we love sharing the love of God with you.

The True Light Project / www.thetruelight.net

Mike Shreve explored eastern religions after leaving the Catholic faith and before encountering the Lord Jesus Christ. He was heavily invested in the practice of yoga and meditation, teaching yoga at four universities and running a yoga ashram in Tampa, Florida, until that blessed day when he was born again. This website was created to share the Gospel with those of a New Age or Far Eastern mindset. It contains personal transformation stories, pertinent articles, and teaching videos full of biblical truths that set people free.

Shreve Ministries / www.shreveministries.org

This is our main ministry website where you will find relevant articles, our speaking itinerary, audio and video teachings, and our complete bookstore, as well as other offerings for the people of God.

Deeper Revelation Books / www.deeperrevelationbooks.org

If you are a Christian writer and would like to become a published author, visit our publishing company website. Our vision is to help you fulfill your vision. Our mission is to change the world one book at a time. Mike Shreve and his associates have a wealth of publishing knowledge that will help you achieve success with your book project. Most importantly, they consider every published book an act of worship offered to God.

Connect by email: You may email Mike Shreve and his staff from any of the websites mentioned in this section or use the address:

mikeshreve@shreveministries.org

Appendix #10 / Other Offerings from Mike Shreve

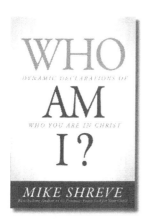

WHO AM I? Dynamic Declarations of Who You Are in Christ—One of the most transformational insights a believer in Jesus can receive is the revelation of our spiritual identity, who we are "in Christ." This is best discovered by studying the names and titles given to the people of God in His Word. Great for personal devotions or group studies.

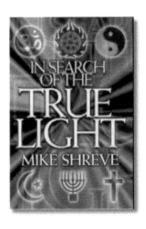

In Search of the True Light—An in-depth comparison of over twenty religions, showing commonalities and contradictions. Mike Shreve also shares his transformation story of coming to Jesus after searching for God in yoga, meditation, and new age spirituality. This is a great book to give someone who is looking for truth in far eastern mystical religions.

25 Powerful Promises from God—There are 7,487 promises in God's Word. This life-changing book highlights 25 of the most powerful with both a biblical teaching and a real life testimony showing the fulfillment of God's Word. This is one of the most encouraging revelations believers could receive!

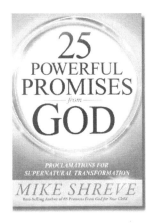

65 Promises from God for Your Child—God has given 65 promises in His Word concerning those things He pledges to do for the offspring of believers who commit their lives to Him. Praying, believing, and confessing these promises over our children is a powerful way of interceding in their behalf.

Endnotes

1.   Information drawn from https://media.ascensionpress.com/2019/01/21/the-other-23-catholic-churches-and-why-they-exist/ accessed 3/12/22. Also, https://en.wikipedia.org/wiki/Latin_Church accessed 3/15/2022.

2.   https://sourcebooks.fordham.edu/basis/lateran4.asp, accessed 8/24/2022.

3.   https://heritagebiblechurch.com/free-literature/anathemas-of-the-council-of-trent/, accessed 8/24/2022.

4.   https://www.papalencyclicals.net/pius11/p11morta.htm, accessed 8/24/2022.

5.   Ibid., accessed 8/24/2022.

6.   https://www.vatican.va/roman_curia/congregations/cfaith/documents/rc_con_cfaith_doc_19730705_mysterium-ecclesiae_en.html, accessed 8/24/2022.

7.   Ibid., accessed 8/24/2022.

8.   https://www.usccb.org/offices/general-secretariat/how-new-pope-chosen, accessed 1/6/2022.

9.   https://theconversation.com/should-catholics-view-the-pope-as-infallible-109548#:~:text=The%20First%20Vatican%20Council%20in,matters%20of%20faith%20and%20morals, accessed 10/3/2021.

10.   https://www.population-security.org/19-CH11.html, accessed 9/5/2022. Also, former priest, Richard Bennet, in his video presentation on YouTube, presented this historical fact: https://www.youtube.com/watch?v=7k-jvWchaXE.

11.   https://uscatholic.org/articles/201105/is-there-a-list-of-infallible-teachings/ accessed 1/6/2022.

12.   https://catholicsay.com/what-is-the-meaning-of-the-title-pope/, accessed 1/7/2022.

13.   https://en.wikipedia.org/wiki/Pontifex_maximus, accessed 3/6/2022

14.   Ibid., accessed 3/16/2022.

15.   Ibid., accessed 3/6/2022.

16.   There are differences of opinion concerning the exact wording that should be used during the baptism ceremony. Some choose to say: "I baptize you in the name of the Father, the Son, and the Holy Spirit" (Matthew 28:19). Others choose to say, "I baptize you in the name of the Jesus Christ for the remission of sins" (Acts 2:38). My purpose in this chapter is not to assess the correct wording, as much as the correct method that should be used: full immersion, not sprinkling. Both wordings are scriptural, so both could be combined in one declaration over the person being immersed. What is most important is the posture of the heart during baptism.

17.   https://www.chabad.org/theJewishWoman/article_cdo/aid/1541/jewish/The-Mikvah.htm, accessed 1/22/2022.

18.   https://www.catholic.com/magazine/online-edition/infant-baptism, accessed 1/23/2022.

19.   https://www.catholic.com/magazine/print-edition/can-infants-be-born-again, accessed 1/23/2022.

20.   https://www.catholic.com/magazine/print-edition/to-explain-infant-baptism-you-must-explain-original-sin, accessed 1/23/2022.

21. CCC 1250, https://www.catholic.com/magazine/online-edition/infant-baptism, accessed 1/14/2022.

22. https://www.catholic.com/magazine/online-edition/infant-baptism, accessed 2/2/2022.

23. https://www.catholicculture.org/culture/library/catechism/index.cfm?recnum=1472, accessed 10/3/2021.

24. https://en.wikipedia.org/wiki/Clerical_clothing, accessed 2/25/2022.

25. https://www.catholic.com/tract/celibacy-and-the-priesthood, 7/9/2022.

26. https://historynewsnetwork.org/article/696, accessed 2/3/2022.

27. https://www.catholic.com/tract/celibacy-and-the-priesthood, accessed 7/9/2022.

28. https://futurechurch.org/future-of-priestly-ministry/history-of-celibacy/, accessed 7/9/2022.

29. https://www.aboutcatholics.com/beliefs/mortal-sins/, accessed 6/30/2022.

30. https://stmaryofthesevendolors.com/prayers-2/list-of-mortal-sins-every-catholic-should-know/, accessed 6/30/2022.

31. http://www.saintaquinas.com/mortal_sin.html, accessed 6/30/2022.

32. https://www.britannica.com/topic/cardinal-sin, accessed 6/30/2022.

33. https://www.catholicculture.org/culture/library/dictionary/index.cfm?id=37060, accessed 6/25/2022.

34. https://www.aboutcatholics.com/beliefs/mortal-sins/, accessed 6/29/2022.

35. https://www.catholic.com/magazine/online-edition/mortal-and-venial-sin, accessed 3/23/2023.

36. https://www.newadvent.org/cathen/11618c.htm, accessed 9/27/2022. This article is a very thorough presentation of the Catholic position on the sacrament of Reconciliation.

37. Ibid., accessed 9/27/2022.

38. Ibid., accessed 9/27/2022.

39. https://www.catholic.com/magazine/print-edition/god-chooses-to-uses-human-intermediaries, accessed 8/31/2022.

40. https://bulldogcatholic.org/wp-content/uploads/2018/12/a-detailed-catholic-examination-of-conscience-2nd-ed..pdf, accessed 9/1/2022.

41. https://www.loyolapress.com/catholic-resources/prayer/traditional-catholic-prayers/prayers-every-catholic-should-know/act-of-contrition/, accessed 8/31/2022.

42. https://hallow.com/2022/04/01/how-to-go-to-confession-the-sacrament-of-penance-reconciliation/#:~:text=Often%2C%20you'll%20be%20able,should%20love%20above%20all%20things., accessed 8/31/2022.

43. https://www.thecatholicthing.org/2017/10/04/penance-after-confession/, accessed 9/1/2022.

44. https://www.catholic.com/magazine/online-edition/is-confession-in-scripture, accessed 2/23/2022.

45. https://canonlawmadeeasy.com/2020/04/30/confession-over-phone/, accessed 2/26/2022.

46. https://www.ncronline.org/news/vatican/francis-chronicles/if-you-cant-go-confession-take-your-sorrow-directly-god-pope-says, accessed 2/26/2022.

47. https://bustedhalo.com/questionbox/what-is-the-prayer-of-absolution, accessed 2/26/2022.

48. https://www.thecatholicthing.org/2016/03/09/penance-absolution-and-forgiveness-of-sins/, accessed 9/29/2022.

49. https://www.catholicculture.org/culture/library/dictionary/index.cfm?id=33481, accessed 10/1/2022.

50. Hardon, John. *The Question and Answer Catholic Catechism.* The Crown Publishing Group. Kindle Edition. #1382, #1384

51. https://en.wikipedia.org/wiki/Self-flagellation#:~:text=In%20the%2011th%20century%2C%20Peter,recite%20forty%20Psalms%2C%20increasing%20the, accessed 2/26/2022.

52. Halley, *Halley's Bible Handbook*, "The Reformation" (Grand Rapids, Michigan: Zondervan Publishing House, 1967) page 787..

53. https://www.ligonier.org/learn/articles/fortress-truth-martin-luther, 2/26/2022.

54. Ibid., 9/2/2022.

55. Ibid., 2/26/2022.

56. Roland H. Bainton, *Here I Stand, A Life of Martin Luther* (Nashville Tennessee: Abington Press, 1978) page 49.

57. https://www.vatican.va/archive/ccc_css/archive/catechism/p2s2c2a4.htm, accessed 11/23/2021.

58. https://en.wikipedia.org/wiki/Penance, accessed 7/30/2022.

59. https://en.wikipedia.org/wiki/Douay%E2%80%93Rheims_Bible, accessed 8/3/2022.

60. https://www.vatican.va/archive/ENG0015/__P4C.HTM, accessed 8/3/2022.

61. https://www.catholiceducation.org/en/culture/catholic-contributions/the-process-of-becoming-a-saint.html, accessed 3/25/2022.

62. https://www.encyclopedia.com/religion/encyclopedias-almanacs-transcripts-and-maps/canonization-saints-history-and-procedure, accessed 9/3/2022.

63. https://www.catholiceducation.org/en/culture/catholic-contributions/the-process-of-becoming-a-saint.html, accessed 3/25/2022.

64. https://www.encyclopedia.com/religion/encyclopedias-almanacs-transcripts-and-maps/canonization-saints-history-and-procedure, accessed 9/3/2022.

65. https://www.pewresearch.org/fact-tank/2014/04/24/papal-saints-once-a-given-now-extremely-rare/

66. https://uscatholic.org/articles/201310/how-many-saints-are-there/ accessed 3/26/2022.

67. https://www.google.com/search?q=what+is+the+devil%27s+advocate&rlz=1C1EJFC_enUS820US820&oq=what+is+the+devil%27s+advocate&aqs=chrome..69i57.4481j1j7&sourceid=chrome&ie=UTF-8, accessed 3/26/2022.

68. https://www.interestingfacts.com/fact/62157c62d64d450007a2189a#621579b99e2b600007588c37, accessed 3/25/2022.

69.   https://www.azquotes.com/quote/671296#:~:text=%22I%20am%20a%20 saved%20sinner,or%20you%20are%20a%20sinner, accessed 4/6/2022.

70.   https://www.learnreligions.com/why-do-catholics-pray-to-saints-542856, accessed 3/9/2022.

71.   https://www.patheos.com/blogs/davearmstrong/2016/05/asking-saints-to-intercede-teaching-of-jesus.html, accessed 3/25/2022.

72.   Ibid.

73.   https://www.cs.cmu.edu/~spok/catholic/rosary.html, accessed 8/3/2022.

74.   Information drawn from https://www.dummies.com/article/body-mind-spirit/religion-spirituality/christianity/catholicism/how-to-pray-the-rosary-192609/ which was compiled by various Catholic theologians, accessed 8/3/2022.

75.   https://www.tektonministries.org/st-dominic-and-the-origins-of-the-rosary/, accessed 9/7/2022.

76.   Ibid., accessed 9/7/2022.

77.   https://stpaulcenter.com/understanding-marys-perpetual-virginity/ accessed 10-26-21.

78.   https://en.wikipedia.org/wiki/Parthenon, accessed 8/4/2022.

79.   https://www.churchpop.com/2016/08/14/why-was-mary-assumed-into-heaven-while-jesus-ascended-the-answer-matters/, accessed 8/6/2022.

80.   https://en.wikipedia.org/wiki/Queen_of_Heaven, accessed 11/10/21.

81.   https://en.wikipedia.org/wiki/Queen_of_Heaven#:~:text=The%20Catholic%20faith%20states%2C%20as,the%20work%20of%20eternal%20salvation, accessed 4/16/22.

82.   https://en.wikipedia.org/wiki/Second_Vatican_Council, accessed 4/16/22, https://en.wikipedia.org/wiki/Mediatrix, accessed 4/16/22.

83.   https://www.catholic.com/magazine/print-edition/is-marys-queenship-biblical, accessed 4/16/22.

84.   https://www.ncregister.com/blog/revelation-12-who-is-the-woman-clothed-with-the-sun, accessed 8/6/2022. All Pope Benedict quotes on this page.

85.   Ibid., accessed 8/6/2022.

86.   https://www.amazon.com/Behold-Your-Mother-Historical-Doctrines/dp/1938983912/ref=sr_1_1?crid=364IFYXOI8RJ5&keywords=behold+your+mother&qid=1676683451&s=books&sprefix=behold+your+mother%2Cstripbooks%2C63&sr=1-1, accessed 10/08/2022.

87.   https://www.britannica.com/topic/Hail-Mary-prayer, accessed 4/23/2022.

88.   https://www.aboutcatholics.com/beliefs/catholic-confirmation-explained/, accessed 4/21/2022.

89.   https://www.catholic.com/qa/we-receive-the-holy-spirit-at-baptism, accessed 4/21/2022.

90.   http://rclbsacraments.com/confirmation/walkthrough-confirmation-rite, accessed 4/21/2022.

91.   For an in-depth explanation, read the article titled "The Baptism with the Holy Spirit" in the biblical teaching section of www.toCatholicswithlove.org or in our comparative religion website: www.thetruelight.net.

92.   https://www.youcat.org/credopedia/gifts-of-the-holy-spirit/accessed 10/20/2021.

93.   https://www.olqoa.org/wp-content/uploads/2018/08/Choosing-a-confirmation-saint-name-.pdf, accessed 4/17/2022. The list of saints at this link shares supposed areas of influence or expertise various saints possess. This is supposed to help a Catholic choose the best patron saint, most fitted to intercede for him/her and most effective as a guide through life.

94.   https://www.bibleinfo.com/en/topics/ten-commandments-list, accessed 4/30/2022.

95.   https://www.cam1.org.au/en-us1/Catholic-Faith/Church-Teaching/The-Ten-Commandments, accessed 4/30/2022.

96.   https://www.catholic.com/magazine/print-edition/the-bible-supports-praying-to-the-saints, accessed 4/30/2022.

97.   Ibid., accessed 4/30/2022.

98.   https://www.ecatholic2000.com/councils/untitled-21.shtml, accessed 2/21/2023.

99.   https://www.mercyhome.org/blog/sunday-mass/why-are-prayer-candles-used-in-the-catholic-church/#:~:text=In%20our%20churches%20today%2C%20we,we%20continue%20on%20our%20day, accessed 5/12/2022.

100.   https://en.wikipedia.org/wiki/Ceremonial_use_of_lights, accessed 5/7/2022.

101.   https://www.washingtonpost.com/archive/local/2003/05/10/for-zoroastrians-a-luminous-home/6753a391-5975-4afe-ab0d-7cc261023a1b/,accessed 5/7/2022.

102.   https://blog.buddhagroove.com/the-significance-and-use-of-candles-in-spiritual-practice/ accessed 5/13/2022.

103.   https://www.nylon.com/life/ask-a-witch-candle-magick, accessed 5/7/2022.

104.   https://en.wikipedia.org/wiki/Ceremonial_use_of_lights, accessed 5/7/2022.

105.   https://www.simplycatholic.com/holy-smoke/ accessed 5/13/2022.

106.   https://adoremus.org/2012/02/holy-smoke-the-use-of-incense-in-the-catholic-church/, accessed 5/14/2022.

107.   https://www.goodcatholic.com/holy-smokes-why-do-catholics-use-incense/ accessed 5/13/2022.

108.   Ibid., accessed 5/13/2022.

109.   https://adoremus.org/2012/02/holy-smoke-the-use-of-incense-in-the-catholic-church/, accessed 5/13/2022.

110.   https://www.ncbi.nlm.nih.gov/pmc/articles/PMC6801997/#:~:text=Buddhists%20regard%20incense%20as%20%E2%80%9Cdivine,26%2C27%2C28%5D., accessed 8/8/2022.

111.   https://en.wikipedia.org/wiki/Religious_use_of_incense#:~:text=The%20use%20of%20incense%20is,such%20as%20Krishna%20and%20Rama, accessed 5/14/2022.

112.   https://en.wikipedia.org/wiki/Religious_use_of_incense#:~:text=The%20use%20of%20incense%20is,such%20as%20Krishna%20and%20Rama, accessed 5/14/2022.

113. https://religion.fandom.com/wiki/Religious_use_of_incense, accessed 5/14/2022.

114. Ibid., accessed 5/14/2022.

115. https://www.interestingfacts.com/fact/62b2100a10a67e00081bf736?utm_source=daily&utm_medium=email&utm_campaign=1540653145#62b20e-6710a67e00081bd7a1, accessed 8/1/2022.

116. https://en.wikipedia.org/wiki/Relic, accessed 5/18/2022.

117. Ad Riparium, i, P.L., XXII, 907.

118. https://en.wikipedia.org/wiki/Second_Council_of_Nicaea, accessed 5/18/2022.

119. https://www.newworldencyclopedia.org/entry/Veil_of_Veronica, accessed 5/18/2022.

120. https://holylandpilgrimages.org/st-helena-the-legend-of-the-true-cross-and-the-holy-sepulcher/, accessed 5/18/2022.

121. https://en.wikipedia.org/wiki/Syriac_Infancy_Gospel, accessed 5/19/2022.

122. https://en.wikipedia.org/wiki/Holy_Prepuce, 5/19/2022.

123. https://historycollection.com/religious-relics-never-found/, accessed 5/18/2022.

124. https://www.buzzfeed.com/tomchivers/how-many-foreskins-does-one-god-need, accessed 5/23/2022.

125. https://www.wired.com/2006/12/whatever-happen/#:~:text=his%20Divine%20Ascension.-,After%20being%20lost%20for%20almost%201500%20years%2C%20Christ's%20foreskin%20(known,become%20the%20rings%20of%20Saturn, accessed 5/19/2022.

126. https://www.cbc.ca/radio/ideas/how-jesus-foreskin-became-one-of-christianity-s-most-coveted-relics-and-then-disappeared-1.6002421, accessed 5/19/2022.

127. Ibid., accessed 5/19/2022.

128. https://www.atlasobscura.com/places/st-anthonystongue#:~:text=Want%20to%20Visit%3F&text=Padua%2C%20Italy-,St.,celebrated%20for%20his%20oratory%20skills, accessed 8/10/22.

129. https://www.history.com/news/saint-john-the-baptist-head-where#:~:text=A%20skull%20identified%20as%20the,artifacts%20from%20the%20Roman%20catacombs, accessed 5/19/2022.

130. Ibid., accessed 8/10/2022.

131. Ibid., accessed 8/10/2022.

132. https://www.thereformationroom.com/single-post/2017/06/04/relics-that-cried-out-for-the-reformation, accessed 5/19/2022.

133. https://freerepublic.com/focus/religion/1050873/posts, accessed 5/21/2022.

134. https://www.famous-trials.com/luther/295-indulgences, accessed 5/21/2022.

135. Ibid., accessed 5/21/2022.

136. https://catholicstraightanswers.com/what-are-relics/, accessed 5/19/2022.

137. https://www.vatican.va/archive/ENG0015/__P2N.HTM, accessed 5/27/2022.

138. https://rcspirituality.org/ask_a_priest/ask-a-priest-why-is-there-Purgatory/, accessed 6/11/2022.

139. https://en.wikipedia.org/wiki/Purgatory accessed 11/12/2021, also https://www.universitycatholic.net/praying-for-the-dead-in-november-book-of-the-dead/, accessed 11/12/2021.

140. https://www.catholic.com/encyclopedia/beatific-vision, accessed 6/11/2022.

141. https://www.catholic.com/magazine/online-edition/does-Purgatory-deny-christs-sacrifice, accessed 6/11/2022.

142. https://www.catholicculture.org/culture/library/catechism/index.cfm?recnum=4704, accessed 5/23/2022.

143. https://www.catholic365.com/article/2909/temporal-punishments-for-sin-what-does-that-mean.html, accessed 6/27/2022.

144. *Manual of Indulgences: NORMS AND GRANTS*, United States Conference of Catholic Bishops, accessed 6/11/2022.

145. https://www.ewtn.com/catholicism/devotions/what-13361, accessed 5/23/2022.

146. https://visitationproject.org/pages/list-requirements-plenary-indulgences, also https://www.ewtn.com/catholicism/devotions/conditions-13362, accessed 6/28/2022.

147. Father Winfrid Herbst, S.D.S., *New Regulations on Indulgences* (Tan Books and Publishers, Inc, Rockford, Illinois, 1970, 1977) e-book version.

148. https://catholicallyear.com/blog/catholic-indulgences-what-they-are-when/, accessed 6/11/22.

149. Ibid., accessed 6/11/2022.

150. https://en.wikipedia.org/wiki/Purgatory accessed 11/12/2021. In Wikipedia it states as the source: Catechism of the Catholic Church § 1030-1031 (section entitled, "The Final Purification, or Purgatory); cf. Council of Florence (1439): DS 1304; Council of Trent (1563): DS 1820; (1547): 1580; see also Benedict XII, Benedictus Deus (1336): DS 1000., accessed 5/27/2022.

151. https://www.catholic.com/tract/primer-on-indulgences, accessed 5/27/2022.

152. Ibid., accessed 5/27/2022.

153. https://catholicallyear.com/blog/catholic-indulgences-what-they-are-when/, quoting from https://www.catholic.com/tract/primer-on-indulgences, accessed 6/11/2022.

154. https://www.famous-trials.com/luther/295-indulgences, accessed 11/15/2021.

155. Ibid., accessed 11/16/2021.

156. https://brewminate.com/forgiveness-for-sale-indulgences-in-the-medieval-church/, accessed 8/11/2022.

157. https://www.britannica.com/topic/limbo-Roman-Catholic-theology, accessed 1/29/2022.

158. https://www.thecatholictelegraph.com/question-of-faith-do-we-still-believe-in-limbo/46903 accessed 11/12/2021.

159. https://www.pewresearch.org/fact-tank/2019/08/05/transubstantiation-eucharist-u-s-catholics/, accessed 8/18/2022.

160. This line of logic is offered by George L. Faull in an article posted on the Summit Theological Seminary website on the subject of "Transubstantiation," http://

www.summit1.org/gun14/gun01.htm, accessed 8/21/2022.

161. https://sourcebooks.fordham.edu/basis/lateran4.asp, accessed 8/24/2022.

162. https://aleteia.org/2017/08/24/why-do-catholics-call-their-main-church-services-mass/, accessed 8/20/2022.

163. https://www.catholic.com/encyclopedia/extreme-unction, accessed 9/2/2022.

164. https://www.learnreligions.com/the-apostles-creed-p2-700364#:~:text=Origins%20of%20the%20Apostles'%20Creed&text=Today%20biblical%20scholars%20agree%20that,into%20being%20around%20700%20AD., accessed 9/18/2022.

165. https://www.catholic.com/encyclopedia/sacraments, accessed 8/20/2022.

166. Ibid., accessed 8/20/2022.

167. https://en.wikipedia.org/wiki/Counter-Reformation, accessed 9/5/2022.

168. https://www.brainyquote.com/quotes/john_knox_378457, accessed 12/3/2022.

169. http://traditionalcatholic.net/Tradition/Council/Trent/Twenty_Third_Session,_Doctrine_and_Canons.html, accessed 11/19/2022.

170. http://www.thecounciloftrent.com/ch7.htm, accessed 11/19/2022.

171. Ibid., accessed 11/19/2022.

172. Ibid., accessed 11/19/2022.

173. Ibid., accessed 11/19/2022.

174. http://www.thecounciloftrent.com/ch13.htm, accessed 11/19/2022.

175. http://www.thecounciloftrent.com/ch14.htm, accessed 11/19/2022.

176. Ibid., accessed 11/19/2022.

177. http://www.thecounciloftrent.com/ch7.htm, accessed 11/19/2022.

178. http://www.thecounciloftrent.com/ch22.htm, accessed 11/19/2022.

179. Ibid., accessed 11/19/2022.

180. http://www.thecounciloftrent.com/ch6.htm, accessed 11/19/2022.

181. https://sb.rfpa.org/the-church-and-the-sacraments-views-during-the-third-period-750-1517-a-d-the-seven-sacraments-penance-continued/, accessed 11/19/2022.

182. http://www.thecounciloftrent.com/ch14.htm, accessed 11/19/2022.

183. Ibid., accessed 11/19/2022.

184. https://www.catholic.com/magazine/print-edition/anathema, accessed 12/1/2022.

185. https://sabbathsentinel.org/canons-from-laodicea/, accessed 12/26/2022.

186. https://bccatholic.ca/voices/graham-osborne/why-do-catholics-believe-in-sacred-tradition, accessed 3/15/2023.

187. https://www.catholic.com/magazine/print-edition/magisterium, accessed 3/23/2023.

188. Ibid., accessed 3/23/2023.

189. http://www.therealpresence.org/eucharst/mir/magisterium.htm, accessed 3/23/2023.

190. https://onepeterfive.com/magisterium-cheat-sheet/, accessed 3/23/2023.

TRUTH IS MORE
IMPORTANT
THAN
TRADITION